T0129732

ALSO BY EUGENE LINDEN

Silent Partners:
The Legacy of the Ape Language Experiments

The Education of Koko
(with Francine Patterson)

Affluence and Discontent:
The Anatomy of Consumer Societies

The Alms Race:
The Impact of American Voluntary Aid Abroad

Apes, Men, and Language

THE
FUTURE
IN
PLAIN
SIGHT

NINE CLUES TO THE
COMING INSTABILITY

EUGENE LINDEN

SIMON & SCHUSTER

SIMON & SCHUSTER
Rockefeller Center
1230 Avenue of the Americas
New York, NY 10020

SIMON & SCHUSTER and colophon are registered trademarks
of Simon & Schuster Inc.

Designed by Irving Perkins Associates, Inc.

Manufactured in the United States of America

1   3   5   7   9   10   8   6   4   2

Library of Congress Cataloging-in-Publication Data
Linden, Eugene.
The future in plain sight : nine clues to the coming
instability / Eugene Linden.
p.   cm.
Includes index.
1. Twenty-first century—Forecasts.   I. Title.
CB161.L494   1998
303.49'09'05—dc21   98-7080
CIP

ISBN 978-1-9821-3494-5

For Gillian, Sofia, and Alec:
My hopes for the future.

CONTENTS

PART III
THE CASE FOR INSTABILITY
245

PREFACE

I ENTER INTO THIS BOOK knowing full well that predicting the future is a fool's errand. As the great Roman orator Cicero put it in a remark to the Roman Senate, "No soothsayer should be able to look at another soothsayer without laughing." It is not hard to collect countless examples of predictions gone awry. Economist Robert Heilbroner looked at the track record of his peers in predicting long-term trends in the decades leading up to the 1970s. None foresaw the advent of multinational companies, the emergence of inflation, or the rise of Japan as an economic power.

The twists and turns of the future are not a bad thing, of course, just a fact of life. Were it not for failure of vision, entrepreneurs would wither and die as massive and ancient corporations extended their reach over new markets and new technologies. The shortsightedness of the tabulating companies allowed IBM to dominate an exploding computer market in the 1950s and 1960s, but IBM's failure to pay heed to the implications of the integrated circuit and the software to program such devices allowed personal-computer makers and software programmers to snatch billions of dollars in business from a giant with near-monopolistic power in the market in the 1970s. Now Microsoft's Bill Gates, who became the richest man in the world thanks in part to IBM's inattention, is frantically searching the Internet for clues to the future of the computer market so that he may avoid his appointment in a technological Samarra.

Unless they involve an asteroid smacking into the planet from outer space, the clues to the future usually lie in plain sight. But someone has to pay attention. So it has always been, in all fields of inquiry. The academic and political elite of the Victorian era believed that science was on the verge of answering all major questions about the workings of the universe, just before Einstein tore apart their universe and prized open the portals to worlds never before imagined. Einstein himself could never completely accept the implications of the paradigm shift he helped bring about.

At all times of transition there are points at which two people look at the same thing at the same time, but with entirely different views of its value. The young man who inherits a brownstone in the ghetto may be willing to unload it at any price because for him it represents pain and deprivation. With no memory of its past, the young architect who buys it sees a fine structure and a greatly undervalued property.

The keys to the future lie hidden in plain sight because we are blinded by the glare of the present, by what paleontologists call "the tyranny of the near past," and by other factors that contribute to the distorting lens of attitudes and biases that mediate our perceptions of the world.

This was one of the great insights forming the basis of *The Structure of Scientific Revolutions* by the late philosopher Thomas Kuhn. In that book, Kuhn recounts an experiment by Jerome Bruner, the father of gestalt psychology. Different people were shown a series of playing cards. At first the cards were flashed for only brief periods, but with each successive trial, the cards were shown for longer and longer periods. Unbeknown to the experimental subjects, salted through the deck were anomalous cards such as a red ace of spades or a black four of hearts.

At first, the subjects saw all the cards as normal, blithely identifying a red six of spades as a six of spades, etc. As they had more time to look at the cards, they began to see something wrong, but could not put their finger on it—"That's the six of spades, but there's something wrong with it—the black has a red border." Eventually, with even longer exposure, some would recognize the anomaly, but others would lose all confidence, even in their ability to recognize normal cards.

Once we have formed a vision of the way the world looks and works, it is difficult to accept change; it is even difficult to recognize it as it happens. This is all the more true of intellectual elites (or, in the corporate world, the managerial establishment of large corporations), who, being masters of the present, are perhaps the least qualified group to predict the future. Naturally, they are also the first group that the media and policy makers turn to for an expert opinion on where the world is heading. Thus we have in place an almost foolproof mechanism for guaranteeing that we will always prepare for a future that never comes about, and always be unprepared for the future that does.

In retrospect, what threats were obscured and ignored during the West's fifty-year obsession with communist expansion? What future should we be preparing for today? Which of today's events today will eventually come into focus as revealing the contours of the next century? What clues to the future now lie in plain sight?

I cannot pretend to have any special advantage over anyone else in predicting the shape of things to come. Rather, I propose a way to think about the future. I suggest that we will know much about the future if we can answer one question: Will life in the next century be less stable than it is now? Stability and instability are fundamental characteristics of life, and past episodes of instability tell us how people and societies act in both stable and unstable times. If we can make an informed guess as to whether the future will be more or less stable than the present, we can then try to imagine the ways in which changes in stability might transform the way we live and think. To make that informed guess, we must try to see the clues lying in plain sight today that mutely point toward the future.

INTRODUCTION

TODAY'S BABY BOOMERS HAD the privilege of growing up in one of the most stable periods in the vast sweep of human history. As of this writing, more than fifty years have passed without catastrophic conflict between great powers. This fifty-year hiatus falls within a period of 150 years of extreme climate stability that has only recently begun to change. Finally, the 150-year stretch falls within an eight-thousand-year period in which climate has been relatively clement compared with the record of the past million years or so. Since our distant ancestors last saw real instability, humans have invented agriculture, writing, cities, and commerce, flown to the moon, and multiplied from some few million souls to roughly 5.6 billion.

The world we know is one of stability nested in stability nested in stability. As a species, however, *Homo sapiens* was forged by instability, and for the first 95 percent of humanity's time on the planet, our ancestors regularly had to cope with rapid change brought about by severe climate change and its resulting impacts on the landscape and food supply. Even in the brief snippet of time that constitutes recorded human history, civilizations have collapsed repeatedly before invasions of armies, microbes, and ideas.

The current period is truly extraordinary, but most of those born after World War II consider it the norm. This might turn out to be a dangerous delusion should instability return. Can that happen? What would it mean for humanity? The first order of business is to define what is meant by stability.

Like pornography, stability is in the eye of the beholder. It is an elusive term that all understand until they try to agree on a definition. Unlike pornography, however, the definition of stability has benefited from a huge body of scientific inquiry in biology and physics as well as such arcane disciplines as systems dynamics and the study of artificial life, fields in which the meaning of stability has formal significance. Though the jargon differs from field to field—physicists talk about "strange attractors," biologists about "homeostasis"—certain common elements recur through these definitions. They have enough in common so that we may extract some of the characteristics of life you would expect to see in stable times.

Ecologists, for instance, use words like "persistence" and "resilience" to describe stability. Persistence means that the stable state tends to continue in the face of disturbance, whereas resilience is the property of stable systems that enables them to recover from shocks. Also, stable biological systems are characterized by firm linkages between their various components even as things change around the system.

The cod population off the Georges Bank in New England, for instance, has risen and fallen over the millennia, absorbing shocks as food supply varied, but until recently the cod have remained in dynamic equilibrium with other major fish in the ecosystem. Biologists use the word "homeostasis" to describe the complex feedback mechanisms that help keep the system in balance. Thus a stable system is not dormant but, rather, buzzes in a type of dynamic tension, like a vibrant and healthy organism, as it encounters, absorbs, and recovers from shocks from without and within. These characteristics of stability apply to individual organisms, to communities of species, to ecosystems, and, if James Lovelock, the author of the Gaia concept, is to be believed, to the entire biosphere. He sees the biosphere as a system that blindly regulates itself through feedback to maintain conditions favorable to life. Leaving Gaia aside, the list of design features used to characterize stable biological systems very nicely describes the global situation of the past half-century.

Obviously, some will disagree. It's not hard to find pockets of instability scattered around the globe: ethnic and religious conflict afflicts the Balkans, Algeria, and the Sudan, among other places; the pressures of human migration stir resentment and hostility in regions as disparate as the U.S., Europe, Asia, and Africa; peasant uprisings rattle Mexico; hugely powerful international gangs have proliferated and push around governments in Latin America, Russia, and Asia; and so on and so forth. It is doubtful that the people of Zaire, Liberia, Albania, Uzbekistan, Somalia, Pakistan, or a dozen other countries would characterize life as stable.

Stability will never be ubiquitous, nor does it have to be. The past fifty years have been remarkable for what has not happened. There has been no serious global economic contraction since the Great Depression started almost seventy years ago (in the century before it, panics and depressions tended to roil the markets every twenty years or so). The last armed conflict between great powers ended over fifty years ago. The last great killing epidemic was the swine flu of 1918, which killed twenty million people—more than died on the battlefield in all of World War I—in twelve months. It was only in the late nineteenth century, when the Frenchman Louis Pasteur, the Englishman Joseph Lister, and the German Robert Koch successively laid the groundwork for the germ theory of disease and prompted an attendant focus on sanitation, that societies gained sufficient mastery over infectious disease so that cities could grow past a population of one million without periodically collapsing from the ravages of cholera and other plagues.

These long gaps between destabilizing events have provided humanity with breathing room. They allowed time for the building of infrastructure like roads and ports, for vaccination programs, for investments in agriculture, for market and political reform, and for other improvements that have lengthened life spans and lifted incomes around the globe. Human population itself is a solid indicator of stability. It tends to rise during periods of climate and geopolitical stability, and it stalls or falls during upheaval.

After the 1996 election, President Clinton's advisers fretted openly that there was no great issue either internationally or domestically which he might tackle to define his second term, the theory being that great presidents need great problems. Despite our national proclivity to see disaster around the corner, Americans are beginning to entertain the notion that things might not be so bad right now. Crime rates are plummeting in most American cities. After all the ink spilled over its negative consequences, even corporate downsizing has begun to get some positive press; supposedly, the payroll trimming of the 1990s has made America the best prepared of the industrial nations to compete in an integrated global economy.

Around the world, nations are struggling toward democracy, strengthening property rights, privatizing, and opening their markets to attract investment. In sub-Saharan Africa, long the basket case to end all basket cases with its declining incomes and food production, growing rates of infectious disease, rampant corruption, and tribal strife, new leaders are emerging who preach discipline and self-reliance.

"Resilience," that other attribute of stable systems, very aptly describes the way the world community has absorbed shocks that in other times might have led to spirals of economic collapse and disorder. The power of OPEC loomed over the 1970s, the third-world debt crises terrified policy makers and financiers in the early 1980s, but neither has brought down the international banking system. Japan has not taken over the world economy, as feared by futurist Herman Kahn in 1970 and novelist Michael Crichton in 1992; nor did the collapse of Japan's real-estate-driven, bubble economy lead to economic meltdown. Neither the financial doomsayer Paul Erdman's prediction of a crash in 1979 nor the biologist Paul Ehrlich's predictions of coming famines have yet materialized.

If the present stability continues, the U.S. may be able to avert the new suite of potential doomsdays, such as the increasing burden of Medicare, the bankrupting of Social Security, the burden of the national debt, the deterioration of the nation's infrastructure. With continued breathing room, the world community may be able to take effective action to control nuclear proliferation and the spread of biological and chemical weapons before such means of mass destruction are again used in anger. It is even possible that nations might act to tackle global environmental problems such as deforestation; the poisoning of land, air, and water; the destruction of ecosystems; desertification; the looming threat of mass extinctions; and human-induced climate change.

As the biological definition suggests, stability tends to beget more stability—at least for a while. Some eminent students of history are willing to say that the world has entered a new era. The British historian Paul Johnson boldly made this point in an op-ed article for *The Wall Street Journal* in 1995: "Not a single leader of any of the Great Powers . . . has a program in which major war plays any part. As a historian I can confidently say that this is unique: There is no precedent in world history for war being ruled out of calculations at such a high level." He links this happy state of affairs to an emergent practicality and the decline of absolutist ideologies. After the search for perfection brought us the mass destruction of Hitler, Stalin, and Mao, humanity has turned to democracy, capitalism, and the notion of incremental improvements, supposedly reducing both the stakes and the risk of conflict.

Continued tranquillity and growth led the *Journal* in 1997 to publish a front-page article, "Global Growth Attains a New Higher Level That Could Be Lasting," which noted that the world may be entering a new era in which "several trends are coming together to fuel a global growth wave that is unprecedented in size and scope." Indeed, global economic expansion, which now approaches 4 percent a year, has attained levels considered inconceivable just a few years ago. World figures such as UN Secretary General Kofi Annan and Domingo Cavallo, an economist who was the architect for Argentina's transition from hyperinflation to stable growth, use the phrase "Golden Age" to describe the new era; Cavallo has predicted, "Historians will come to see the 1990s as the time of its birth." Even that most sober journal *Foreign Affairs* joined the giddiness, publishing an article suggesting that the business cycle, according to which recessions inevitably followed booms, no longer applied.

In good times, everybody has sound reasons why the good times will continue. Economist Lawrence Kudlow argues that information technology and other high-tech productivity improvements mean that the U.S. can sustain both high economic growth and low unemployment for years without running the risk of renewed inflation. Others suggest that information technologies now keep retailers, distributors, and manufacturers in such intimate contact that the elements of production and sales instantly adjust to changes in the marketplace, so that recessions will be a thing of the past.

On the global scene, some argue that international stability will continue because the power of an integrated global marketplace has sufficient clout to force nations to settle their differences short of conflict, and also the power to discipline or isolate those renegade states that pursue beggar-thy-neighbor policies. Technological optimists such as the late economist Julian Simon believe that mankind's ability to develop and deploy technology has reached a point where we can predict increases in material well-being and health regardless of whatever curve balls nature might throw at us. Dennis Avery, an agricultural expert at the conservative Hudson Institute, flatly states, "Politics, not droughts or overpopulation, causes hunger."

Human initiative has certainly contributed greatly to the stability of the present era. As noted, the germ theory of disease and the discovery of antibiotics blessed humanity with a honeymoon from infectious disease. Then there was the so-called Green Revolution. It bloomed in the 1950s, after plant geneticist Norman Borlaug figured out how to combine strains of wheat that produced a heavy head of grain in a dwarf variety that had a sturdy enough stalk to support the weight without falling over. This enabled farmers to take great advantage of fertilizer. As plant breeders created high-yield varieties of rice and corn, the Green Revolution contributed to stability around the world by improving the incomes and diets of hundreds of millions of poor people.

It would be a mistake, however, to underestimate the importance of the global context within which this progress took place.

The relatively good weather of the past 150 to 200 years, a period that encompasses much of the industrial and information revolutions, has allowed farmers around the world to increase production. As Charles Kellogg argued in his 1941 classic *The Soils That Support Us,* this fundamental source of wealth provided the capital for other forms of investment and development. Relatively clement weather makes it easier to maintain a sound financial system, which in turn makes it easier to foster political and social stability, bolstering those firm linkages between the components of the system. Families prosper and grow—and therein lies the rub.

In nature, when climate is favorable and food plentiful, a species tends to proliferate. The population curve is similar whether it applies to bacteria in a petri dish, fruit flies, lemmings, or caribou. Numbers increase until they reach some threshold and crash. Humans are not fruit flies, of course, but the example shows how steady advances can bring a system past some tipping point beyond which the system descends into instability. The boom-and-bust cycle is typical of the rhythm of nature, not just markets.

Christopher Langton, a systems theoretician based at the Santa Fe Institute in New Mexico, is a pioneer in the field of artificial life. This discipline, analogous to artificial intelligence, attempts to replicate large-scale patterns of life on computers. Langton has focused on major events in evolution, such as the tendency over time for such basic building blocks of life as molecules to organize into ever more complex systems, first cells, then multicellular communities, then organisms, and ultimately social units that use technology. The whole process involves shifts between one stable system and another as life evolves. Langton and his colleagues have thus given a good deal of thought to the transitions between stability and instability.

Langton describes the process of boom and bust succinctly. Faced with new ecological opportunities, various competing organisms try different strategies to exploit the system. Over time, this chaos resolves itself into a stable system as the competing groups sort things out. This persists until someone comes along with a special advantage, or something changes the ecology of the system. The favored competitor prospers, driving out rivals, until the whole system becomes unstable and crashes. There follows a new period of chaos, until the surviving competitors stabilize around a new game. This, for instance, is where the Georges Bank fishery is now. Human overfishing of cod has tipped the system over the edge, and the community has been replaced by a bizarre agglomeration of species.

This paradigm is generic across systems, argues Langton, applying to phenomena as diverse as market crashes and extinction events. Indeed, he notes that this archetypal pattern describes the geopolitical situation that produced the Cold War, whereby collective interests kept the more aggressive tendencies of some nations in check. Israel was on the point of completely crushing Egypt's army in the Sinai during the 1973 war until the Soviet Union threatened a wider war unless the U.S. intervened to halt the impending carnage. Yet, in the aftermath of the Cold War, the world has entered a period in which no one instrument, even the discipline of the integrated global marketplace, can control renegade nations like Iraq.

Stability thus does not beget more stability in perpetuity. After some elusive point, stability begins to unravel, often because a species (or, in the case of markets, a corporation) continues to adhere to a reproductive (or market) strategy even after it becomes maladaptive. In 1997 the Korean economy is on the point of collapse, for instance, in part because its hypercompetitive manufacturers went on a building spree, developing industrial capacity financed by foreign investors, in the process driving down prices so far that a number of Korean debtors can no longer service their loans. Stuart Kauffman, one of Langton's colleagues at the Santa Fe Institute, notes, "What does it say about stability and wisdom when your best adaptive strategy may ultimately hustle you off the evolutionary stage?"

What are the exterior factors that can cause a system to tip into instability? One of them, again, is the weather. Severe drought in Central Asia that began around 300 A.D. destroyed vital pasturelands along the Great Silk Road, causing the abandonment of this caravan route linking the Middle East and China. Some historians believe that continuing drought caused barbarian tribes from the Steppes to migrate westward and into conflict with the Roman Empire.

Although Ellsworth Huntington made this argument in 1907 in his book *The Pulse of Asia,* the study of climate as it affects history is a relatively new field. It draws its practitioners from archaeology, biology, geophysics, and chemistry, and concerns itself with the links between weather patterns and historical events. In the past few years, the field has gotten a shot in the arm from breakthroughs in the understanding of long-term cyclical weather patterns as they have recurred in the period since the last ice age. Indeed, only since 1993 have scientists had a sufficiently precise record of climate to compare changes in civilizations with changes in climate. These records come from ice cores drawn from Greenland, from sea-bed sediments in the Gulf of Oman, and from bottom sediments from Lake Van in Turkey. According to archaeologist Harvey Weiss of Yale University, this last record permits comparisons on an annual basis going back fourteen thousand years.

Climate has been relatively stable for some eight thousand years since the reverberations of the last ice age finally subsided, but the findings in Greenland and other recent data suggest that even in historical times there have been periods of abrupt change in global weather patterns. The big cycles that affect global climate result from factors as large as the variations in earth's orbit as it hurtles around the sun to an ultra-low-frequency ringing set in motion in the atmosphere by changes in the ice sheets and oceans. These cycles appear with frequencies ranging from every seventy thousand years or more to events that recur every 1450 years, and as they ripple around the globe, the harmonics of these planetary-scale waves can plunge whole continents into periods of drought lasting hundreds of years.

When, for instance, the 1450 event arrives, it brings about changes in both the atmospheric pressure over the North Atlantic and the vast deep ocean currents that redistribute heat from the tropics to the poles, changes that lead to drier and perhaps colder weather throughout Europe and the Middle East. The changes are not so dramatic as during an ice age, but they are sufficient to bring down empires. Though current fears about global warming center on temperature changes, Harvey Weiss notes that accompanying changes in precipitation can have more to do with the rise and fall of civilizations.

One such occurrence of a drying cycle happened forty-two hundred years ago, and, according to archaeologist Weiss, the climate change led to the collapse of the Akkadian Empire, a culture that arose on the Habur Plain in northern Iraq. This was the first documented civilization in the region to form a central government and establish an organized system of agricultural centers, but over a period that may have been as short as fifty years or as long as three hundred, the empire dwindled to nothing as people starved and abandoned lands. Weiss believes that the beleaguered people wrote of their plight in the "Curse of Akkad," forty-one hundred years ago:

> *The large fields and acres produced no grain*
> *The flooded fields produced no fish*
> *The watered gardens produced no honey and wine*
> *The heavy clouds did not rain*
> *On its plains where grew fine plants,*
> *"lamentation reeds" now grew.*

Weiss and Paul Mayewski, director of the University of New Hampshire's Climate Change Research Center, are exploring links between climate change and other major historical events as well. These start eighty-one hundred years ago, with a dry period that occurred at the same time as the decline of a prepottery Neolithic culture in Western Asia, continue through a period of economic and political collapse in the Mediterranean that began around 1315 B.C., and also include the so-called Century of Trouble that saw the end of the Byzantine Empire in the eighth century A.D.

The most recent cooling event had devastating effects beginning about 1250 A.D. The "Little Ice Age" overwhelmed the Viking colonies in Greenland, which had proliferated during the clement weather of the previous two centuries. This set the stage for the later conquest of the New World by more climatically favored southern neighbors such as England and Spain. The disruption continued for centuries. According to the historian H. H. Lamb, it was in response to the severity of the winter of 1564–65 (the coldest since the 1430s) that the Flemish painter Pieter Brueghel the Elder launched a new artistic tradition by making the severe winter landscape a focal part of his painting *Hunters in the Snow*. As the harsh weather continued, such landscapes became a leitmotif of European art.

As one of its most recent acts, the Little Ice Age may have helped launch the American Revolution. Two U.S. historians, David Smith and William Baron, argue in "Growing Season Parameter Reconstruction for New England Using Killing Frost Records 1697 to 1947" that a succession of bad growing seasons in the thirty-seven years before 1776 placed an enormous burden on the food supply in the colonies, particularly after Britain stationed six thousand troops in the Northeast in 1765 and demanded that the colonists provide for them.

Since the mid–nineteenth century, climate has been warming, although there is disagreement about whether the Little Ice Age is really over. There is scant comfort in moderating temperatures, however, since continued warming carries its own risks—an increase in hurricanes, floods, and droughts. Moreover, along with an understanding of these new climate cycles has come the disturbing suggestion that climate may have a tendency to flip, bringing about extreme change in an extraordinarily short period of time. Ten thousand years ago, at the end of one of these cycles, temperatures rose in some places by eighteen degrees Fahrenheit or more in just a few years. To put this in perspective, the chaos wrought by the Little Ice Age came about with just a two-degree drop in regional temperatures.

Another powerful horseman of instability is disease. The

Black Death of the fourteenth century helped bring down the feudal order that had arisen seven centuries earlier, when the isolated survivors of a previous plague pandemic organized themselves into defensive communities. The outset of this earlier series of epidemics in turn had speeded the end of the ancient order, killing ten thousand people a day in Constantinople at its peak in the years 541–44. Across the Atlantic, disease, principally measles, spread by conquistadors helped bring down the Aztec and Inca empires.

And then, of course, a system can topple because of the proliferation of one of its members, a metaphorically powerful idea with its implication that success carries with it the seeds of its own destruction. This may have happened on Easter Island. Polynesian numbers soared to seven thousand by 1600. In the ensuing years, the Polynesians stripped the island of trees, depriving themselves of the material from which to construct fishing boats. A brutal competition for resources started a descent into cannibalism and barbarity from which the Polynesians on the island never recovered. By 1722, when Europeans arrived, only three thousand Polynesians remained, living in extremely primitive conditions. So complete was the collapse of this civilization that the survivors had forgotten the purpose of the great stone heads their forebears had erected during the civilization's glory days.

Loss of biological diversity, one byproduct of runaway population growth as humans overtax ecosystems, also threatens stability. A study led by G. David Tilman of the University of Minnesota examined a number of plots of American prairie, and the findings suggested that, the more diverse the plot, the more resistant it was to disease and pests. Also, the more diverse a system, the better it may be able to adjust smoothly to external changes such as climate. No clear measure directly links declines in diversity to instability. Some ecosystems can lose half their species and remain robust, others may collapse with the loss of 1 percent of the total number of species. Many of the species inhabiting coral reefs, for instance, depend on parrot fish, whose grazing prevents algae from smothering the corals.

The tributaries of destabilization nourish each other in a matrix of decline. Crowding and famines produce conditions favorable for epidemics, as do war and social upheaval. These positive feedbacks of negative forces then create a situation in which instability begets more instability. This has been the norm through most of human history as a species. For all but a tiny fraction of the time humans have been on the planet, the promised land of stability has lain just beyond the horizon. Perhaps as a result, we are superbly equipped to deal with upheaval.

Indeed, *Homo sapiens* is the product of climate instability, which drove our ancestral species to seek new food supplies during several periods of cooling and drying within the past five million years. The shift from digging for roots to hunting meat, and then the demands of organized hunting, both favored hominids with bigger brains. Hunting particularly required larger groups working together, and a bigger brain to sort out the complexities of social relationships and planning.

Adaptation to instability has continued during the modern era. Out of episodes of financial, political, and epidemiological instability have come reserve banks, the United Nations, the Centers for Disease Control, and other institutional attempts to learn from past upheavals so that their impact might be less when they recur.

Instability and change have also spurred the human imagination. An Asian volcanic eruption beginning in 1815 loaded ash into the atmosphere, causing global temperatures to plummet (the winter was so cold that vendors used horses and sleighs to deliver supplies over the frozen salt water to Nantucket Island, thirty miles off the coast of Massachusetts, an event that has never happened since). That summer, a party of houseguests in Switzerland responded to the weather by staying indoors and telling each other stories, one of which became the core of Mary Shelley's *Frankenstein.* We can see the gaudy sunsets this ash produced in the paintings of Frederick Turner.

That humans can cope with instability, however, does not necessarily mean that humans have prospered during times of upheaval. Successful adaptation to instability is measured by the durability of the species, not the individual, and it simply means that humanity has the capacity to recover from calamitous drops in population. Economic instability makes it difficult to attract investment; social instability makes it difficult to deploy new technologies; and poverty, which increases during unstable times, limits the options of both people and their political leadership, even when they know what they must do.

Egypt today imports about 40 percent of its food. For the sake of political stability, the government must insulate the poor from the vagaries of a volatile world grain market. Egypt needs better yields from its farmers, but this requires increasing farm incomes, and President Hosni Mubarak cannot do that without increasing the price of the heavily subsidized bread that is the staple of tens of millions of poor urban Egyptians. Thus the Egyptian government faces a choice between further fueling unrest in a population already flirting with Islamic fundamentalism, and risking calamity should a bad Egyptian harvest coincide with a tight market for grain exports in the future. Analogous constraints limit the policy options of leaders of Mexico and Haiti, among other countries. Much is possible when bellies are full, borders quiet, and incomes growing that is not possible when a nation, a region, or the entire globe is in turmoil.

Moreover, the growth in human numbers, a byproduct of stability, and the leveraging of human impacts by technology have changed both the stakes and the nature of the game. Humanity has proliferated to the point where we now have the capacity to destabilize global systems that were beyond the reach of our ancestors. The spiderweb of links connecting peoples and economies around the world can spread ill as well as good. Even in the limited sphere of finance, the scale and connectedness of global markets make a return to instability a frightening prospect. Stability has produced a situation in which we can no longer afford instability.

Since stability and instability are fundamental conditions which have profound effects on all other aspects of life, it is worth asking how long this current halcyon period might continue, and what might bring it to a close. Even today, glimpses of renewed instability peek out. Since 1982, trends in infectious disease have been on the rise. Also since the early 1980s, the weather has taken a turn for the worse. Four of the five warmest years recorded since data collection began in 1866 have occurred just since 1990. Extreme weather events have increased, particularly winter cyclones in the Northern Hemisphere. The warming oceans have expanded, forcing sea level to rise by nearly a foot in the last century. A two-degree-Fahrenheit warming of the cold waters off California since 1949 has caused a 40-percent drop in zooplankton, the shrimplike creatures that sustain the oceanic food chain. This in turn decimated populations of seabirds such as the sooty shearwater. According to a study published in *Global Change Biology,* four million birds, amounting to 90 percent of the shearwater population, disappeared between 1987 and 1994.

Another troubling portent is the ever-increasing strain on freshwater resources. Freshwater supplies impose a very hard limit on agriculture and life, because water is too expensive to create or move in large volumes. Today, usable supplies are shrinking fast even as demand rises.

Are these signals from the future, or more temporary irritants that will be shrugged off in this new era of stability? Is it possible that lurking beneath the surface today are the stirrings of change even as Paul Johnson and others write about the dawning of a new world order of tranquillity and civility? Some nervousness about the future is in order if for no other reason than that the doomsayers are in retreat and the optimists rule the day. In the past, widespread optimism has always been a good indicator that disaster is around the corner. Looking back at the present from the vantage point of the year 2050, will historians be talking about the 1990s as the dawn of a new Golden Age, or will they be making comparisons between Bill Clinton and Herbert Hoover, and asking how his administration could have failed to take action to head off the coming chaos?

Actually, President Clinton is probably off the hook. If widespread instability returns, it will come about more likely because of global forces that are not within the control of a president than because of some policy misjudgment (unless, of course, that policy misjudgment leads us into economic collapse or nuclear war). This perhaps offers a clue about where to look.

Murray Gell-Mann, the Nobel Laureate in physics who discovered the quark, the first subatomic particle to be identified, has a helpful suggestion in this regard. In a 1995 speech at a Tufts University symposium on the next century, Gell-Mann noted that in physics the transition from liquid to solid is very complex but can be understood in terms of just a few variables. He wonders, similarly, whether just a few variables control the complex transition that will happen in the next century as the curves of population growth and consumption flatten.

Turning Gell-Mann's thought around, we can ask, What are the events and anomalies in the present that connect to forces that we are least able to do something about, and how might they affect the future? Gell-Mann mentioned one: the increase in human numbers. The nature of demographic lag—a product of the huge number of young people just coming into their childbearing years—means that human numbers will continue to grow regardless of policy decisions for decades to come—unless nature intervenes.

Population trends merit a brief digression, because they are so important. In recent years there has been much comment in the press about the implications of a surprising drop in fertility rates, which are now plummeting around the world. This drop is a function of many different factors, including massive migration to the cities in the developing world, lower infant mortality, rising material aspirations of many young people, and perhaps even a dawning awareness that the neighborhood is getting kind of crowded. Despite the drop in fertility, however, global population is increasing at its highest rate ever—roughly ninety-five million people a year—and this increase will continue and even rise for at least a couple of decades to come, as huge numbers of girls enter their childbearing years. Even Ben Wattenberg, author of *The Birth Dearth,* who argues that the population explosion is over and a population bust is imminent, acknowledges that global population is likely to grow by another two billion people before 2050. Other estimates are higher, but even two billion people is equivalent to total human population in the 1930s. At this point in human history, with human population at unprecedented levels and most wildlands occupied, it is safe to say that an additional two billion souls added to human numbers will have profound effects on the globe, regardless of future technological break-throughs.

Where and how those effects will be expressed is a trickier question. In some countries, like Haiti, a rapid increase in human numbers has been accompanied in lockstep by a decline in forests and other ecosystems. In a very few places, such as the is-land nation of Mauritius, a long-standing conservation ethic has enabled people to preserve a good portion of their wildlands even as population grows. The issue facing humanity, however, is not how population pressures will play out in any given country so much as the broader question of how such pressures are likely to affect how long the overall stability of the present will con-tinue.

I believe that a fresh look at the present-day landscape reveals clues that speak to this fundamental question of whether the fu-ture will be stable or unstable. The clues to the next century I have chosen derive from basic driving forces, such as population. This is my path around the minefield of prediction. Rather than address whether we will all be living to the age of 120, or travel-ing to meetings in personal flying machines, I hope to answer a question about the most basic characteristic of life. It gives noth-ing away here to say that I will argue that humanity has set the stage for a return to instability. But what will that mean?

The answer forms the heart of this book. Following a de-scription of clues that point the way to the return of instability, I attempt to envision how these changes will rework the fabric of life in the twenty-first century in a thought experiment that unfolds through a series of scenarios set in the year 2050. I hope to capture the spirit of times that will be very different from those we know today. Obviously, this is dangerous territory (it's just possible that I might be around to have these scenarios flung back in my face, although I'm not sure how much, at age 103, I will care about being right or wrong), but here again I will draw from past and present for examples of the ways in which people react to extreme circumstances.

The scenarios in this book will explore some of the ways in which instability might rework values, as well as how instability will change the way we live. I assume that the people of 2050 will be recognizable to us today, just as we recognize our commonalities with those who came of age in the early 1940s. Whether our great-grandchildren coming of age in 2050 look back on us with amusement or horror depends in no small measure on the stability of the world we bequeath them.

Before getting to 2050, however, let us look at the present. Many of these clues are at first unsurprising, but it is my hope that looking at the obvious in a new light will bring the future into focus. In the last century, for instance, geologists looked at the familiar Himalayas and Andes and saw the mountain ranges as the product of some poorly understood vertical force. Only years after the theory of continental drift was first proposed, geophysicists came to recognize that the Himalayas were not the result of some vertical force pushing upward but, rather, of a horizontal force as great plates collided. Now every high-school science student who looks at the San Andreas Fault can envision the great plates of the continents sliding over each other.

Most of the clues I have chosen are as familiar features of the present-day landscape as the San Andreas Fault or the Himalayas. The collapse of the Mexican peso in 1994 prompted endless analysis in the months following the event. Similarly, the resurgence of infectious disease has spurred articles, best-selling books, and several movies, including *Outbreak* and *Virus*. The extraordinary growth of the developing world megacities, recent changes in climate, the loss of biodiversity, and volatility in the global food system are also well-trodden ground. A few of the clues—the resurgence of slavery, the automation of knowledge, the rise of ecomigration—are perhaps more obscure, but certainly not unknown.

This book will attempt to take such events, familiar and obscure, and put them in a new light. For instance, at one level the currency crises that hit Mexico in 1994 and then Southeast Asia in 1997 amounted to nothing more than specific investors reacting to specific events. It is not the Thai baht and Mexican peso crises themselves, however, that offer a clue to the next century, but, rather, the shifting market tectonics that produced them, and that also produced subsequent currency crises in Malaysia and Indonesia. If we step back, it becomes clear that the timing and nature of investors' reactions in these episodes exposed an instability intrinsic to an integrated global market that will very likely recur in the future. It has also become clear that there is not much governments or financial institutions can do to eliminate such instability.

Human migration, an issue as old as humanity itself, is another phenomenon easy to dismiss as a clue to the future. Through history, people have sought out new resources, jobs, or areas to settle, and have been pushed by warfare, economic collapse, political upheaval, prejudice, drought, or crowding. Because migration redistributes labor to where it is needed and reduces crowding and stress, many economists look at it in a positive light.

Today, however, migration continues to increase in the developing world even though more and more nations and cities are putting out "no-vacancy" signs, suggesting that migration is increasingly a function of push rather than pull. Upon closer inspection, it becomes clear that deep, inelastic forces like environmental degradation and population pressure play an ever more prominent role as both direct and indirect factors in creating the conditions that drive migration. What is important about migration as a clue to the twenty-first century is its links to these deep, difficult-to-reverse forces I mentioned above. This means migration will increase in the coming years; and as the number of safe havens and refuges continues to shrivel, instability increases as well.

It is my hope that the list of clues in the following section will bring into focus the design of the future now hidden in the familiar face of the present, and in so doing also reveal the box that humanity has created for itself. If we know one fundamental attribute of the future, we may not be able to avert it, but perhaps we can prepare. Though it is very late in the game, there is still much that humanity can do to moderate the instabilities that lie ahead and prepare for those that are unavoidable. The following list of clues is not meant to be exhaustive—it could have been much longer—but, rather, provocative. And so let us try to consider the obvious, the familiar, and the easily dismissed in a new light.

PART I

NINE CLUES TO THE FUTURE

Chapter 1

HOT-TEMPERED MARKETS

DURING AN EXTRAORDINARY FOUR-month period starting on June 27, 1997, the currencies of Thailand, Malaysia, the Philippines, Singapore, Indonesia, Taiwan, and Korea all went into a free fall. Even places like Hong Kong, whose currencies escaped the pummeling, suffered stock-market collapses. The contagion, nicknamed "bahtulism" after the Thai baht, the first currency to swoon, spread also to Latin America, where markets in Mexico and Brazil suffered precipitous declines. Then, in neat symmetry, exactly four months after it began, the Asian financial flu hit the United States, as American investors began to realize that an integrated global economy entails risks as well as rising profits and low inflation. On that day, the Dow Jones Industrial Average suffered its biggest one-day drop ever as the index fell 554 points (although in percentage terms this roughly 7-percent plunge was but a third of the 22-percent drop in the Dow during the crash of 1987). The damage done to markets and economies could be measured in the trillions of dollars, and the economic meltdown has tempered talk of a "new Golden Age" for the world economy, but the most unsettling and telling aspect of this debacle is that it was not supposed to happen.

The international community had supposedly learned lessons from the collapse of the Mexican peso two years earlier, and set in place measures to prevent its recurrence. These responses included efforts to monitor emerging economies for early-warning signals of distress, so that institutions like the International Monetary Fund and industrial nations could coordinate a timely response. In fact, the world did have early warning that a crisis was brewing in Asia, and right after it broke, the IMF, in concert with Japan and other powers, did frame a coordinated response. Nonetheless, the crises rolled on, gathering steam. A combination of factors overwhelmed the market-calming efforts of the IMF and others. One of these factors was the desire to cut losses in an area that suddenly became questionable. This sudden shift of perception exposes a powerful destabilizing force in the world economy, a force that is an inherent attribute of the integrated global marketplace. The power and unsettling nature of this unwanted side effect of globalization first became apparent with the fall of the Mexican peso.

As late as the fall of 1994, Mexico's economic prospects seemed positively glowing. A poll of business confidence by Dun and Bradstreet indicated that Mexican businessmen expecting higher sales in the coming quarter outnumbered pessimists by nearly 90 percent—the highest percentage in any of the fifteen countries surveyed at that time. On December 9, U.S. President Bill Clinton singled out Mexico as a development success story.

Eleven days later, on December 20, the mood changed in the blink of an eyelash. The government devalued the peso by 13 percent in a futile effort to slow the outflow of its fast-shriveling supplies of foreign exchange. Instead, in just a few hours, institutional investors, an anonymous but powerful group of players, responded by pulling roughly $5 billion out of Mexican stocks, bonds, and short-term securities. Before the end of the month, another $5 billion fled the country, bringing the nation to the brink of collapse. Other Latin American currencies, such as the Argentine peso, began to teeter, while investors turned cautious on countries as far away as India and Thailand. Thailand rebounded quickly from the 1994 events; its collision with the brutal calculus of an integrated global economy was still two and a half years away. The Mexican capital hemorrhage continued until February 1995, when the U.S., the IMF, and other industrial nations put together a package of $52 billion in guarantees to stabilize the currency and qualm the fears of foreign investors.

In the months following the initial debacle, the undertaker beetles of international crises—pundits, politicians, and economists—went to work trying to decipher its causes and what lessons it held for the future. Some analysts cited the political pressures that spurred the Mexican government to keep printing pesos so that consumers could pay for imports during an election year even as foreign reserves were rapidly disappearing; others cited worries about the stability of the country in light of a persistent uprising in the state of Chiapas, and indications that high officials were involved in drug smuggling and the assassinations of prominent politicians Luis Donaldo Colosio, Mexican President Carlos Salinas' hand-picked successor, and opposition leader José Francisco Ruiz Massieu.

Jeffrey Sachs and two Harvard colleagues, Andrés Velasco and Aaron Tornell, laid much of the blame on Mexico's adherence to a policy of pegging the peso to a particular range of the dollar, and its refusal to devalue the currency in March, following the Colosio assassination, which, the Harvard economists argue, would have reassured investors by providing higher returns, and would have been accepted by the international financial community as a necessary act during a political crisis. Mexican officials were faulted by others for being slow to report the free fall of foreign reserves in the months prior to the devaluation.

All of these analyses were relevant to the specifics of the Mexican crises. But the lasting significance of the panic was that it offered a preview of what lay ahead in the short term, and what lies ahead for years to come. The peso collapse exposed attributes inherent in an integrated global market that portend huge destabilizing swings in the coming decades. Two years later, the currency collapse that rippled through Southeast Asia underscored the importance of the fault lines exposed by the peso crisis.

Common characteristics of both crises were: the power of

perception; homogeneity underlying the appearance of diversity; the synchronicity of markets; and a tendency of investors to jump ship in a crunch, even when it would be in their long-term interest not to do so. As will become clear, these attributes, all first exposed in the weeks following the peso debacle, have broad salience to larger issues looming over the global financial markets.

Ironically, one contributing factor to the Mexican crisis was a belief among Mexican finance officials that growing international confidence in the Mexican economy would soon lead to more favorable long-term borrowing rates. Reluctant to issue long-term debt until rates dropped, the government issued billions of dollars in short-term notes called *tesobonos* that were pegged to the dollar. Between January and December 1994, the total amount owed on these obligations skyrocketed from $1 billion to roughly $18 billion, all of which was soon to come due. Mexico also had to find the foreign-exchange reserves to cover another $10 billion in dollar-denominated financial obligations. At the same time, foreign-currency reserves had dropped from $28 billion in March to little more than $6 billion in December.

This raised the possibility that the Mexican government was illiquid and would default on its obligations. According to Sachs and his colleagues, this in turn caused foreign investors to pull back and created a self-fulfilling prophecy. Without new funds, Mexico could not roll over the obligations coming due. Fears rapidly became reality, and a financial panic ensued.

Most of the information that produced the panic had been available to investors for months. Presumably, institutions and other foreign investors would have been following the declining reserves of foreign currency and the increase in the dollar-denominated debt. Presumably, they could themselves conclude that a crunch was coming. In an efficient market, these investors would have responded to different cues or bits of information, and they would have pulled back from the markets in an orderly fashion, probably prompting Mexico to respond with a series of moves to restore investor confidence.

This did not happen. Indeed, the Mexican government was

clearly surprised by the reaction to the devaluation. Who would have predicted that this single action could bring a nation to the point of economic collapse? What happened on December 20 that made the world different from December 19? Certainly, Mexico did not change overnight from a development "success story" into a banana republic.

Simply put, what happened is that institutional players finally acted. In the months before December, Mexican investors had already decided that a crunch was coming and moved capital to safer havens. This liquidation was scarcely noticed as foreign investors bought up notes that Mexicans were dumping. When foreign investors finally awakened to the problem, it was too late for an orderly evacuation. Institutional investors decided that Mexico did not have the money to meet its obligations and, en masse, decided that they did not want to be left holding the bag. When they came to the conclusion that Mexico was not a safe place for money to rest, they all tried to leave immediately.

Without buyers, however, the huge pension funds and other institutions could unload only a fraction of their holdings. The players found themselves in what in game theory is called a "prisoner's dilemma." This is a situation in which a prisoner who sells out his accomplice stands to benefit from leniency, unless his accomplice separately sells him out as well. The third option is that neither sells the other out, and each serves a sentence longer than if he sold the other out, but shorter than if they were sold out. Had the players decided to stay with Mexican investments in the reasonable belief that the country would find a way to honor its obligations, there would have been some suffering but no crisis.

They did not. For all the sophistication of the supposedly heterogenous group of investors who control the vast pools of institutional capital, they reacted like a herd. The diversity of the marketplace, which should have modulated wild swings, turned out to be an illusion.

Perception, as much as hard financial data, seems to determine the direction and stability of the marketplace. The decline in Mexico's foreign reserves in 1994, for instance, was not steady, but marked by a series of steps punctuated by rapid declines. Among the things that this suggests is that foreign investors pay close attention only at selected moments.

In fact, this financial version of an evolutionary model called "punctuated equilibrium" seems to be a property of markets in general. Players will stay with a particular course even as tension builds and circumstances change. Ultimately, some signal—a devaluation of the peso, the Federal Reserve chairman's testimony before Congress—causes people to act en masse. Thus there is a type of homogeneity that underlies the apparent diversity of the market players. That markets are subject to various degrees of mob psychology is not news, of course, but changes in the scale and integration of the world's markets make herd behavior much more destabilizing.

When the peso crisis hit, U.S. Treasury officials had to consider both the consequences of an economic meltdown in Mexico and the possibility of a domestic calamity as the huge institutions that supply the liquidity for American capital markets were forced to absorb tens of billions in losses. Thus the $52-billion bailout had the dual function of protecting American investors and stabilizing a neighboring country.

What would have happened had not American investors been at risk? What would have happened had the crisis hit some country that did not share a border with the U.S.? The world got part of the answer in the summer of 1997, when Thailand and then in quick succession Malaysia, the Philippines, Singapore, Indonesia, Hong Kong, Taiwan, and Korea all suffered currency routs or market collapses with eerie similarities to the peso crisis.

But also differences. The Mexican crisis surprised the international speculative community, that amorphous group of investors who prowl the world's markets looking for opportunities for a killing in speculative bubbles and other sins against financial probity. Thailand, on the other hand, was a planned hit. On June 27, 1997, Thailand gave up its attempt to defend the baht after spending billions in foreign-exchange reserves in a losing effort to keep the currency within a narrow trading range. The Thai action effectively conceded the impossibility of going against the mood of the marketplace. The baht promptly dropped by 20 percent, and then fell another 25 percent by early September. As currencies in the other Southeast Asian economies suffered similar free falls, the region's markets followed suit. By the end of 1997, the Dow Jones World Stock Indexes for Malaysia, the Philippines, Indonesia, and Thailand showed respective year-to-date declines of 70 percent, 62 percent, 63 percent, and 76 percent in U.S. dollar terms. In just a few months, foreign lenders and investment banks slashed new commitments by $100 billion. The contagion spread to Hong Kong during the business week ending October 24, whereupon fears of a regional banking collapse and economic chaos in Asia spooked the American markets, producing the 554-point drop in the Dow before trading was suspended on October 27.

The U.S. market recovered quickly but remained turbulent for the rest of the year. As this book goes to press, however, the Asians continue to wallow. Only extraordinary intervention by the World Bank in the week before Christmas 1997 prevented Korea from defaulting on its obligations, and Moody's listed many of its loans in technical default in early 1998. As Indonesia's currency continued to plummet in December, new worries surfaced about its ability to repay an estimated $200 billion in public and private dollar-denominated debts. By January, the Indonesian currency had fallen so low that in dollar terms its GDP (Gross Domestic Product) had fallen from a peak of over $220 billion to a mere $85 billion. In effect, the currency crisis had wiped out twelve years of Indonesian growth in just a few months.

Here again, emerging economies shifted from economic tigers to economic turkeys in the blink of an eye. In the aftermath of the peso crisis, numerous analysts dismissed an early attack on Thailand's currency because, as the conventional wisdom then held, in Thailand's case foreign investment and imports were supposedly serving the cause of building an economy rather than unproductive consumption. In the aftermath of the collapse of the baht, investors forgot about their earlier euphoria vis-à-vis Thailand and pointed out the vulnerability of banks in an overheated real-estate market. Similarly, Indonesia shifted from being a low-wage Mecca for foreign investment to a fragile economy whose competitiveness is hampered by protectionism, inefficiency, corruption among the elite, and the question of who or what will succeed the regime of seventy-six-year-old President Suharto. As was the case in Mexico, the next casualty of this crisis will likely be economic growth in the region, as capital scarcity forces governments and businesses to put development plans on hold.

One other gestalt shift that came out of the Asian crisis was a new respect for the importance of honest governments and markets. The collapse of the Southeast Asian currencies exposed the dark underbelly of the "Asian miracle": cronyism, corruption, lack of honest government regulation, and a stifled press allowed a huge buildup of bad loans. Once the scale of the problems became apparent, governments found themselves limited in what they could do to fix the problems, because officials were sandwiched between the elites, who resisted devaluation because they owed dollar-denominated loans, and the public, who tolerated repression and corruption only as long as their incomes were rising. With riots in the streets of Thailand, and stirrings of unrest elsewhere, foreign investors realized that the "Asian Way" had problems that went far deeper than something that could be fixed by the IMF. Suddenly Asia switched in the minds of investors from a place with hard workers and high savings to an area suffering from a "democratic deficit," as one hedge-fund investor put it—a place where lax supervision, cronyism, and repression of the free flow of information abrogated the checks and balances of the marketplace and allowed a bad situation to spin out of control.

That the Southeast Asian crisis came about only two years after the international community had supposedly learned the lessons of the Mexican crisis speaks volumes about the inherent volatility of an integrated global market. Bankers and policy makers can set up bailout funds or an international bankruptcy court, improve the flow of financial information, and take other actions designed to soothe markets, but these will not work. Both the Mexican and Southeast Asian examples demonstrate that market instability is about not only information and systems but perception and human nature. If the story is that Thailand or Mexico or Indonesia is a good place to get good returns on money, the relatively homogeneous investment community will put money into that country, ignoring warning signals until it is too late. Then they will all try to leave.

Capital controls will not work either, as Malaysia learned during the summer of 1997. As the value of the ringgit plummeted, Malaysian Prime Minister Mohamad Mahathir railed against George Soros and other hedge-fund operators and then imposed restrictions on capital flows in an effort to fight the speculators. He might as well have written them a check: the market reaction to his move was a drop in the Kuala Lumpur Stock Exchange Composite Index of 4.2 percent in one day, further enriching those who were already short the market. *The Wall Street Journal* quoted Peter Churchouse, a market strategist with Morgan Stanley, as saying, "There are enough problems in these markets without the authorities changing the rules of the game. There are lots of other equity markets . . . to invest in. You don't have to be involved in Asia." In a nutshell, this summarizes why the so-called circuit breakers will not work. "Hot-money" investors will shy away from any country that tries to place limits on when outsiders can sell their holdings.

Ultimately, even bailout funds will not work. In the aftermath of the peso crisis, Mexican industrialists proposed setting up a fund of private money that would show their confidence in the economy and help prevent runs on the peso. The few billion dollars mentioned is not nearly enough money to convince foreign investors to stay should there be a repeat of the events of December 1994. The larger issue, however, is that, to the degree that bailout funds insure speculators against failure, they also impede market adjustments and political reforms, and thus set up bigger crises in the future.

This is a subject very much on the minds of central bankers in the aftermath of Mexico and Southeast Asia. Economists and philosophers call the problem "moral hazard." With the U.S., the IMF, or Japan ready to act as sugar daddy, global investors may take more risks than they otherwise would, reducing pressures on Thailand to improve accounting standards, or on Indonesia to open its markets and tackle corruption. On the other hand, the volatility of the world markets means that investors tend to over-react to bad news, driving nations closer to insolvency than might be warranted by the facts.

Without the $52-billion bailout in Mexico, a cascade of bank-ruptcies and bank collapses could have plunged the nation into complete anarchy, fostering an immense wave of migration to the United States. The question facing Mexico, Southeast Asia, and the global investing community is whether these bailouts have bought nations time to institute necessary reforms, or merely postponed a much more painful day of reckoning. As we shall see, this ques-tion pertains to markets in the industrial powers as well.

Emerging economies must face the fact that if they are to enjoy the fruits of the integration of the global economy they must maintain relatively free markets, and this means they must also be willing to face the prospect of being whipsawed as capital flows occasionally fall prey to mob psychology. (On the other hand, it should be noted that many reform-minded thinkers in emerging economies ranging from Indonesia to Mexico welcome the power of the international marketplace, even with its costs, because those who control the flow of capital are relatively intolerant of corruption and rigged markets.) At any given moment, markets are driven by moods punctuated by rapid change, and not the collective interpretation of information. As Mexico discovered, when these moods involve like-minded people precipitously moving huge blocks of money, small countries can find them-selves facing financial and political collapse.

The same attributes of investors exposed by the Mexican peso crisis—the power of perception, the homogeneity underlying apparent diversity, the synchronicity of mood swings in the market, and, perhaps most important, the behavior of investors faced with a prisoner's dilemma—apply to big economies as well. And, of course, the stakes are much higher.

The U.S. got a taste of this in 1987, during the October crash, when the New York Stock Exchange's Dow Jones Industrial Average fell by 22 percent in one day. The market overseers subsequently instituted a package of reforms, including circuit breakers, to prevent computerized program trading from blindly driving down prices in the future. Share prices recovered from that setback, and the bull market that had begun in 1982 resumed its unprecedented march upward.

Many bankers, however, were left with a lingering malaise. What was so scary about the crash was not the immediate losses, but a glimpse of the abyss which yawned open the day after Monday's plunge. On that Tuesday, the network of settlements and guarantees that support the markets almost broke down entirely. As stocks gyrated through the day, well-known players placed huge orders that in ordinary times would have had traders salivating. On that day, however, it was sometimes impossible to know what real prices were at any given moment. Nor was it possible to know whether the tycoon placing an order was solvent, bankrupt, or doubling up his purchases because he had nothing to lose.

Although stock-market regulations then required that a buyer put up at least 50 percent of the money for a purchase, the very big players, such as the so-called hedge funds, found ways to borrow up to 75 percent of their purchases. This meant that, if they bought a stock on margin and it dropped more than 25 percent, the burden of risk shifted from the buyer to the broker who allowed him to buy on margin. Since the buyer had up to five days to deliver the money to settle the purchase, big players could bet with their brokers' money and double or triple their buys as prices fell, in the hope of covering their losses. Even if they bet wrong, their own immediate risk was limited.

The situation looked very different for those brokers who were ultimately responsible for paying the sellers. Being stuck with one bad debt on a multimillion-dollar trade could wipe out the capital of a small firm; indeed, a number of companies went under. For this and other reasons, the New York Stock Exchange, the epicenter of the financial universe, very nearly imploded that Tuesday. Traders looked into a void with no handholds on the way down, and faced the sickening realization that this fantastic engine of wealth that matched buyers and sellers was based almost entirely on intangibles like trust. Earnings, dividends, assets—all the hard information that supposedly informed prices—receded into the background when the simple issue before you was whether the person on the other side of a transaction was willing to take you down with him. Had not the Federal Reserve opened the spigot for low-cost money to provide liquidity on that Tuesday, a series of bankruptcies could have rippled through the world financial markets, toppling the entire system.

Although everybody breathed more easily as the markets stabilized, the successful resolution of that crisis might have been a mixed blessing, again because of the knotty problem of moral hazard. The lesson that investors took away was that central banks and other institutions could manage any financial crisis. This notion was reinforced when the U.S. successfully negotiated the savings-and-loan crisis (although at a cost of hundreds of billions of dollars) in the late 1980s; and then again in 1994, when the bailout assuaged international anxieties about the collapse of the Mexican peso.

With Uncle Sam, other industrial giants, and the world's 171 central banks ready to act as lender of last resort, the message for investors was that the world was entering a new era in which global financial catastrophes were a thing of the past. Acting on this presumption, investors poured ever more money into ever-riskier markets in the hope of higher returns. Or, as the intelligent and pessimistic market observer James Grant put it in an article in *The New York Times,* "Believing devoutly in central banks, investors have assumed more risk than they would have taken in a more suspicious frame of mind."

Pensioners and ordinary workers poured hundreds of billions of dollars into mutual funds, which in turn sought the highest returns. Like the monetary equivalent of an El Niño, money sloshed toward the riskier side of the financial ocean, piling up in high-yield bonds, developing economies, emerging technologies, real-estate developments, and other tempting but dangerous investments. The figures were astonishing. As of 1996, Americans had invested more than $3 trillion in mutual funds. By 1997, 50 percent was allocated to higher-return, higher-risk investments, reaching levels that had not been seen since the 1960s, which marked the end of the last great bull market. This time around, however, a much broader segment of the population had their fortunes tied to the market. In a type of generational forgetting, pensioners and coupon clippers alike became plungers with their life savings. Noting the shift in mood, one Wall Street veteran remarked that when he began his career, in the 1950s, New York State pension funds were not allowed to invest in stocks because they were too risky, and that just before he retired, in 1997, he saw a news-wire report that a California pension-fund manager was fired for putting some of the fund into bonds and not entirely in stocks.

Obviously, high-risk investments pay high returns because there is a greater chance that they will not be repaid. At the peak of the 1990s bull market, however, investors acted as though risk were eliminated. Many "junk"-rated bonds in 1996 were priced at levels very close to those of the most conservative, established, and solvent corporations. Similarly, the debt of nations with real question marks hanging over their future traded at levels not significantly above U.S. Treasury obligation. Before the Asian crisis erupted in the summer of 1997, Republic of China ten-year bonds were paying just .7 percent more than Treasury bills backed by the world's dominant economic and military power. Such a tiny premium implied that China, a nation that faced major transitions in the coming years and which had a history of playing hardball with foreign investors, was only slightly more risky than the U.S. as a place to park money.

This situation is ripe for adjustment, and in theory the adjustment should be orderly and smooth. But as the unfolding events in Asia are showing us, theory is not practice. Keep in mind the lessons of Mexico. Inevitably, the real price of risk will make itself felt in the United States as well, and the market will shift in mood. With so much money piled up in risky investments, massive redemptions of mutual funds could cause stocks to plummet. If mutual funds are forced to sell into a falling market, they might discover that they, like Mexico, have become illiquid. If a crash were to get out of control, investors could discover that even supposedly safe money-market funds might not be able to deliver cash on demand.

The quixotic nature of markets is such that this shift in mood could result from events ranging from an election to a financial crisis brought about by bad credit-card debt, the collapse of an insurance or banking giant, or some event abroad (it is worth noting that in 1987 the trigger for the crash was a credit tightening by the German Central Bank). Unless human nature or the nature of markets has changed, that mood swing would be rapid, and, given the amounts of money now under the discretion of individuals, any shift out of risk toward security could overwhelm the absorptive capacities of the U.S. markets.

The United States is not Mexico, of course, and that is both reassuring and disturbing. The U.S. market is so big and the dollar so important that it is inconceivable that authorities would allow a crisis to get out of hand. On the other hand, the U.S. market is so big, and so fundamental to global financial stability, that if it did get out of hand it is equally hard to imagine who or what short of a very rich Martian would have the liquidity and authority to restore balance.

The circulatory system that connects the U.S. economy to the financial stability of the global monetary system is the U.S. dollar. Only the American currency is large enough and liquid enough to act as the "reserve" or basic currency to support the world economy. In 1997, U.S. dollar securities accounted for $423 billion out of the world's $762 billion in foreign-currency reserves held by governments around the world, according to IMF statistics. More than 55 percent of foreign-currency reserves in industrial nations were in dollars in 1996, and the figure for developing nations was more than 62 percent. Actions that the U.S. might take in response to a market crash or severe economic downturn affect the economic health of virtually every nation on earth, and thus the dollar responds nearly instantaneously to moves by the Federal Reserve. (So do equity markets: in his testimony the day after the 554-point drop in the Dow Jones Average on October 27, 1997, Federal Reserve Chairman Alan Greenspan was handed updates on how the Dow was reacting to his remarks almost on a minute-by-minute basis.) Testimony to the global importance of the U.S. dollar was that, despite the supposedly inflationary pressures of extraordinarily low unemployment rates in the U.S., the Federal Reserve did not dare raise interest rates in the fall of 1997, because the attendant strengthening of the U.S. dollar might have driven several Asian nations closer to the brink of defaulting on their foreign loans.

The future stability of the dollar is hostage to other factors as well. One of the most important is who is holding American obligations. Today, the largest dollar hordes, much of the wealth in the form of foreign-held Treasury bills, are cached in the emerging economies of Asia and Latin America, where central banks do not share the historic sense of responsibility to the reserve currency of the European banks. Dollar accumulation in the exporting nations has been accompanied by some resentment; the price of the dollar as a reserve currency has been such that these high-growth economies have had to enter into a bargain in which they agreed to finance America's budget deficits. The alternative would be converting export earnings to yen or other local currency, which would drive down the dollar, pricing these countries' exports out of the market and decreasing the value of their U.S. investments.

The exporting countries also realize that any panicked attack on the dollar exposes the international bond markets to the same type of domino effect the stock market experienced in 1987, with traders forced to make billion-dollar decisions without clear information about real prices or the solvency of their counterparts. On June 23, 1997, a casual remark by Japanese Prime Minister Ryutaro Hashimoto that was interpreted to mean Japan might sell some of its $220-billion hoard of U.S. Treasury bonds caused the New York Stock Exchange to drop by 192 points in just a couple of hours, as traders contemplated a market flooded with dollars. The Japanese hastily clarified the prime minister's comment, and the stock and currency markets quickly stabilized. As the Asian financial contagion further weakened Japan's already wobbly banks toward the end of 1997, market players once again began to worry that Japan would be forced to liquidate U.S. T-bills to rescue its foundering financial institutions. It should be noted that, as of this writing, U.S. Treasury obligations are a beneficiary of Asian financial problems as investors seek a safe refuge for money. Moreover, the reduction of the U.S. budget deficit has slowed the increase in the supply of Treasury bills. Still, events in the rest of the world have demonstrated time and again that investor perception of risk can change rapidly and unpredictably.

What would it mean if the dollar suffered a rout analogous to the peso collapse of December 1994? Is it even possible?

The triumph of capitalism in this century has set the stage for an integrated global economy. As trade barriers fall, this global marketplace offers fabulous opportunities for nations, corporations, and individuals with the nimbleness to exploit it. The globalization of markets is supposed to spread risks and reduce volatility. Instead, it actually increases the likelihood of violent swings, because of the homogeneity and synchronicity that characterize the actions of the institutions governing the flows of capital.

This is why the collapse of the peso and the Thai baht provides a clue to the future. What trader who has become a student of how markets react to information is going to go against his instincts if the market decides on one unfortunate day that the Mexican peso, the Korean won, or even the U.S. dollar is toast? What happened in Mexico was but a dust devil on a summer day compared with what will happen ever more frequently in the coming decades.

Such episodes are an unavoidable product of the scale and interconnection of the global economy. The global economic situation resembles a herd of elephants crowding onto a high wire. A precipitous drop in the dollar could be handled by the international community—but only as long as no country with major dollar holdings decided to go it alone. Unfortunately, the pattern of history is that at some critical point someone always decides to go it alone.

The invisible hand of the marketplace may smoothly allocate capital and evenly respond to information in theory, but in the real world the process is herky-jerky, as imperfect, inattentive, and shortsighted financiers and politicians react and overreact to events. Shocks and adjustments are an inevitable part of any economic system, but as the scale of the integrated market grows, these jerks will only increase in frequency and amplitude, promising more instability in the future.

Chapter 2

KARACHI AND CURITIBA

IN THE POORER NATIONS of the world, the latter part of this century has seen a massive, unprecedented migration to the cities. The percentage of population living in cities in the richer countries increased by about 37 percent between 1950 and 1995, but the percentage of urban dwellers more than doubled in less developed nations during that same period and more than tripled in the least developed nations, according to UN statistics. The way in which the world's cities absorb this influx will have a profound impact on world health, the stability of nations, and the state of the biosphere in the coming decades.

To the degree that urban migration relieves population stresses on overburdened rural areas and gives people access to health care, clean energy sources, and efficiently constructed housing, this move to the cities is positive. In countries ranging from China to Rwanda, families have been forced, over generations, to subdivide their land holdings until the tiny plot a son inherits can barely support a family's needs, much less produce an income. Urban migration offers a possible soft-landing for these mounting pressures in the developing world. On the other hand, it could just as easily spur social, political, epidemiological, and environmental collapse.

Urban migration is one of those clues to the future that hide in plain sight. Few things on earth are more obvious than the exploding cities of the developing world. What they say about the future is more difficult to decode, however, because the signal is obscured by the cacophony and complexity of cities. Still, a signal is there.

Cities, more than any other human artifact, embody the indomitable human spirit. Again and again human aspiration will raise a city out of its own ashes, or foist order and art on anarchy. Any rise from the ashes, however, presupposes a prior collapse, and when cities collapse, havoc reigns. Today, even as the world's nations make an ever-larger bet on an urban future, there is no reason to believe that this rhythm of history has been interrupted. Consequently, the question is, Which part of the cycle are the megacities of the developing world now entering—renaissance or collapse? Since the great explosion in urban population in the developing world has occurred in this century, much of it since World War II, an enormous number of cities find themselves in a similar fix, and thus the answer will bear heavily on the future stability of the world. There is evidence for both answers, but ultimately I fear that the odds weigh overwhelmingly against a smooth maturation of the cities of the poorer nations.

In city after city, the urban poor have defied seemingly insurmountable obstacles to improve their lives in the face of hardship and indifferent government officials. In Karachi, Pakistan, the Orangi Pilot Project has mobilized people block by block to install a sewer system in a district of over one million souls. Other heartening stories about private initiatives launched by the poor in such megacities as Jakarta, Mexico City, and Calcutta have led to the development of a reassuring mythology about the unprecedented stampede to the cities that has occurred during this century. Get government out of the way of business, let the poor own their plots and homes, and watch human resourcefulness do the rest, goes this argument, which resonates harmoniously with the libertarian mood of the times. The argument is fine as far as it goes, but it does not go far enough.

In Karachi's case, success at upgrading the city's sanitation stops at the edge of the district where the Orangi sewer system dumps its wastes into low-lying areas and the sewage becomes someone else's problem. The project was started in the early 1980s by Akhter Hameed Khan, an architect, but it has not led to copycat successes elsewhere in Karachi, in part because bureaucrats, many of them from the dominant Sindhi ethnic group, have a long-standing enmity toward the district. It is largely populated by Mohajirs who emigrated to Pakistan from India. Moreover, OPP's successes are overshadowed by Karachi's wobble toward chaos. Although sanitation has dramatically cut Orangi's infant-mortality rate, as they mature Orangi's children must survive in a city plagued with epidemics, contend with the highest murder rate on earth, and then compete with four million unemployed for jobs. A city is more than a series of adjoining neighborhoods, and even if a spirit of self-reliance among the poor is a tremendous asset, it will not by itself secure the future of a metropolis.

If Karachi is to offer its citizens more than gunfire, disease, and blighted slums, it needs competent leadership that can find some accommodation between Karachi's trigger-happy ethnic factions; it needs professional police and courts; it needs to rid itself of a corrupt and incompetent bureaucracy; it needs open and honest markets; it needs laws and regulations that last beyond one administration; and it needs prosperity elsewhere in Pakistan to lessen the burden of a constant stream of migrants. With all these elements in place, the city might achieve the stability necessary to lure foreign capital and make the necessary massive investments in infrastructure. Then Karachi would only have to worry about such threats as climate change, the possibility of huge new tides of migrants loosed as population growth in the region continues to overtax economic and ecological resources, and the prospect of new plagues and resistant strains of old diseases that have profited from the new microbe-friendly environment created by human activities in the developing world in this century.

Karachi, of course, is but one of the developing world's megacities. Question marks also hang over Rio de Janeiro, São

Paulo, Mexico City, Calcutta, Delhi, Jakarta, and tens of thousands of smaller cities in Asia, Africa, and Latin America. The fastest-growing cities on the planet are not the giant metropolises, but anonymous secondary cities, agglomerations such as El Alto, a sprawling collection of five hundred thousand people in Bolivia that, siphoning people from the surrounding countryside, grows by 9 percent a year, with virtually no planning and the most haphazard infrastructure. These amorphous settlements must deal with all the problems facing a Karachi or a Jakarta without the claim on national attention and international assistance that flow to the more visible megacities.

Why should the West care what happens in the slums of the third world? With the ever-increasing integration of the world economy, problems that arise in one city can very quickly become global. The health of first-world cities depends in some measure on the success of developing nations in controlling the diseases incubating in slums. The West ignores these issues at its own peril.

Although the future of humanity is intimately joined to the fate of its cities, there is little in the way of hard information about the nature and sustainability of the world's vast conurbations. The one indisputable fact is that this century has seen a massive acceleration of the growth of cities. At the turn of the century, roughly only 5.5 percent of the world's population lived in cities with populations of over one hundred thousand. Between 1950 and 1995, the number of million-plus cities in the developed world more than doubled, going from 49 to 112. In that same period, however, the number of million-plus cities in the developing world rose by a factor of six, from 34 to 213. The UN estimates that rural numbers will remain virtually steady from now on, but urban populations will continue to explode. By how much is open to debate; the UN estimates that by 2025 more than five billion people, 61 percent of the projected population, will live in cities.

Given the continuing growth in human numbers, this concentration of people may well be the only efficient way to house humanity while still preserving agricultural acreage and wildlands. To determine, however, what steps governments might take to lessen the perils of this coming era of giant cities requires basic information not available today. It is difficult, for instance, to get a good fix on something as elementary as the size of the larger cities, because so many of the poor remain outside the formal economy of jobs and taxes that provides the statistical basis for government estimates. So many of the poor in Mexico City steal electricity by tapping into power lines that even electrical hookups fail to provide a reliable indicator of population. In 1992, some estimates put the population of Mexico City at twenty million; today the UN fixes the number at roughly fifteen and a half million; the difference between these figures is greater than the population of Baghdad.

If the world's megacities are perhaps smaller and less anomalous than popularly feared, the bad news is that the situation for the poor may be significantly worse than conventional wisdom holds. The general picture of the last half of the twentieth century offered by institutions such as the United Nations Development Program and the World Bank is one of tremendous improvement in health and income in the developing world: child mortality has been halved in the latter part of this century, and incomes in the developing world have more than doubled, according to the bank. Moreover, it has long been thought that, no matter how nasty and brutish are the living conditions facing the poor in cities, life there is still better than in the hinterland, where the poor traditionally have had little access to medicine, public-health services, or education. Anthropologists have long argued the contrary. Some public-health experts are now beginning to believe that the statistical portrait of the advantages of urban life does not capture dramatic declines in living standards for large numbers of the poor, who have become worse off than their counterparts in the countryside.

Studies of such disparate cities as Accra, Ghana, and São Paulo, Brazil, reveal that the poor bear a double burden of disease, finding themselves weakened by infectious water-borne diseases as well as the chronic problems, such as heart disease and cancers, traditionally associated with affluence. Thus the urban poor have to face the added stresses of urban life in a weakened state (in Africa, between 40 and 80 percent of urban dwellers are afflicted with one or more parasite at any given time; the resurgence of infectious disease will be discussed in detail in chapter 8), drinking and bathing with expensive and often bad water, surrounded by casually disposed-of toxic materials and chemicals, eating unhealthy, high-fat street food, breathing foully polluted air, and contending daily with ever more resilient microbes.

In many cities, the combination of disease, squalor, unemployment, and hopelessness conspires to aggravate another health hazard of urban life. Violence accounted for 86 percent of all deaths of teenage boys in São Paulo in one study conducted in the mid-1990s by Carolyn Stephens, an epidemiologist affiliated with the London School of Hygiene and Tropical Medicine. With roughly four million unemployed, many of them teenagers, Karachi has an endless supply of recruits for its ethnic militias and drive-by assassin teams. "You have a lot of people sitting around idly, and a lot of guns," said one World Bank official; "all you need is a little ideology and you can get your own army." The combustible combination of idleness, young men, and squalor is erupting throughout the developing world. In Algeria, it fuels the Islamic uprising; in Rio, a crime wave that has driven the middle class into garrisons and fostered vigilante justice; and in Mexico, a wave of kidnappings. The affluent can no longer move freely, for fear of assault. Ultimately, crime, disorder, pollution, and disease can reach a point where foreign investors retreat and a city begins a spiral into chaos. Karachi has flirted with that threshold in the past, and after a few years of growth, it may be approaching that tilt point again.

Kinshasa, the capital of the Congo, which from 1965 to 1997 was known as Zaire, has long since passed that threshold. Apart from the horrors its collapse has inflicted on its residents, its slow contraction offers a glimpse of how a city dies when its distress is caused not by war or civil strife but by the corruption and incompetence of government at all levels.

Kinshasa, a city of roughly four million people, began the

1990s with an excellent water system, cheap, reliable electricity, and a functioning system of public transportation. Then, in September 1991, unpaid government troops started a riot and looting spree that was quickly joined by ordinary citizens; the city was pillaged. During this unstructured shopping spree, roughly $1 billion in goods changed hands. Most expatriates fled the city in the subsequent confusion. Few expats have returned, and for the past three years the city has seen its formal economy shrink by 40 percent. Thousands of government jobs have disappeared; the city's water, electricity, and transportation infrastructures have slowly crumbled; and Kinshasa's businessmen have replaced store windows with concrete fronts and steel gates in anticipation of fresh looting and civil disorder. In the mornings and the evenings, the main roads often look like the scene of a forced march, as thousands of malnourished Kinshasans commute by foot in and out of downtown; most people can no longer afford to ride the few buses that still ply the potholed roads.

It is extremely difficult to get an accurate picture of the food and health situations, because of the default of the government at all levels. Still, representatives for several donor groups as well as the accounts of knowledgeable outsiders portray a city in which huge numbers of people eat only every other day, in which long-vanquished diseases such as the plague are returning, in which AIDS, tuberculosis, malaria, sleeping sickness, cholera, and river blindness spread, and, in the words of one recent visiting health professional, "health workers are encountering postoperative infections not seen in a hundred years." It is unrealistic to believe that resistant or newly virulent microbes flourishing amid the breakdown of health care and sanitation will remain confined to the city or region.

What most amazes visitors is that the city has continued to function at all. The true test of Kinshasans' resilience may come soon. Kinshasa's decline took place under the ostensible political stability of the late dictator Mobutu Sese Seko's government of crooks and cronies. Now the city is in the hands of Laurent Kabila and his revolutionary government. Even if his loyalists have the discipline to restore honest government, it remains to be seen whether Kinshasa's slide toward a public-health catastrophe can be halted.

Until recently, urban populations regularly rose and fell as disease, changes in trade and technology, and shifting political fortunes rewarded some cities and penalized others. Alexandria, one of the great cities of the ancient world, had shrunk to just a few thousand souls by the time Napoleon landed on Egypt's shores. One of today's remarkable changes has been that urban populations in the developing world now seem only to rise, driven by the seemingly infinite tide of humanity coming from the countryside. Even as its economy collapsed, Kinshasa's population continued to rise (although hard figures are impossible to come by). The economic and electoral might of the world's major cities already casts a long shadow, and as urban centers continue to absorb the great majority of those born in the coming decades, their power will only grow, as will the threat of turmoil when cities protect their interests.

Despite these dangers, many see movement to the cities as a positive development. Urbanization has long been viewed as a necessary step in economic development, although studies of Brazil and Mexico have shown that it need not lead there. Urban living carries with it built-in incentives to use mass transit, recycle refuse, use energy, water, and space efficiently, and do other things deemed desirable in an increasingly crowded world. In fact, the shift to the cities may be a major contributing factor in the rapid drop in birthrates now occurring throughout the developing world. Rural people moving to the city very quickly learn that extra children are an expensive liability when space is at a premium.

More than anything else, cities serve as a prism for the genius of civilizations. As Lewis Mumford put it, they are a "symbol of the possible," and this is true in the developing world no less than in the West. Faced with budget restraints and capital scarcity, some developing-world cities have experimented with creative solutions to their fundamental problems. Curitiba, Brazil, managed to increase parkland and improve sanitation and housing even as its population more than doubled during the past twenty-five years—and despite the limitations of a per-capita annual income of only $2,000. The key was leadership from a visionary mayor, Jaime Lerner, which has been carried on by his successor. One of Lerner's tenets has been to demand that people meet him halfway, so that they are actively engaged in solving the city's problems. For instance, he began an innovative plan to exchange surplus vegetables for garbage at designated points in those precincts of the city that could not be reached by municipal sanitation trucks, but one key aspect of the program has been the requirement that the neighborhoods collect, sort, and carry the garbage to pickup points.

Curitiba, Bangalore in India, and a few other cities are continually cited at conferences on the plight of urban areas as evidence that the problems facing the poorer cities are not so much their rate of growth or resource base but, rather, the absence of competent leadership. However, the extreme rarity of success stories set against a vast array of struggling municipalities suggests that, just as self-reliance in the poor is not sufficient to bootstrap a city, the lack of competent leadership cannot explain why so many cities are having difficulty creating an environment in which their citizens and businesses can prosper.

In fact, crucial to recognizing the role that cities will play in the future is an understanding of the degree to which their fortunes are ever more hostage to factors beyond their control. Population pressure and the increasing integration of the world economy have unleashed forces that can overwhelm a city no matter how well managed. To a degree, all poor cities today are at the mercy of that same restless $4 trillion in institutional capital that destabilized Mexico, and which roams the world like some giant pelagic bird searching for temporary and profitable places to alight.

As limits on supplies of water or food begin to appear, or, equally important, are perceived to appear, the potential for strife and disorder rises, particularly if there are huge disparities in wealth within a city or society. Other threats loom in the future. Sometime in the next century, cities may have to deal with the consequences of climate change. Even if this threat proves to be a chimera, population pressures have raised the stakes of ordinary climatic variations. More and more people live in harm's way. Many foreign investors already steer clear of Bangladesh because of the low-lying nation's vulnerability to typhoons.

Around the world, an estimated three hundred million people are directly at risk from a one-meter rise in the oceans. Should the world see more frequent and intense storms in the coming years, hundreds of millions more stand to suffer, since thirty of the world's fifty largest cities lie near coasts.

City dwellers have proved their resilience many times over. Beirut is now booming again, Kinshasa refuses to die, and Monrovia in Liberia and Mogadishu in Somalia still limp along despite years of civil war and hellish upheaval. Throughout history, however, cities have collapsed. It is possible to envision a future in which the world's urban population swells from three hundred million in 1950 to perhaps six billion in 2050 without massive collapse, but, unfortunately, it is not likely. As the population grows and cities become more crowded, the margins for error narrow, and the cost of mistakes rises.

In some cities, the right mix of inspired and honest leadership and public intolerance for squalor and corruption will provide the ingredients for some great urban experiments. On the other hand, there is little evidence in the present to suggest that such happy accidents will be the order of the day. Too few examples of such turnarounds exist in the developing world, against a vast tableau of urban failures. It is not a good idea to bet on a scenario that requires a new human being; to envision peaceful, functioning cities in 2050, one must also envision a law-abiding, harmonious, hardworking, ecology-conscious citizenry, supported by enlightened leaders.

The answer to the question whether cities will be part of the problem or part of the solution is that they will be both. There will be more Curitibas and Bangalores, as the resourceful poor strive for a better life throughout the developing world. Unfortunately, there will be many more cities plunging into decline, if only because coping with the stresses of urban crowding demands that people behave better than they can. Unstable cities project instability beyond their boundaries through the incubation and dissemination of microbes, through political and social disorder that can also spread as a contagion, through the disruption of national and regional economies, and through the launching of new tides of migrants—the subject of the next chapter.

Chapter 3

NO "VENT FOR SURPLUS"

If the exploding cities of the developing world are one indication of how demographic pressures will destabilize life in the next century, human migration is another. The urban migration which has fueled the growth of megacities mostly takes place within the borders of a nation, but migration also occurs on a regional and even a global scale. Though such mass movements of people are an obtrusive fact of modern life, the phenomenon is as old as humanity itself. *Homo sapiens* peopled the world in a vast radiation that probably started in Africa about two hundred thousand years ago. When sea levels temporarily dropped, beginning some thirty thousand years ago, the ancestors of today's Amerindians made their way across the Bering Land Bridge to populate two continents. In the nineteenth century, the potato famine drove hundreds of thousands of Irish to abandon their native land in a great migration that ended for many in the United States. Migration's relevance to the next century lies in subtle changes in the matrix of forces that push and pull people from their home country. War, political upheaval, and ethnic rivalry will continue to uproot people, but a whole new mix of pressures is contributing to migration as well, even as nations stiffen their resolve to bar the door to unwanted newcomers.

The potential for upheaval in these irreconcilable trends has captured the attention of the intelligence community. Deep in the recesses of the State Department and the CIA, analysts have been puzzling over a new form of campaign map. Plastered with thick black arrows, these charts seem to depict a world plunged into war. Some arrows lead from Ethiopia into Sudan, others from Somalia into Ethiopia, a series from Mexico, Haiti, and El Salvador into the United States, from Myanmar into Bangladesh, and from Bangladesh into India. The arrows do represent invasions, but the armies are composed of prey rather than predators: legions of the powerless, who must run a gauntlet of bandits, con men, and corrupt police and border guards. Their only weapon is the compassion they can inspire in others.

Refugees are a familiar presence in the world scene, but these migrants are different. Called "ecomigrants," they find themselves forced from their homes by two of the great forces of our age: environmental degradation and the dramatic increase in human numbers. Each arrow on these campaign maps represents tens of thousands of people. Perhaps twenty million worldwide have, in the course of the previous year, been forced to leave their homes because their lands have become too small, too barren, or too poisoned to sustain them.

History has shown that people tend to move when they find themselves squeezed for space, but what happens when there is no place to go? In the past, wildlands and new territories provided what the economist Adam Smith called a "vent for surplus." Migrants today are finding that there is no "vent for surplus" even as the population pressures and environmental degradation force greater numbers of people to uproot their families in search of new places to settle.

The U.S., which famously welcomed the world's tired and poor at the beginning of the twentieth century, has stiffened its resolve to control its borders, a decision driven by practicality as well as politics. If the U.S. opened its borders to ecomigrants, it would find itself besieged with petitioners from around the world. Haiti tries to support 7.2 million largely rural people on a denuded landscape that many experts estimate might at best sustain

3.5 million. The Immigration and Naturalization Service has compiled a list of fifteen other nations where environmental degradation and crowding play a significant role in spurring illegal immigration to the U.S.

In 1994, the United States, a nation whose current population is composed of people almost entirely of immigrant extraction, began forcibly returning to Haiti illegal immigrants intercepted at sea. Also in 1994, California passed Proposition 187, which denied many nonemergency services to illegal aliens. In 1995, the U.S. began returning Cuban rafters to the island they were trying to escape. In 1996, the U.S. Congress passed an act that eliminated many aid programs for illegal immigrants. Indeed, one of the fears that prompted the U.S. to guarantee a Mexican bailout was the possibility that economic collapse would prompt a massive increase in illegal immigration to the United States. As it now stands, an estimated one million illegal immigrants enter the United States each year, amounting to roughly a third of the nation's annual population growth.

Australia and Canada, two nations that in the past have encouraged immigration, have also moved dramatically toward more restrictive policies. In Europe, where there has never been any pretense of welcoming migrants, anti-immigrant sentiment is even stronger. In 1994, Italy forcibly returned boatloads of Albanians fleeing that nation's slide into economic and political chaos, nipping a burgeoning exodus in the bud; in France, which fears the prospect of an invasion by millions of Algerians should that nation further descend into anarchy, politicians all but pledge allegiance to anti-immigrant platforms before seeking national office.

The developing nations match the first world step for step when it comes to anti-immigrant attitudes. Gabon and the Ivory Coast, two reasonably stable sub-Saharan nations, have periodically forced wholesale expulsions of illegal aliens, who crowd locals for both jobs and living space. Nor is it only relatively prosperous nations that find aliens battering at the gates. Assam, India, has several hundred thousand illegal migrants from Bangladesh, and Bangladesh is coping with tides of migrants from

Burma. In the Himalayan kingdom of Bhutan, migrants from Nepal may soon outnumber the local ethnic groups; Tibet itself now has more Chinese than Tibetan residents. Until Russia took measures to stem the tide in 1994, Chinese from overcrowded, environmentally degraded Manchuria were crossing into the Russian Far East by the tens of thousands. Russia and China, two nuclear powers, have fought two border wars in this century.

Some of these movements have already contributed to conflict. Rwanda, one of the most densely populated African nations, still has one of the continent's highest birthrates. With finite amounts of land, families in this almost entirely rural nation are forced to subdivide their holdings with each successive generation. Competition for land between members of the Tutsi and Hutu tribes in Rwanda was a factor in tensions that led to a genocidal rampage against the Tutsi in 1994 by the majority Hutu. Once Tutsi rebels led by Paul Kagame took control of Rwanda, about one and a half million Hutu fled into neighboring Tanzania and Zaire. The impact of these refugees destabilized the eastern region of Zaire, and actually contributed to the unraveling of Mobutu's regime after thirty-two years in power.

In a bizarre series of events, Zaire, goaded by Hutu extremists they were supporting, decided to expel forcibly Tutsi settlers who had lived in eastern Zaire for generations. After a couple of massacres, the Tutsi joined forces with longtime Zairian rebel Laurent Kabila and very quickly routed both the Zairian troops and their Hutu compatriots, launching another exodus through the jungle for the miserable Hutu refugees who had not yet returned to Rwanda. Aided by a sympathetic population and by the incompetence of Zaire's army, which seemed to know only how to loot and flee, Kabila very quickly expanded his sights to include all of Zaire.

The example of Rwanda and Zaire shows how migration can set in motion ripples that in turn destabilize an entire region. The potential for catastrophic collisions of migrants and residents will only rise in the future, as the population continues to increase by roughly a hundred million a year.

*   *   *

Migration in response to population pressures is not a new phenomenon. Vast herds of bison and mammoth beckoned the ancestors of Amerindians across the Bering Land Bridge, linking Eurasia and the Americas, but these migrants were also pushed eastward because the land behind them was in all probability fully occupied. Similarly, the massive, three-hundred-year-long European migration to the Americas was impelled in part by the desire of immigrants to escape the repeated famines that bedeviled the European continent. Through much of this century, however, refugee movements have been attributed largely to warfare, political upheaval, and ruinous economic policies; only in recent years have experts on migration begun to look again at the role of population and environment.

The study of ecomigration falls within a new discipline called "environmental security." One of the new field's pioneers, Thomas Homer-Dixon of the University of Toronto's Peace and Conflict Studies Program, describes it as the study of the interactions of demographic pressures, environmental scarcity, economics, and politics in order to elucidate the connections between environmental degradation and political upheaval.

It is not an easy task to predict where environmental scarcity or pollution will be the dominant force driving migration. Time and again, humans have proved able to overcome limits seemingly imposed by resource scarcity and crowding. Countries ranging from South Korea to Singapore have shown that they can, to use Homer-Dixon's word, "decouple" their development from limitations imposed by land and resources, which means, simply enough, that they base their economic growth on the processing or trading of resources mined or harvested elsewhere. Moreover, many economists view migration as a positive thing. The movement of people from the farm to jobs in industry and services is fundamental to the process of development, and a mobile workforce will redistribute labor to where it is needed, lessening the potential for conflict.

Not every country, however, can "decouple" its economy from land and food; someone has to produce the food to sell to countries that, because of crowding or environmental degradation, can no longer grow their own. Food production failed to keep pace with population growth in seventy-five countries during the 1980s. In per-capita terms, fish production, fresh water, and arable land have all declined during the past fifteen years. Moreover, Homer-Dixon argues that scarcity can breed a chaos that in turn perpetuates scarcity.

Just as cities can pass some tipping point that sends them spiraling toward chaos, so can entire nations. Crowding and environmental scarcity can make it impossible for a nation to develop the stable markets and judicial structures that are essential if a society is to decouple its economy from natural limits. "The limits of a country are determined by both ecology and the intelligence of a society," said Homer-Dixon. "The poorer the resource base, the smarter you have to be. The wrinkle is that a society's capacity to be smart is in turn influenced by a nation's ecology."

This interaction makes migration a clue to life in the next century, for lifting an economy by its own bootstraps through the application of human ingenuity is no longer an option in such situations. Instead, a nation can find itself in a spiral of decline that cannot be remedied by either economic or political reform, except in very rare cases. Driven to extremes, people vote with their feet, through internal migration destabilizing both their home countries and neighboring lands. Three countries—Haiti, Mexico, and China—illustrate how population pressures, environmental degradation, and migration interact to foster political and economic upheaval.

Once a lush island nation that bewitched Spanish and French explorers with its fecund forests, Haiti has been transformed into a Mad Max landscape of stark, eroded hills. From space, it is easy to spot Haiti's border with the Dominican Republic: a line runs right across the island of Hispaniola, brown on the Haitian side and green on the other. During the rainy season, Haiti looks as if it were bleeding, as topsoil reddens the lagoons. All but 2 percent of the nation's dense forests have been cut, aggravating erosion and reducing the available water. Population pressures have driven people to clear and plow steep, erodable twenty-degree slopes. Laws requiring that land be equally divided among heirs have forced families to subdivide plots to the point where farmers cannot allow land to lie fallow or be reforested. Even with continuous working of the exhausted soil, most per-capita rural incomes remain stuck at a tiny $50 per year. Half of Haiti's farmland is considered unreclaimable.

Bad as things are now, they are likely to get worse. Even as agricultural production declines, the rate of population growth has risen in recent decades from 1.83 percent in the early 1980s to more than 2 percent now. While population grows, Haiti's economy has been contracting at about 1.3 percent a year for over twenty-five years. If the trends hold, thirty years from now there will be thirteen million Haitians, forced to eke out a living with even less arable land. What will the additional millions do for a living, what will they eat, where will they live?

Most likely they will try to live elsewhere, as 1.3 million Haitians did in 1995. Few observers disagree that the pressures for migration will continue, but the conventional wisdom holds that Haiti's problem is bad government, bad policies, and corruption, not population pressures and environmental degradation. Optimists like the late Julian Simon of the University of Maryland argue that the real resources of a country are its humans, not natural riches, and that, the more people there are, the more likely it is that human ingenuity will find a way to produce wealth. Once Haiti establishes honest police and courts, reduces tariffs and regulations, privatizes government enterprises, and clarifies ownership of property, goes this argument, the country will attract capital from investors seeking to take advantage of low wages and a business-friendly environment. A plan to promote these market-friendly initiatives is being pushed by the World Bank and other major donors.

But Haitian governments have been slow to implement these reforms. Part of the problem is that neither democratic leaders nor the elite still deeply embedded in Haiti are eager for these changes. In situations dominated by scarcity, notes Homer-Dixon, strong men tend to grab control of resources and have the power to prevent reforms from taking hold. This describes the situation in Haiti, where the feared Tonton Macoute, the auxiliary secret police who spread terror during the Duvalier dictatorships, still control the marketing of rice in Haiti's most fertile areas, according to sources in the U.S. government.

The Mexican landscape is in far better shape than Haiti's, but inexorable demographic forces still create an inevitable push for migration. The government estimates that nine hundred thousand people a year are forced off the land by desertification, as erosion and overuse renders agricultural lands unfit for farming. These legions must compete for jobs with another 950,000 young Mexicans who enter the labor market each year as a result of population growth, and the 1.5 million wage earners who lost their jobs in the economic crisis that has followed the collapse of the peso in December 1994. Compounding this situation has been a drought in the northern states, entering its fourth year in 1997. José Gómez de León of Mexico's National Population Council says ruefully, "It is a valid question as to whether policy can abate the pressures for migration."

Where will they go? Years of economic dislocation and powerful ties to the U.S. have left Mexico with well-established migration routes. In the past, roughly two-thirds of those thrown off the land would have migrated to a Mexican city, and the other third would have made their way legally or illegally to the United States (an immigration official wryly notes that in 1994 arrivals at the Tijuana airport outnumbered departures by 1.5 million, suggesting that much of the difference can be accounted for by people crossing on foot from Tijuana into the U.S.).

Mexican cities are reaching their absorptive capacity, limited by fundamental necessities such as access to fresh water. At the same time, migrants are finding it harder to cross into the U.S. as immigration authorities put more effort into policing America's borders. Thus, at a point when the number of potential migrants in Mexico is soaring, there are ever fewer places to go. Mexico is still contending with Indian discontent in Chiapas, spurred in part by conflicts over land between the Lacondon Indians and Mexican and Guatemalan migrants. Violence also flares up sporadically in Oaxaca, Guerrero, and other poor rural states. Indian and peasant uprisings could spread rapidly should millions of Mexicans find themselves in desperate circumstances with their traditional escape routes closed off.

Mexico's plight illustrates the ways in which environmental issues interact with political and economic issues. Because of uprisings in Chiapas and unrest in other states that were directly tied to land scarcity and desertification, Mexico's leaders were forced to pay attention to the needs of the poor at the expense of prudent monetary policy, particularly since 1994 was an election year. The government's limited policy options set the stage for the December 1994 crisis, and the result has been increased pressures for migration even as options for migration diminished.

Clearly, the potential for a huge new tide of illegal immigrants was yet another factor on the minds of policy makers in the United States when the Clinton administration put together the $52-billion package of loan guarantees following the peso crisis. Despite the urgent need to protect U.S. financial institutions and the potential for a mobbing of the border, President Clinton had a difficult time mobilizing political support for the bailout, in part because Republicans were questioning the concepts of safety nets and foreign aid. It is doubtful that other countries that find themselves facing an analogous spiral toward instability can count on the U.S. to help out.

Looming across the Pacific is a case in point. China, the world's most populous nation, faces building pressures for internal migration that terrify the government. Despite the economic boom that has given China one of the fastest-growing economies on earth, the communist government sits on top of a powder keg of forces that could produce mass movements within the country on an unprecedented scale. The outside world is treated to visions of skyscrapers and luxury hotels rising in Shanghai and Beijing, but in the northwest of the country millions of farmers try to grow crops on a plateau that is made of dust blowing in from the steppes of Eurasia. China's history is marked by a series of collapses brought about by uncontained population growth, according to Jack Goldstone, an expert on the history of revolution and rebellion. He argues that the stage is set for this cycle to be played out again.

The cycle, argues Goldstone, has been for China to outrun its resource base, collapse, and then, with the benefits of new technology, reach even higher human numbers before collapsing again. Between the fifteenth and seventeenth centuries during the Ming dynasty, for instance, the amount of available land per capita was nearly cut in half. Treasury receipts fell as hard-pressed peasants failed to pay taxes. In the early 1600s, rebellions joined by unpaid soldiers and peasants began to tear the dynasty apart.

During the ensuing chaos, so many people died that the successor Manchu dynasty had abundant lands at first. By 1850, however, China's population was 50 percent larger than it was in 1770, and land was even more scarce than it had been when the Ming dynasty collapsed. Massive migration in search of land destabilized the frontiers. By the middle of the nineteenth century, China again fell apart. Revolts culminating in the Taiping Rebellion, from 1850 to 1863, killed tens of millions of people.

The crucial elements for a new breakdown are in place today. In the past, says Goldstone, the mechanics of China's meltdowns involved a combination of prosperity and poverty. Merchants and landowners resented ever-increasing claims on wealth by the central government in Beijing, while arid regions in the northwest and the overpopulated Sichuan plain would rise up out of frustration and desperation. Migration helped catalyze this combustible mix, as the poor fought over land in the frontiers and low-paying jobs in the cities. In fact, internal migration driven by the search for land and jobs has been key to this cycle of breakdown and rebirth.

It is dangerous to generalize about a country as immense and complicated as China, but the nation today faces extreme pressures on land, growing disparities in prosperity between the booming coast and the crowded inland rural regions, and ever-growing internal migration on a vastly larger scale than has ever occurred before. Though the size of the country makes it difficult to amass reliable statistics, a few basic numbers starkly portray China's predicament. At present, between 70 and 75 percent of China's population remains rural, which means that the massive worldwide urban migration in this century has only just begun in the most populous nation on earth. In the ordinary course of development, hundreds of millions of people will likely shift to China's cities.

Exacerbating migration will be the environmental degradation and pressures on land. With 22 percent of the world's population, it has only 8 percent of the farmland. Even as its agricultural population of five hundred million grows by more than eight million people per year, the country continues to lose farmland to erosion, desertification, hydroelectric dams, and urban sprawl. Václav Smil, an expert on Chinese migration at the University of Manitoba in Canada, estimates that during the past three decades China has been losing as much as 1 percent of its arable land a year.

To find work for tens of millions of Chinese squeezed off the land by mechanization, population pressures, and environmental degradation, the central government has been promoting so-called township and village enterprises. These government-sponsored businesses typically involve small industries, such as brick factories or metal-plating installations. Many such ventures have been quite successful, but water and power scarcities limit their development.

The difficult trade-offs imposed by these scarcities offer a vision of what much of the world will be like as population figures continue their inexorable climb. Dam building provides power, but it floods precious farmlands and forces resettlement, fueling migration; water diverted to industry comes at the expense of farm production and domestic use.

These looming limits could exacerbate the disparities between the prosperity of China's cities and its huge rural population. That would mean more people attempting to migrate, first to rural cities and towns, and then to the coast. Should the cities bar the gates, Smil has estimated, the central government will have to contend with an army of two hundred million desperate unemployed rural people within twenty-five years. Goldstone notes that, if the central government instead allows unfettered migration to the cities, there will be vast increases in the groups over which the regime has the least control, ranging from entrepreneurs to the floating population. Another question is how many people the cities can absorb, given the growing problem of water scarcity.

Will these stresses, expressed by ever-increasing internal migration, tear China apart again, as they have in the past? At the least, Goldstone thinks they will bring about the fall of the communist regime. In a study of conflicts arising out of China's environmental problems, Goldstone speculates, "Once the glue of unified communist rule dissolves, China may once again, as it has so often in its history . . . experience a decade or even century-long interregnum of warring among regional states."

If the science of understanding ecomigration is still imperfect, the problem is becoming ever more visible. For all the uncertainties surrounding migration, it is clear that population and environment are rapidly moving up the ladder of influences on migration, even as the number of migrants steadily increases. It is unlikely that the world can prevent the continued rise of ecomigration. The image of vast armies of the wretched poor, surging around the globe and clamoring at the borders of the rich nations, will probably become more familiar in the coming decades.

The rich nations will face difficult choices. Because of declining birthrates and an aging population, many might benefit from an infusion of youth and vitality into the workforce and the ranks of consumers. On the other hand, the industrial nations have reached population stability at very crowded levels, and none has yet shown a desire to become known as a haven for the hundreds of millions of potential migrants. Moreover, even where there might be a need for workers, the French, the Germans, and the Japanese do not wish to become minorities in their own home-lands.

The potential for conflict rises even more if climate change begins to rework coastlines and rainfall patterns. Even a modest sea-level rise of one meter would force a hundred million people to flee river deltas and coastal lowlands in countries such as Bangladesh, Indonesia, and India, according to Stephen Leatherman, director of the Laboratory for Coastal Research at the University of Maryland. On higher ground, climate change could force a vast redistribution of humanity as changing rainfall patterns, ocean currents, and atmospheric circulation penalized some regions and rewarded others. Indeed, some models estimate that changing rainfall in Mexico could depress agricultural production by as much as 60 percent.

The increasing number of migrants forced to wander the globe is but one of the ominous indicators that the effects of overpopulation may already be appearing on the global stage. Another is the sheer scale of human suffering that occurs when things go awry, as they have in Rwanda, the Sudan, Ethiopia, Somalia, Liberia, Zaire (now the Congo), Iraq, Haiti, Cuba, Angola, and many other countries. Still other symptoms of the effects of growing human numbers are that humanitarian emergencies have become more frequent and longer-lasting, as well as more complex and dangerous. According to a State Department study of humanitarian emergencies, the number of complex emergencies— e.g., those involving drought as well as civil war—rose from an average of five a year in the late 1970s and early '80s, to more than twenty a year in the mid-1990s.

The enormous growth in human numbers is beginning to have an effect on attitudes toward suffering. Recent history has shown that, regardless of whether the world community has the capacity to respond to each new eruption of human misery, the number and complexity of events produce a type of empathy fatigue that dulls the sense of urgency crucial to mobilizing public support for humanitarian assistance. Public outcry over images of starvation in Somalia prompted President Bush to send U.S. troops to help restore order and prevent widespread looting of relief supplies. But American resolve was short-lived. It evaporated completely after subsequent television footage showed Somalis cheering as a dead American soldier was dragged through the streets of Mogadishu. As of this writing, Somalia is still in disarray. More than a million of its people were at risk in 1995, but there was no public clamor for the U.S. to act. In 1997, flooding destroyed crops and put half a million Somalis at risk of starvation, but, again, there was no public pressure for the U.S. to act. Nor is much attention paid to the three million Sudanese, 4.3 million Ethiopians, 1.6 million Eritreans, 3.7 million Angolans, 2.1 million Liberians, or the millions of Afghanis, Burmese, Sri Lankans, Yemenis, and other peoples who lived at risk of starvation in the mid-1990s. Though television and other media bring these catastrophes to the public attention, people can absorb and respond to only so much misery.

What will happen as the earth becomes more crowded while images of suffering become ever more available? Will people tune out and turn inward, if only to preserve their humanity? Very likely. Will xenophobia and various forms of racism become resurgent as those living in favored regions search for ways to rationalize their inability to help the millions who seek aid or entry? Also very likely. The point, however, is that population pressures affect societies in many surprising ways, putting huddled masses at the gates of their neighbors, yet fueling atavistic antagonisms that can dehumanize even those nations that feel smugly insulated from the overcrowded world. The rise of ecomigration offers a disturbing preview of coming upheavals.

Chapter 4

THE UBIQUITOUS
WAGE GAP

THIRTY YEARS AGO, POLITICAL scientists warned that a widening gap between rich and poor threatened to produce political and social upheaval. At that point, the richest 20 percent of the people on earth earned thirty times more than the poorest 20 percent. Instead of narrowing, however, that gap has expanded, so that the better-off now earn sixty times as much as the poorest.

This gap has widened despite statistics that show huge improvements in incomes, educational opportunities, and health care in the developing world, where the bulk of the world's poor live. How can this be? Part of the answer is a synergy between population growth and technological change, which rewards the educated and adept and marginalizes everyone else. Despite much-trumpeted improvements in nutrition and infant health, in 1996 more than 2.4 billion people—a number greater than the total world population in 1945—still lived on less than $2 a day. Despite an integrated global economy, two billion people, more than a third of the earth's human population, still live unconnected to the grid of the industrial world by either electricity or oil.

A country such as Indonesia can attract manufacturing jobs to the Jakarta area with labor priced at $1.50 a day, but industries can easily pick up stakes and find highly motivated workers elsewhere, should either workers or their governments make demands for higher wages or better working conditions. In the meantime, unrelenting migration from overpopulated agricultural regions gives workers ever-declining leverage over employers. In Egypt, where five hundred thousand new job seekers enter the market each year, per-capita income has fallen from $750 to $620 in eight years.

As these surplus workers become more desperate, the line between freedom and slavery begins to blur. In northeastern Brazil, agricultural workers live in perpetual indenturement to landowners who pay them so little that, no matter how hard they work, they only fall deeper into debt. In Africa, an organization called the American Anti-Slavery Group has produced evidence of the return of outright slavery in Mauretania and the Sudan. The group reported in *The New York Times* that, as supplies of slaves secured by raids increased, the price of a woman or a child dropped from $90 to $15 between 1989 and 1990.

The return of slavery is noteworthy because it is the extreme expression of a trend toward the marginalization of those at the bottom of the global economy. In an integrated global economy, consumers will have increasing power over how products are produced, so slavery is unlikely to return on a large scale, since the concept has become morally abhorrent in most of the world. Of course, there is no guarantee that the global economy will remain integrated fifty years from now, or that slavery will still be morally repugnant. If it does return to any significant degree, it is more likely to be camouflaged by the paternalism of landowners, corporations, or the state.

Around the world, 4.5 billion people live in conditions that James Gustave Speth, administrator of the United Nations Development Program, describes as "deplorable." Of that number, one billion live in absolute poverty. In 1996, Speth wrote that every day sixty-seven thousand babies a day—twenty-five million a year—are born into families so poor their parents cannot afford sufficient food to perform normal work. The International Labor Organization estimates that 750 million of the world labor force of 2.5 billion people are either unemployed or underemployed.

Thus the fruits of worldwide economic growth disproportionately accrue to an ever-smaller percent of the population. As a trend, this cannot continue without producing violent reactions from those left behind. The forces driving this widening gap—the population explosion, the integration of the world economy, and the automation of work—are fundamental. Moreover, two of these forces, technological advance and the increasing integration of the global economy, are the keys to present economy. So the world faces a dilemma: the widening income gap between rich and poor may be integral to continued economic growth as capitalism extends its reach and human numbers expand.

This widening gap is not confined to the developing world. In the U.S., twenty years ago the average CEO earned thirty-five times more than the average worker; now it is 150 times more. In that same period, the poorest 20 percent of U.S. workers have seen their real earnings drop by 24 percent, and the upper 20 percent have increased their real income by 10 percent. And in the wealthier nations alone, there are thirty million jobless. Speth describes the situation as a "famine of jobs" amid economic growth.

It is not just blue-collar workers who find themselves forced from their customary livelihoods. Whereas population pressures are a force driving unemployment and underemployment in the developing world, technology impels change in the richer nations: the information revolution is completing the automation of the workplace that began two hundred years ago with the industrial revolution.

First armies of blue-collar employees were swept away by efficiency improvements, but now hundreds of thousands of clerical, managerial, and other white-collar workers who never dreamed they might be out of a job are being laid off. Between 1979 and 1993, 18.7 million white-collar jobs disappeared in the United States. New jobs have been created as well, millions of them, but often at lower pay, with fewer benefits and less security. Many paternalistic and bureaucratic companies that resisted the trend for white-collar layoffs during the 1980s used the recession of 1991 and 1992 as an excuse to achieve workforce reductions that were in fact driven by technological change.

If the future were a simple projection of the past, most of these dislocated employees would find new opportunities after an initial period of turmoil. This time around, such happy endings are improbable for many. Computers can now analyze sales data, perform credit analyses, and allocate discount seats on airlines, and workers who developed such esoteric expertise are finding themselves out on the street with unmarketable skills. Sandwiched between a younger generation and well-educated, cheaper labor abroad, they have nowhere to go but down.

This picture of the future is at extreme variance with the conventional wisdom in the booming economy of 1997. With the global economy growing at nearly 4 percent a year, and the U.S. economy in its fifth year of sustained growth, both downsizing and integration were beginning to look like flat-out wins. U.S. productivity was climbing, and by December 1997, the 4.6-percent unemployment rate was the lowest in thirty years and below the 5-percent level considered to represent full employment. The unprecedented bull market created a lot of paper wealth as well.

If there was a troubling sign on the horizon in the U.S., it was that consumer debt in 1997 reached an all-time high at $1.2 trillion. This represented a 50-percent increase since 1991. Total household debt, which includes mortgages, reached $5.4 trillion, and by 1997 the average person was spending 18 percent of income just to service debt, the highest level since the mid-1980s, but in terms of burden, the highest level ever, since consumers no longer had the ability to deduct interest on debt from their taxes. Personal bankruptcies were also at an all-time high. By the middle of the year, credit-card delinquencies reached 7 percent, also near record levels; since most credit-card debt is repackaged by the card issuers as asset-backed bonds, rising delinquencies can rapidly spread through the financial system, undermining the liquidity of the card issuers as well as the institutions that trade the obligations.

Perhaps more significantly, the rising delinquencies revealed a fault line in the otherwise rosy economic landscape. A lot of different reasons account for the rise in bad credit, ranging from bad judgment on the part of credit-card issuers, to the declining stigma of bankruptcy, to the failing efforts of those with downsized incomes to maintain their former standards of living. But the combination of full employment with rising indebtedness and delinquency suggests that people are working harder, yet not making enough money to meet their material aspirations.

This fault line was also indicated by low inflation, conventionally interpreted as an indicator of the robustness of the economy. Ordinarily, low unemployment would be an indicator of future inflation, because, with labor scarce, employees could demand raise hikes and also pour money into the economy, driving up prices. In the 1990s economy, however, years of low unemployment and a booming economy did not result in wage hikes or in strong increases in consumer spending (except in services—a further indication that people were working harder, and thus forced to eat out more often and pay for functions like child care and laundry that housewives used to perform, before the advent of the two-income family). Savings continued their long-term downward trend. In the post-downsizing era, workers had nowhere near the perks, the guarantees, or, in many cases, the incomes they had in previous decades. Moreover, even with labor theoretically scarce, employers could turn to a steady supply of immigrants willing to work for very little. This is exactly what has happened. As the boom of the mid-1990s created a demand for new employees at the bottom end of the wage curve, Hispanic workers, many of them immigrants, joined the workforce at four times the rate of black or white workers.

The Federal Reserve Bank worried about inflation, but the combination of job insecurity, decreasing family incomes in the middle class, and global overcapacity in most industrial sectors created a strong momentum toward disinflation, if not deflation. Even as goods were getting cheaper in the U.S., thanks to imports, many Americans found that their discretionary income was relatively flat. The rising credit-card delinquencies reflected the reality that borrowers can suffer in deflationary times, particularly since real interest rates in 1997 were at a very high 4 percent and above.

With inflation, which tends to guide wage increases, hovering at 2 percent, many people were steadily falling behind in their ability to pay bills. If inflation and raises continue to fall because of global overcapacity on almost all goods, then the indebted will fall behind even faster, unless interest rates come down as well.

The entrepreneurial and gifted will still thrive in these harsh times for workers, but a growing population of white-collar workers whose fortunes have turned sour depresses the prospects of a country as a whole. In the U.S., consumer spending drives the economy, accounting for two-thirds of GDP. As mentioned earlier, layoffs in recent years have focused on professionals, managers, and administrators, the segment of the middle class that traditionally has the most discretionary income. Even those who escaped the recent rounds of downsizing have cut back on spending, out of fear for the future. In 1997, the U.S. had the strange situation of unprecedented peacetime growth, but a workforce made up of individuals who were scared to death about their own future. Businessmen who have slashed their workforce are now faced with the irony that their very strategy to improve profits poses a threat to their long-term prospects by contributing to a climate of consumer caution that puts a damper on spending.

A disenfranchised managerial class could pose a real threat to stability in the future. One need only look to the chaos of Russia in the early 1990s to see how difficult it is for white-collar workers with obsolete skills to adapt to new conditions, and how much mischief this politically sophisticated class can cause when it finds itself stripped of its perks.

Given such dangers, the first instinct of social planners has been to call for retraining programs, but this offers only a partial solution. The Information Highway allows employers to tap into a global talent pool. Mid-career Americans must compete for jobs with the European Community, which had 17.4 million unemployed in 1995, as well as legions of engineers, administrators, and accountants in Asia and Latin America who also must scramble for jobs as the trend toward corporate downsizing spreads around the world. Software companies can now hire low-cost teams of programmers in India to write code, and in the near future even these workers may find themselves automated out of jobs. The growing pool of modem-accessible workers may act as a cap on wages and job availability in the U.S. for years to come. A substantial percentage of America's white-collar workers face an indefinite future of limited prospects.

This means that a large pool of voters will have more reason to remain angry and dissatisfied, becoming fertile ground for radical and xenophobic causes. The danger to society comes not so much from extreme events such as the 1995 bombing of the Alfred P. Murrah Federal Building in Oklahoma City, which was the product of paranoid fantasies about government conspiracies, as from ever-wilder oscillations in political positions, in which moderates lose influence and the more passionate extremists take control of the political agenda.

This is one reason why the widening gap between the top and the bottom income groups cannot continue to widen indefinitely. The few can maintain their wealth only with the permission of the many. If the middle continues to stagnate in the developed countries while the top prospers, the majority will demand action, and politicians, being politicians, will give it to them. But what can they offer the middle and the poor, given the ceilings imposed by an integrated global economy?

One thing politicians can deliver is inflation. As a policy tool, inflation is always tempting, because it redistributes wealth from those who lend to those who owe, while camouflaging who did what to whom. Again, however, the potential negative reactions of the integrated global market means this is not really a policy option for the U.S.—which is not to say that it will not happen anyway. Responding to public anger, a populist or a demagogue might well come along promising a new New Deal brimming with deficit-financed social programs. This domestic policy would likely spook foreign holders of dollars, who would see it as inflationary and thus a de facto write-off of U.S. debts. If an economic downturn produced protracted misery, demagogues might call for an outright repudiation of the U.S. debt burden, and the mere threat of this could spur a panic. Alternatively, U.S. politicians like Pat

Buchanan or Ross Perot who call for more protectionist trade policies might have their day; as other nations respond—enacting tariffs and other barriers to protect favored industries—the world
could descend into a cascade of mercantilism that would be as
destabilizing as a panicked run on the dollar.

In the developing world, the resolution of the widening gap
promises to be even more unruly, as the examples of Mexico and
China cited earlier suggest. Many of the countries with the widest
gaps between rich and poor, such as Russia and Venezuela, have
fragile democracies. One conclusion of a confidential CIA-spon-
sored study of the nations that collapsed over the past forty years
was that emerging democracies were more unstable than dictatorships when times turn bad, because people can give voice to frustrations for the first time yet democratic institutions remain too
weak to address the underlying causes of the misery.

Could the widening gap between rich and poor resolve itself
painlessly? Theoretically, this could happen if a global economic
boom outpaced both population growth and the application of
productivity improvements. However, even with global economic
growth at nearly 4 percent a year in 1997, the gap continues to
widen.

The gap might also narrow if labor became scarce again. With
the global workforce growing by over fifty million people a year, this
is not likely barring some catastrophe or radical social change. The
latter happened in Afghanistan, where the Taliban has enforced a
harsh version of Islamic law and forced women to abandon jobs for
home life, greatly reducing the number of professionals.

The gap between the rich and poor cannot widen indefinitely
without producing instability, and it is difficult to imagine it shifting
toward a more equitable distribution of wealth without instability.
The forces marginalizing both ordinary labor and knowledge workers derive from deep, long-term trends, including the automation of
the workplace, the integration of the global economy, technological advances that permit companies to tap a global labor market for
many types of work, and the inexorable expansion of human numbers. None of these trends will change without upheaval.

Chapter 5

A WARNING FROM
THE ICE

THE MESSAGES THE WORLD has been getting from its atmosphere and climate have been hard to ignore, even if they are difficult to interpret.

In the early 1980s, Joseph Farman of the British Antarctic survey began getting unusual readings of stratospheric ozone above the skies of Antarctica. Ozone, a form of oxygen, is a pollutant in the lower atmosphere, but in the stratosphere it shields life on earth from lethal forms of ultraviolet radiation. The readings Farman saw during the Antarctic spring suggested that there was virtually no ozone in the skies above his station. At that time, scientists knew that man-made chlorofluorocarbons (CFCs) could destroy ozone, but all the models for ozone depletion then being used predicted a slow decline, not the catastrophic numbers Farman was looking at. Initially, he dismissed his readings, thinking that his instruments were in error. It was not until 1985 that atmospheric chemists began to realize that the Antarctic skies were sending a message.

The message was that humanity had unleashed an entirely new chemical reaction in the atmosphere, a process powerful enough to punch a hole the size of North America in a shield that protects life itself. Seven years after these first readings, the international community acted, forging an agreement for the phasing out of the chemicals that jeopardized the ozone layer. Because of the long life (sixty years) of these chemicals in the atmosphere, however, humanity will be living with the still-unknown consequences of continuing ozone depletion until well into the next century.

More recently, the ice continent sent out a new signal, but this one may prove much more difficult to decode. On March 26, 1995, a massive iceberg—measuring forty-eight by twenty-three miles—broke off from the Larsen Ice Shelf in Antarctica. At the same time, the three-hundred-foot-thick ice shelf that bridged the Prince Gustave Channel, between Antarctica and James Ross Island, disintegrated, allowing ships to circumnavigate the island for the first time in recorded history. Elsewhere on the frozen continent, rocks poked through ice that had been buried under nearly two thousand feet of ice for more than twenty thousand years. Since the 1950s, the Wordie Ice Shelf, Antarctica's most northerly stretch of permanent sea ice, has disappeared, moving the upper limit of the ice dramatically southward. And one gigantic river of ice within the West Antarctic Ice Sheet seems to be surging toward the coast.

Some of these events, like the huge calving of bergs off the Larsen Ice Shelf, are part of the normal dynamics of ice flow. Others, however, may be signaling that human actions are beginning to have an impact on this vast and icy realm.

The cause of the breakup of the peninsular ice shelves is clear. Since the 1940s, parts of Antarctica have warmed by nearly five degrees Fahrenheit, as evidenced by records at the United Kingdom's Faraday Station. The reason for the warming is far less clear, but these rapid changes in Antarctic ice must give pause to hundreds of millions of coastal dwellers around the world. The West Antarctic Ice Sheet is half the size of the U.S. and more than three miles thick at its deepest point. Were it to break up or slide into the ocean, sea level around the world might suddenly rise by twenty feet, imperiling billions of people, inundating ports, drowning megacities like Jakarta, putting almost the entire Florida peninsula under water, and flooding millions of acres of prime coastal agricultural lands.

That is not likely to happen, but there are other, more subtle changes afoot in the world's climate. For the past few years, scientists at Germany's Max Planck Institute have been puzzling over what some believe to be a steady increase in the size of waves in the North Atlantic. Waves are a creation of winds. Given the world's limited view of what takes place across the vast reaches of the world's oceans, it is difficult to determine whether waves are getting bigger, and if they are, for what reason.

Glaciers are also melting rapidly throughout the middle latitudes and the tropics, where they exist at very high elevations. It was the melting of Alpine glaciers in Switzerland that in 1992 uncovered the famous "Ice Man," who had been entombed for five thousand years. Warm-weather plants and insects are marching up mountain slopes as the freezing line moves higher. Spring is coming earlier in Siberia, and birds are migrating northward earlier through Great Britain. If breezes are stiffening, glaciers retreating, and ice sheets melting, the question arises whether earth's vast systems for distributing energy are beginning to respond to human tampering with the biosphere.

This question, and the uncertainty it injects into human affairs, has crucial bearing on the future, whether it is humans or normal fluctuations in climate that are responsible for the changes. The issue of wave size alone forces people around the world to reappraise their prospects. Actuaries charged with determining insurance rates for shipping companies must estimate whether there is increased probability of shipwrecks, coastal surveyors will have to recompile their estimates of future beach erosion, and millions of home buyers will think again about how close to the ocean they really want to be. And this is just one of myriad issues raised by the prospect that the gases released into the atmosphere by humans in this century will produce climate changes that will affect life on earth in the next.

Will climate change warm the oceans, raising sea level and inundating coastal areas; will warmer water in the tropics lead to longer hurricane seasons marked by more frequent and intense storms? Will changes in earth's heat budget alter atmospheric and oceanic currents, plunging some areas into drought and leaving others awash with rain? Will change be rapid, or slow enough that crops, forests, and creatures can adapt? If climate change should arrive, will it be noticeable at all?

Such are the complexities of climate that, long after global warming arrives (should it arrive), scientists will probably still be arguing about whether changes in climate have come about because of natural variation or because of human impacts on the atmosphere. But that has nothing to do with the impact of the *prospect* of climate change. Climate change has already affected the way people think about the future.

People must now live with uncertainty. Given the relationship between global temperatures and levels of greenhouse gases, people cannot ignore the possibility of climate change in planning for the future. Those whose livelihoods are affected can no longer rely on the past as a guide to determine what will likely happen to the climate in the future.

The world is already beginning to see the consequences of this uncertainty. No industry has more of a stake in knowing whether the world climate is entering a period of instability than the $670-billion global property-insurance industry. Insurance rates are prospective, meaning that they are based on estimates of risk over the coming years. Until recently, insurers looked at past incidence of hurricanes and other extreme natural events for guidance in setting rates, but an unprecedented series of natural disasters have shaken the industry, bringing a number of companies, including the giant syndicate Lloyd's of London, to the brink of insolvency. From the industry's point of view, climate change is already here. Natural disasters during the 1980s, for instance, were 94 percent more frequent than in the previous decade.

So far, the 1990s promise to be even worse. Hurricanes Andrew and Iniki together caused $19.5 billion in insured losses in 1992 and left twelve insurance companies insolvent. Hurricane Andrew's insured loss of $15.5 billion—the total damage caused by this monster storm amounted to $30 billion—wiped out premium income collected during the previous twenty years. The combination of Hurricane Gilbert in 1988, which cost Lloyd's of London about $1.8 billion, and Hugo, which in 1989 hit Lloyd's for $3.3 billion, and a series of other costly windstorms almost brought down the venerable insurance syndicate. The drought-intensified Oakland, California, fires of 1991 produced $1.7 billion in insured losses; more wildfires in Los Angeles two years later caused $600 million more in losses. The 1993 floods in the Midwest caused $13 billion in damage, and 1995 saw more "floods of the century" in the Southeastern U.S.

In just a five-year period, the U.S. suffered two "hurricanes of the century" (Andrew and Hugo), a "five-hundred-year flood" (the 1993 Midwestern floods), at least two "floods of the century" (the 1995 floods in the Southeast and in the Red River Valley in 1997), and "a drought of the century" (in California). And that was just the United States. A 1993 study by Munich Re, a giant reinsurance firm, estimated that windstorms and other natural disasters in 1990 produced losses of roughly $50 billion and killed fifty thousand people worldwide.

Unusual weather has indirect effects not tabulated in insurance losses. An extraordinarily long spring monsoon in India in 1994 was followed by ninety days of temperatures above a hundred degrees Fahrenheit—a "heat wave of the century." Rodents driven into town by the extreme heat proliferated in stores of grain donated to ease suffering following an earthquake, bringing with them an outbreak of pneumonic plague that briefly panicked the city of Surat and ultimately cost India $2 billion, as tourists and businessmen alike canceled trips. The flooding and heat also spurred a dramatic increase in cases of malaria and dengue fever.

Any of these specific events could be the result of chance and normal fluctuations in climate, but other changes seem to be happening on a global scale. Nine of the warmest years in this century have occurred during the last eleven years. During the past century, sea level worldwide has risen between four and ten inches, driven by an increase of one degree Fahrenheit in average temperatures and the melting of glaciers around the world. Stephen Leatherman notes that sea level is now at the highest mark in the past five thousand years, and is rising at a rate ten times faster than the average during that period.

The rate of rise over the last century has been two millimeters a year. This does not sound like much, but it is enough to be causing erosion of 90 percent of America's beaches. The one-foot rise in sea level, as has happened along much of the Eastern U.S. because of accompanying subsidence of the land, causes beaches to recede an average of two to three hundred feet, reducing the barriers that protect the $2 trillion in insured property along the Atlantic and Gulf coasts of the U.S. Thus insurers must worry about an apparent increase in the severity and frequency of storms at the same time that beach defenses are disappearing and seas are rising.

Many scientists don't expect global warming to begin to show its effects for a few decades, but some of the changes in the current global climate provide a vivid preview of what is to come. On September 16, 1991, Typhoon Mirielle swept across Japan, the first severe storm to hit that nation in thirty years. The storm left behind $5.4 billion in insured losses, and gave the Japanese insurance industry religion about global warming. A study by the Tokyo Marine and Fire Company asserted that the storm had several unusual features, including extremely low central air pressure, extreme speed, and a path that diverged from the customary track of typhoons in that region. The insurance company suggested that storms similar to Mirielle might become more frequent with global warming.

Some scientists are convinced that changes in the weather already bear the signature of human impacts. Thomas Karl, director of the National Climatic Data Center, headed a study that examined one very likely consequence of the greenhouse effect—an increase in the frequency of extreme rainfalls. As temperatures rise, there is more potential energy for storms, and the atmosphere's ability to hold moisture increases as well. Defining as "extreme" storms that produced more than two inches of rain in a twenty-four-hour period, Karl found that, since 1976, such events have occurred roughly 3 percent more frequently in the U.S. than during any comparable previous period in this century. The period from 1980 to 1994 showed a 4-percent increase over previous fourteen-year periods.

Karl, who is taken seriously by all sides of the debate because he launched his study as a skeptic of predictions of global warming, is 90–95 percent certain that this steady increase in extreme weather events provides evidence that the greenhouse effect is beginning to alter the world's climate. From an insurer's point of view, the cause really does not matter. What matters is that the world seems to be changing, and if these changes persist, insurers face the prospect of ever-increasing losses. A study by Travelers Corporation of Hartford, Connecticut, estimates that even a modest .9-degree-Fahrenheit increase in global temperatures by the year 2010 could produce a twenty-day extension of the hurricane season, a 33-percent jump in hurricane landfalls in the U.S., and a 30-percent rise in catastrophic losses. Even a small strengthening of storm winds can produce dramatically higher insurance claims. By one estimate, a wind-speed increase of only five knots would have doubled the $3 billion in losses incurred during a 1987 storm in Europe.

No wonder insurers are retreating from coastal properties and islands around the world. Following a series of costly hurricanes, Allstate and Prudential stopped writing homeowner policies in coastal areas of Florida. Travelers, which lost $240 million because of Andrew, stopped writing policies in parts of Florida and pulled out of coastal areas in Connecticut and New York as well. Where, for political reasons, insurers cannot pull out, they have raised rates. Between 1989 and 1993, the price insurers pay to protect themselves against catastrophic losses rose 400 percent in the U.S., 650 percent in the U.K., and 1,000 percent in Japan. In the Pacific and the Caribbean, major insurers have pulled out of many island markets altogether; this in turn has cooled the ardor of banks to write mortgages, since lenders risk losing their investment with the next storm.

One ironic, and telling, aspect of the insurance industry's reaction to the prospect of global warming is that in this case the business world is far less cautious about predicting more intense and frequent storms as a consequence of global warming than is the scientific community. Though few scientists dispute Karl's assertions about rainstorms, some, like J. D. Mahlman of the National Oceanic and Atmospheric Administration, argue that an increase in the number and intensity of major weather events is possible, but not yet supported by evidence. The reaction of the insurance industry shows, however, that such "possible" future consequences have very real effects on present-day behavior: nature provides an industry in the line of fire with a preview of how costly those consequences might be in the years to come.

Inevitably, insurers' and banks' changing attitudes toward climate will begin to affect the purchasing and political behavior of ordinary people, changing their views both of nature and of risk. As the costs of extremes in climate ripple through society, people in the developed world will also rediscover that climate, fair or foul, is the context for all human activity, and that nature is more than a backdrop. This reorientation will have profound effects on everything from demographics to religion.

Chapter 6

A BIOSPHERE
IN DISARRAY

A FEW YEARS AGO, biologist Thomas Eisner and colleagues came upon a curious plant in the mint family that grew in only a few hundred acres in central Florida. Despite the fact that *Dicerandra frutescens* had tempting, succulent leaves, the plant was not bothered by insects. Subsequent investigation revealed that, to protect itself, the plant produced a powerful insect-repellent, and that it had developed an arsenal of antifungal compounds as well. Like a midget R&D laboratory, this one plant, growing on a mere speck of land, may lead to new products for the multibillion-dollar insect-repellent and antifungal industries. Who knows what other chemical miracles were produced by neighboring species but have now disappeared because of urbanization and agricultural development? Development might well have wiped out this species as well, except that the tiny niche where it grows lies in a biological preserve.

A happy story? Just the opposite. Although the succulent is protected for the moment, most of Florida is an ecological disaster. Development-driven decisions to tame the Everglades and turn the land to agriculture have led to the collapse of its bird and mammal populations, and contributed to the destabilization of Florida Bay, which now suffocates under regular algal blooms. There are still wood storks and white ibises, but their numbers have dropped by 90 percent in this century. Each of Florida's indigenous species adapted to perform some role in the maintenance of the system. When populations collapse, the system falls into disarray, and ultimately that disarray affects humans as well.

This is the clue camouflaged by the more dramatic problem of extinction. Extinction has been sold to the public as a problem for humanity because drug companies lose valuable sources of new pharmacologically active agents. That impression has been bolstered by the negotiations surrounding the Biodiversity Treaty, which came out of the vaunted Earth Summit that took place in Rio de Janeiro in 1992. The treaty was supposed to be an international accord to protect species and ecosystems, but it has degenerated into a squabble over issues of intellectual property.

The loss of biodiversity, however, is much, much more than a problem of intellectual property, or even of protecting individual species. It cannot be fixed by protecting representative samples of earth's biota in preserves, or simply giving people rights to benefit financially from the wonders nature creates as species struggle to survive. Long before creatures begin to go extinct, the ecosystems that support them can get so fragmented or diminished that they become dangerously spastic, as both symbiotic and predator-prey relationships break down.

Earth has gone through five major extinction crises during the past few billion years, including the Permian extinctions of 245 million years ago, which wiped out three-quarters of the life forms on earth, and the cataclysm of sixty-five million years ago, which spelled the doom of the dinosaurs. It is going through one now, and this promises to be a whopper.

Previous extinction crises resulted from titanic geophysical changes that precipitously changed earth's climate, such as epic episodes of volcanism, or the catastrophic aftereffects of comets crashing into the planet.

Today's crisis is the product of the direct and indirect effects of human activities. Destruction of habitat is the biggest culprit. Migratory birds find they have no place to land or breed as wetlands and forests vanish. In Africa, brilliantly colored mouthbreeding fish called cichlids are losing their species diversity and merging into a dull-colored mongrel because human contamination of the lake waters has made it too difficult for females to distinguish the markings of their proper mates. Almost all the great apes in Africa are now endangered, in part from hunting, in part from disease, and in part from habitat destruction as land is converted for agriculture. With the great apes, the social upheavals of these changes can be as destructive as the loss of habitat itself, argues Lee White of the Wildlife Conservation Society: logging is driving chimp bands into neighboring territories, setting off fierce chimp wars in which as many as four out of five animals die in hand-to-hand combat.

Whereas many previous extinction events developed over time scales of many thousands of years and more, the present loss of biodiversity has accelerated in just a few decades. On any future chart plotting species diversity over time, the loss of biodiversity will appear instantaneous, as though some awful contagion swept around the globe indifferently extinguishing species. Not only rare, precariously specialized species like the river dolphin are succumbing, but also some of nature's most ubiquitous lines, such as frogs and sea turtles; the latter had survived the aftershocks of comets, the reign of volcanoes, and twenty ice ages, but not the combined effects of air and water pollution, ozone depletion, human encroachments on habitat, and the diseases unleashed by all of these disturbances.

Fictions like *Jurassic Park* notwithstanding, extinction is irreversible. Even if it were possible to bring extinct forms back to life, their importance to life on earth is the role they play in an ecosystem. As scientists have discovered, it is extremely difficult to restore a damaged ecosystem, even when all the parts are still available.

No one really knows how many species are disappearing, because no one really knows how many species there are. Scientists have documented only 1.4 million species of plants, animals, insects, fungi, etc., but the full range of the diversity of life on dry land and in the oceans may include between thirty and a hundred million species if bacteria and other microscopic life forms are included. Skeptics openly ridicule the notion that humanity should worry about saving every bacteria, gnat, or salamander, noting that nature herself has done in countless species down through the ages without jeopardizing life on earth.

This is true, but not the issue. The loss of biodiversity puts humanity in the position of assuming that we know exactly which species we can do without. This is dubious, since scientists have only the most rudimentary notion of what makes an ecosystem work. In just a few cases do scientists know which creatures are crucial to the functioning of an ecosystem. Nor, since values and technology change in unpredictable ways, do we know which species might prove vital to our health and well-being in the future.

Moreover, if the only issue were conserving the greatest number of species, governments could go a long way in that direction by protecting so-called biodiversity hot spots around the world. Most of the world's species live in relatively few places, such as the eastern slopes of the Andes, the island of Madagascar, and the Philippines, through accidents of geography and continental drift. The Geneva-based International Union for the Conservation of Nature estimates that targeting for protection these strategically important ecosystems alone, which cover less than 3 percent of the globe, would ensure the survival of more than 50 percent of earth's biota.

The biodiversity crisis, however, is much more than a simple question of accounting. Animals, plants, and insects do not have to become extinct for an ecosystem to begin a wobble toward chaos. The issue is not simply how many individuals of a given species remain, but where they are—and, equally important for migratory creatures, where they can go. Even though they may persist in large numbers in the aggregate, the disappearance of a species from a given locality can lead to a dramatic decline in an ecosystem.

Consider, for instance, the missing elephants of West Africa. Elephants are not extinct, but they have been hunted out of many of the forests of the Ivory Coast, Sierra Leone, Cameroon, Nigeria, and a host of other sub-Saharan countries. Today, they persist in any concentrations only in a corner of central Africa where the Congo, the Central African Republic, and Cameroon meet. (In Kenya, Zimbabwe, and a few other East and Southern African nations, elephant populations have recovered somewhat, but find themselves crowded out of most of their original habitat by farmers.) There is no confusing these forests with those in the region that no longer have elephants. The remote Ndoki region of the northern Congo is crisscrossed with elephant trails. The main trails tend to run north to south, but they intersect with east-to-west trails linking the elephant thoroughfares to favorite watering holes and mud baths. It seems that elephants, like urban planners, favor a grid pattern for their transportation infrastructure. Scattered through the region are *bais*, or clearings, created by the elephants.

Countless animals benefit from the earthworks of this elephant civilization. Terrestrial herbaceous vegetation, or THV, abounds in the gaps the elephants create in the forest, thus providing food for the lowland gorilla, the bongo, and other large grazing creatures. Perhaps because of the transportation infrastructure created by elephants, this region of central Africa has some of the densest concentrations of gorillas on earth. Also, as the only animal capable of passing the large seeds of some species of trees—including some members of the mahogany family, which is prized by loggers—the elephant is crucial to the forest.

When elephants are eradicated, the forest gradually reclaims their roads and clearings, reducing ground vegetation. Over time, gorillas and the large ungulates disappear as well. A number of scientists argue that the trickle-down effects of elephants may explain why Africa's forests abound with large mammals but the tropical forests of South America do not.

Few would doubt that the largest land mammal on earth would play a crucial role in its ecosystem, but smaller, less charismatic creatures also turn out to be surprisingly important. As

noted earlier, parrot fish and other coral-reef grazers prevent algae from covering corals. When parrot fish are overharvested,
corals suffocate, and the whole reef ecosystem begins to collapse.

Innumerable such dislocations are occurring around the
world, always accompanied by unanticipated consequences. The
disappearance of predators in the Northeastern U.S. led to a huge
increase in deer populations and their attendant deer ticks. As a
result, Lyme disease, unknown and unnamed two decades ago, is
now epidemic virtually throughout the U.S.

It would seem that saving ecosystems should be an urgent
undertaking that governments would pursue in their own interest.
In reality, most governments treat the notion of ecosystem conservation as an amenity issue, except where wildlands provide watershed or some other function easily reducible to an economic
argument.

Even if the international community made the preservation of
earth's life-support systems the world's most urgent priority, the
nature of ecosystems makes them ill-suited for the neat, system-
atic attempts at preservation favored by bureaucrats. What is an
ecosystem anyway? Is it Yellowstone Park, or the swamps, pine
deserts, wetlands, and other distinct biomes within the park, or is
it the park and the surrounding forests and mountains that provide its watershed, corridors, and buffers? According to the current theory of ecosystem viability, if Yellowstone Park and its
surrounding protected areas were not sufficient to protect the
ecosystem, over time species populations would diminish. They
have not, suggesting that Yellowstone, at least, is big enough to
remain vital. Yellowstone, however, is the largest park in the
lower forty-eight states. Most of America's other parks show declining populations of key species. This may suggest that the
parks are either too small or too isolated from vital migration corridors.

That is the problem. Life on earth is so complicated that neither scientists nor governments can answer such basic questions
as the minimum size of a protected area necessary to preserve its

life forms in perpetuity; the minimum population of a species before it enters the slippery slope toward extinction; or when a population of a species becomes so isolated that it loses its genetic
vitality, expressed by the splitting of populations into evolutionar-
ily distinct groups.

Even if scientists could answer these questions and impose
ironclad protections for regions vital to ecosystems, both humanity and earth's creatures are now vulnerable to global forces unleashed by humans. For instance, the polluted Arctic front, a curse
laid on the Far North by the industrial world, results from global
air currents that pool the collected contaminants of the Northern
Hemisphere over the polar region during wintertime. The contaminants condense and fall with snow, and then, during the spring
melt, they go into the tundra, where they are taken up by animals
and plants and the people who eat them. Because of the Arctic
front as well as ocean dumping of radioactive and toxic material,
animals and humans in some of the most remote parts of the Far
North carry huge concentrations of mercury and carcinogens in
their fat and hair. Some seals in the Arctic Russian Far East have
radioactive growth-rings in their teeth. The bodies of some whales
that wash up in the mouth of the St. Lawrence Seaway contain
such concentrations of toxins that they would be declared a haz-
ardous-waste site in the United States.

Despite the fact that the pesticide DDT was banned by the
U.S. and most industrial countries in the 1970s, its use in the developing world still threatens bird life. As reported by Les Line in
The New York Times, the reach of the poisons extends to Midway
Island, smack in the center of the Pacific Ocean and thousands of
miles from any industrial or agricultural center; here DDT is one
of several toxins accumulating in the bodies of the black-footed
albatross, a giant pelagic bird with a seven-foot wingspan. The
DDT, which the birds ingest with flying-fish eggs, causes their
own eggshells to thin, leading to crushing and high mortality
among chicks.

There is no part of the globe where species and ecosystems
do not already feel the weight of humanity. A team of ecologists

led by Peter Vitousek of Stanford University published an account of human domination of earth's ecosystems in the journal *Science* in 1997. The figures this group produced are awesome: half the world's mangroves, vital buffers and nurseries of the oceans, altered or destroyed; 66 percent of all recognized marine fisheries either at the limit of their exploitation or already overexploited; half the accessible fresh water on earth co-opted for human use; roughly one-quarter of all bird species on earth driven into extinction; and on and on.

Lurking in the future are the unfolding consequences of ozone depletion, which may be weakening the immune systems of many creatures on the planet, and the dislocations of ecosystems that may come from climate change. Clearly, a changed climate poses a profound threat to any creature that has adapted to a narrow range of temperature and rainfall, but the subtle ways in which climate change might throw ecosystems into chaos were dramatically demonstrated on remote Wrangell Island, in the Russian Arctic, just a few years ago.

The dominant land-based predator in this ecosystem is the polar bear. The white bear is a kind of mirror image of a marine mammal, spending most of its life at sea, albeit on top of the ice rather than below. Over the millennia, polar bears acquired a white coat, which concealed them from their prey; blubber for warmth; and oversize feet, which help them paddle in the water and distribute their weight so that the eight-hundred-pound creatures can walk on ice too thin to support a human being.

Together these adaptations make the polar bear a formidable killing machine. Bears conceal themselves by lying on the ice facing their prey, so that only their noses break the tableau of whiteness. It is said that if an unarmed man sees a hungry polar bear on the ice it is already too late for escape. The animal has been forced to develop its stalking skills because it is a pure carnivore. To survive, an adult bear must kill an animal the size of a seal every week of its life.

Ordinarily, the bears leave the island in the late spring and stay on the ice pack as it shrinks toward the north, returning to

Wrangell with the fall freeze. In 1992, the ice pack retreated dramatically, stranding polar bears and walruses on the island for the summer. The result was bloody carnage, as predator and prey found themselves locked in tight quarters together.

The distinct warming of the past couple of decades has already had perceptible effects on smaller life forms as well. Camille Parmesan, an entomologist at the University of California at Santa Barbara, published a study in the journal *Nature* which detailed local extinctions and changes in the range of a butterfly called Edith's checkerspot, an insect that is very sensitive to climate change. She found that warming temperatures had killed off the butterfly in much of the southern reaches of its range in Mexico, but that it was expanding its range in Canada and cooler areas at higher elevations.

Even without climate change, countless species will continue to decline. Ignorant of the workings of the systems that sustain us, we continue to squeeze them, not knowing whether we are squeezing them too much. There is absolutely no question that there will be a day of reckoning for this mad gamble.

David Quammen, author of *The Song of the Dodo,* which explores the anarchy wrought by the fragmentation of nature, quotes conservation biologists Michael Soule and Bruce Wilcox on the net result of humanity's impact on the biosphere: "There is no escaping the conclusion that in our lifetimes, this planet will see a suspension, if not an end, to many ecological and evolutionary processes which have been uninterrupted since the beginnings of paleontological time."

If scientists do not know how an ecosystem sustains itself, they do know that nature tends to seek equilibrium. As the players or circumstances change in any given ecosystem, nature adjusts, seeking some new equilibrium. That period of adjustment can be quite volatile. It can also take a long time for nature to recover from a spasm of extinctions. Ten million years is the figure that the great Harvard biologist E. O. Wilson uses, and it is useful to keep this figure in mind when those who doubt the seriousness of the fragmentation of habitats and the loss of biodiversity argue that societies can restore their ecosystems once they have made economic progress. Wildlands may be easily convertible into capital, but the reverse is not so easy.

Of all the clues to what lies ahead, the squeezing of earth's life-support system may have the most direct and immutable ties to future instability.

Chapter 7

LIVING WITH LIMITS:
A PREVIEW

As FOLLOWERS OF THE eighteenth-century British thinker Thomas Malthus and his like-minded twentieth-century counterparts have discovered, specific predictions that humanity will outrun its food supply are a fool's errand and may be dangerous to a scientist's reputation. So far, technology and human initiative have pushed back many predicted days of reckoning. With sufficient capital and energy, food can be grown almost anywhere. Countries like China have greatly improved their efficiency, and there is still vast room for improvement in much of Asia, Africa, and Latin America. The unchecked application of fertilizers, pesticides, and irrigated water can of course produce ecological calamities that ultimately affect food production. A long-heralded biotech revolution in agriculture has yet to deliver on its promise to increase crop yields beyond levels reached during the Green Revolution, which introduced high-yielding hybrid crops and fertilizers to the farmers of the world.

A variety of signals suggest that the next round of improvements in food production are not going to be as easy as the gains achieved during the Green Revolution. Nor are there now great stretches of wildlands ready to be brought under plow, as there were decades ago, or great sources of untapped fresh water that might be used for irrigation. All of these factors, plus the stresses of producing enough of five basic crops—corn, wheat, soybeans, barley, and rice—to feed six billion people, have conspired to produce a compelling clue to the future: an increase in the volatility of the global food system.

Between May and December 1995, the United States Department of Agriculture lowered its figures for World Grain Carryover Stocks—in essence, the world's grain surplus—four times. In May, government estimates predicted a surplus of fifty-three days' supply. By September, that figure had dropped to forty-nine days. At first, this may seem like an ample cushion, but the figure represents the smallest surplus since the USDA began tabulating these in 1961. Then the estimate dropped again, to forty-eight days. This contrasts with the eighty-day cushion that characterized many of the past thirty years. On the one hand, huge surpluses tend to depress prices, and thus investment in improvements in agriculture. On the other hand, the world will now get a glimpse of the consequences of seeing the surplus vanish.

In 1973, when carryover stocks fell to fifty-five days, world grain prices gyrated wildly, throwing the markets into chaos. The global food market is much more efficient now, but the shortages of 1996 drove corn prices to stratospheric levels before massive planting and good weather brought them back down. In 1997, it was wheat's turn to experience market gyrations, as prices were whipsawed by promises of good weather followed by predictions of huge crop losses from bad weather and floods.

The shortages of early 1996 prompted some observers to argue that the food equation had finally tilted in favor of suppliers, after forty years of steadily dropping grain prices. The reassuring response of the market gave comfort to those who believe that food production is a function of research and capital more than acreage. Indeed, by the fall of 1997 economic contraction in Asia led to a temporary glut of agricultural commodities.

Still, the extraordinary price rise of 1996 prompted farmers to plant every available acre of land, and even though the crisis disappeared temporarily, many sober experts were left wondering how many times more the global agricultural system could pull the rabbit out of the hat, particularly since with every passing year farmers have to feed an additional ninety-plus million people with less land and an increasing competition for water.

One of those experts is George Rothschild, until 1997 the director general of the International Rice Research Institute in Los Baños, the Philippines. This scholarly Australian was as responsible as anyone for the well-being of from two and a half to three billion of the world's people, most of them poor. Unless the institute manages to find ways to keep increasing rice yields by at least 2 percent a year, rice production will fall behind consumption, and tragedy will result.

Rice has a special place in the world food system, because it is the staple of people in warm nations who are too poor to afford anything else. If these three billion people cannot afford rice, they have nowhere to turn for food. What worries Rothschild is that, to keep pace with population growth, rice production has to increase by more than 70 percent in the next thirty years. This means that the institute must come up with ways to double the gains produced for rice during the Green Revolution. Unfortunately, the curve that describes yield increases has been flattening. On the horizon are new strains of biotech hybrid rice and a high-yielding "super rice" now in development, but Rothschild estimates that these improvements might ultimately increase the rice harvest by only 25 percent. Somehow rice growers must find another 45-percent increase. Where that will come from is not obvious at the moment, particularly given the trends in the world today.

The amount of irrigated land around the world has not significantly increased since 1992, and erosion, the salinization of fields, and other forms of desertification are taking millions of acres out of production each year. Farmers themselves are taking land out of the production of staple crops as they move to higher-value crops and sell their fields to land developers. Free-market advocates dismiss the dangers of this trend, arguing that as these nations develop they earn the foreign exchange to buy rice and other crops on the world market.

Someone has to produce this rice, however, and the danger is that, in a tight market, prices will rise beyond the means of the poor to buy food. For the eighty poor food-importing nations, increased volatility increases the danger that food will be the least affordable and available when it is most needed. Economic powerhouses such as China have the economic and political clout to bid for supplies on the world grain markets; nations such as Egypt and Mozambique do not. These are the circumstances under which riots occur and governments fall.

As this book goes to press, a preview of this linkage is becoming apparent in Indonesia, the fourth most populous nation on earth. The combination of a strong El Niño, a periodic oscillation in weather patterns around the world, and the collapse of the Indonesian economy left the nation short of rice and other staple crops at the very point that Indonesians could least afford to pay for imported food. The 1997 El Niño inflicted severe drought on the country's rice-growing regions, delaying plantings at a time when Indonesia was already importing 10 percent of its rice. Since the spring of 1997, food prices have already risen by 24 percent, with further increases inevitable as more shortages appear. The specter of future shortages has already spurred rioting in many Indonesian cities. Meanwhile, with its economy in shambles and its policy options limited by the terms of an agreement with the IMF, the Indonesian government will be hard pressed to subsidize food costs in order to mollify the restive poor.

Domestic instability makes it difficult to make the capital investments necessary to deploy technological breakthroughs in agriculture, starting a vicious cycle. Even without political instability, increasing volatility can breed a type of conservatism that actually worsens the problem. In the Philippines, farmers know that higher-yielding strains can bring them more income, but are afraid to make the necessary investments because of ruinous price swings in the marketplace.

There are other instabilities inherent to the production of crops themselves. Developing an agricultural system to feed an expanding and increasingly urbanized world population involves a number of trade-offs. The need for standardized, easily transportable foods has tended to focus attention on just a few crops, creating a self-reinforcing cycle in which farmers look to increase yields and increase focus on ever-fewer varieties, grown in ever more similar ways. Bangladesh, which once grew ten thousand variants of rice, now relies on just five. Agriculture, however, needs diversity no less than natural systems. A food system can insure itself against blights, floods, frosts, and droughts by using a variety of production techniques, offering a broad diversity of crops, and growing many different variants of each crop.

Primitive variants of basic crops such as wheat and corn carry with them adaptations to an enormous variety of threats. Some corn varieties that originated in high-altitude regions of Mexico, for instance, have purple tassels that may store heat, providing protection from frosts and some defense against ultraviolet radiation; the latter issue may prove important as the ozone layer continues to deteriorate under assault by man-made chemicals. These and countless other varieties of staple crops are disappearing, as farmers abandon traditional crops in favor of higher-yielding standardized brands. The danger is that pests, blights, or climate change may produce an emergency in one of the staple crops to which scientists cannot respond.

As more and more high-yielding crops are grown, the swings in production because of droughts get bigger, simply because the higher the yields, the more stands to be lost in any episode of bad weather. Like the world's capital markets, the world food system is becoming more synchronized. More and more farmers are doing the same things, and since most of the world's production is in the Northern Hemisphere, more and more of them are doing those same things at the same time. In any system, the more elements become synchronized, the bigger the amplitude of waves when these elements converge—and the larger the crash when they break.

And then there is water. Whether or not climate becomes more unstable, water scarcity looms as a huge limit to future increases in productivity. The International Food Policy Research Institute estimates that 338 million people live in countries now suffering water stress, which means that the region suffers major problems during drought years. IFPRI estimates that by 2025 roughly fifty countries, with a total population of three billion people, will suffer water stress. This projection represents a nine-fold increase in water scarcity in just thirty years.

As per-capita supplies of fresh water diminish, global demand increases at 2.4 percent annually, a rate faster than population growth. This sets up a no-win competition between industry, agriculture, households, and ecosystems for ever-smaller amounts of water. According to Thomas Homer-Dixon, in Taiyuan, in China, the competing claims on diminishing water supplies have forced farmers to poison fields knowingly with irrigation water polluted by carcinogenic industrial wastes, simply because they have no other source. Some industries must shut down in summer so that water supplies can be maintained for homes.

In the poorer nations, agriculture already uses more than 90 percent of available fresh water, so future improvements will have to come out of more efficient use of existing supplies. Since IFPRI estimates that as much as 75 percent of the water used in the developing world is wasted, there is room to increase supplies without tapping new sources. But Mark Rosegrant, who wrote the IFPRI study, notes that, even if one sector is wasting water in the developing world, chances are that someone is capturing that waste, rendering the total efficiency much higher than the figures suggest. This would imply that the gains from future efficiency expenditures may not be that great. Moreover, these investments are not cheap. Instead, water-poor nations will be tempted to divert to agriculture water that now supports vital ecosystems, or that now flows to their neighbors.

All of the largest freshwater wetlands in the world are now under threat from diversion projects. The Pantanal, which encompasses parts of Brazil, Bolivia, and Paraguay, is threatened by Hydrovia, a plan to create a transport waterway reaching deep into the interior of the continent, as well as plans to drain parts of the wetland and open it to agriculture. Angola plans to divert the Okavonga River to supply water to itself and Namibia, but this

would kill off a vast array of animals, including elephants and lions, that now depend on the swamps the river feeds. In the north,
Sudan has long planned to build a channel through the Sudd,
which would increase the downstream flow of the Nile but in so
doing starve the flood plain that is now the most productive
ecosystem in North Africa.

Such trade-offs will typify the coming decades, because water
supplies cannot increase, and water is too expensive to move except by gravity. Given the needs of hungry people, ecosystems
are very likely to lose out first. Ultimately, the people surrounding
these drained water-sources will lose out as well, since the loss of
the wetlands changes the local climate.

This was the harsh lesson imposed on Kazaks and Uzbeks by
the Soviets when, in a blind rush to increase irrigated acreage,
they diverted the tributaries of the Aral Sea, leaving the world with
a ghastly monument to the consequences of shortsighted central
planning. As what was once one of the largest inland bodies of
water on earth shrank to one-third its original volume in a matter
of decades, concentrated salts killed off its once-rich fishery, and
temperatures around the diminished body of water soared to
crop-killing levels during the summer. Residents of local villages
are now plagued by respiratory ailments and other diseases, since
the winds have picked up salts and other poisons from the lifeless
salt pan that remains around the now dead lake.

The competition for water also raises the likelihood of conflict between nations. Turkey controls the headwaters of both the
Tigris and Euphrates rivers, and its past actions to dam the rivers
have prompted its bellicose downstream neighbors, Iraq and
Syria, to threaten war. Tensions could flare again as Turkey moves
to complete its $21-billion Greater Anatolia Project, which would
divert water to irrigate 1.65 million hectares of agricultural land.
The possibility of conflict over water extends to dozens of countries in Asia, Africa, and the Middle East, and at the heart of the
tensions will be the issue of food security.

The experience of recent years suggests that the shrinking
margin for error that comes with diminishing surplus stocks and

humanity's ever-greater dependence on a small range of seeds and diminishing supplies of fresh water will foster ever-greater turmoil. The issue, then, is not so much whether the global agricultural system can continue to expand supplies to meet demand, but whether increasing volatility in both price and supply indicates that the world has passed a threshold so that continued improvements in food production will come at the price of environmental and political instability.

Once again, looming over any scenario for the future is climate change. Even as the global system becomes more synchronized and volatile, global climate has in recent years become more unstable. Climate instability, should it continue or worsen, will further increase the likelihood of a crash and could exacerbate volatility in food supplies. Some climate specialists ask whether world population could have grown to its present size if the previous 150 years had been marked by the climate instability that characterizes the present. As yet no one has attempted an answer, but the question hangs in the air. What does climate instability portend for the food supply as population continues its trajectory toward eight to ten billion souls? Even food optimists agree that any kind of turmoil, whether it be extreme weather or political upheaval, nullifies forecasts of increased production. All too easily, the world could tip into a spiral in which shortfalls beget instability, which beget more shortfalls. The doomsayers have been wrong in the past, but there is no reason to believe that they will be wrong in perpetuity.

Chapter 8

INFECTIOUS DISEASE RESURGENT

NOT FOR NOTHING DID the Bible's Book of Revelation make pestilence one of the Four Horsemen of the Apocalypse. Down through history, plagues and epidemics have brought low great empires. Measles and other diseases, not conquest, brought down the civilizations of the New World and Polynesia, and a virulent strain of influenza that circled the world in 1918–19 killed more people than World War I. Disease is an indicator of instability, but it is also a precursor to future instability. When ecosystems are out of balance, microbes tend to benefit; when populations of any given species explode, disease can bring them back into balance with brutal efficiency. Humans have vastly more weapons at their disposal than other species in the battle to keep microbes at bay, but disease will always be with us, lurking in the shadows, seizing opportunities whenever they arise.

When microbes find an opening, their depredations can lead to profound social change. If we could know trends in disease in the future, we would know a lot about how people will live. But trends in infectious and chronic disease are one of the trickiest clues to the future, because trends are not destiny, and because the rise and fall of disease represents a response to an enormous range of factors. Climate change, tropical deforestation, poverty, education levels, trends in agriculture and international trade, even an individual's psychological state bear on disease. Because of its strong linkages to instability, it is the mother of all clues to the future, but it is difficult to tease its message from the cacophony of the present. Once again, however, profound, hard-to-reverse changes in life on earth in this century suggest that disease and the instability that comes with it will play an ever more important role in the coming decades.

Microbes are configured to respond extraordinarily quickly to any environmental change. They have in their favor a particular reproductive strategy, dubbed the "R-strategy" by those who study population dynamics. R-strategists secure their perpetuation through massive reproduction in very short periods of time. The creatures that prey on microbes and the mosquitoes and other vectors that spread disease tend to be so-called K-strategists (the "K" refers to the German word for "culture"). These species have fewer offspring but protect and nurture them, so that they are more likely to survive. In the normal course of life, the two strategies tend to remain in balance, but when weather, human activities, the loss of biological diversity, or some other upheaval upsets that balance, the R-strategists are better poised to exploit the opportunity and proliferate.

This is happening today on a massive scale around the world, as human activities and human movements transform the globe. Each of the clues discussed in earlier chapters contributes in some way to the resurgence of infectious disease. The vast migration of people to the cities in this century, for instance, has perfected the ideal nursery for incubating more virulent forms of old diseases as well as strains that resist formerly effective treatments.

Indeed, urban migration in the developing world threatens to undo one of the great victories of the twentieth century, the first period in which it has been safe to live in cities. Previously, plagues and epidemics periodically decimated cities once they grew past their capacity to dispose of wastes and maintain clean water. Unfortunately, future historians may look back upon the respite of the past few decades as the last period in which it was safe to live in cities. In squatter settlements and favelas, inade-

quate sanitation, air pollution, poverty, malnutrition, and the mis-
use of antibiotics combine to pave the way for infectious diseases.
As HIV has swept through Africa, tuberculosis has followed, finding newly hospitable surroundings in the weakened immune systems of AIDS sufferers. Malnutrition also weakens people, leaving
them susceptible to a host of other resurgent bugs.

Human migration has helped spread disease since the dawn
of the species. According to Ross McPhee, chairman of the mam-
mology department at the American Museum of Natural History,
as humans invaded new environments—such as the Americas ten
to twelve thousand years ago, or Madagascar one thousand years
ago—they brought with them diseases that killed off larger animals with lower reproductive rates. Adapted to an existing range
of pathogens, goes this argument, these large, slow-to-reproduce
animals were thus unprepared for the microbial onslaught that
piggybacked on the human interlopers and the other animals they
brought with them. Microbes have proved to be equal-opportunity
destroyers, and during the Age of Discovery native populations of
the Americas and the Pacific died by the millions as a result of infections imported by explorers. In the five centuries since the
Spanish first set foot in the New World, an estimated fifty-six million natives have died from diseases introduced by Europeans.

Now, having radiated into every corner of the globe spreading contagion with it, humanity is discovering that there is a symmetry to the spread of disease. People are becoming the preferred
target of countless diseases that are new to mankind but to which
other species have already adapted. Periodic outbreaks of hemorrhagic fevers such as the lethal Ebola virus provide a glimpse of
the horrors waiting in forests and fens for opportunities to establish themselves in earth's dominant mammal.

Ebola is a "jumper," a zoonotic disease that can move from
one species to another, but it is not the only jumper that people
have to worry about. As humans domesticate wildlands, they
lower the diversity of environments, and diseases formerly held in
check flourish. This is the story of another hemorrhagic fever, the
Machupo virus, which surfaced in Bolivia after farmers converted

rain forest to farmland, leading to an explosion in rodent populations. Rita Colwell, a microbial ecologist at Johns Hopkins University, argues that the loss of diversity at the microbial level
contributes to the emergence of virulent strains of a disease.

Even in the developed world, humans have altered the environment to favor the microbes. The incidence of skin rashes has
risen dramatically in recent decades, causing some scientists to
wonder whether the cumulative impact of toxins in the air, water,
and diet are beginning to overwhelm the body's defenses. Equally
puzzling has been the rise of asthma in the U.S., even as the air
has gotten cleaner. Is this growing health threat the result of exposure to some toxin related to the proliferation of cockroaches,
the weakening of immune systems burdened by the stresses and
pollutants of modern life, or both?

When a new microbe emerges from the jungle or a resurgent
bacteria emerges from a favela, it finds that humans have provided a perfect system for its spread. A drug-resistant strain of
plague that emerged in 1997 in Madagascar could make it from
the African island to the U.S. in a day and a half, hitching a ride on
some unwitting traveler. Other bacteria might hop a ride on co-
conut milk from Thailand, cantaloupes from Mexico, or raspber-
ries from Guatemala.

News of resurgent microbes comes as an unexpected surprise
to ordinary Americans, who share the widespread belief that medical science and modern sanitation have conquered infectious disease. Smallpox was vanquished, tuberculosis nearly so, and as
sanitation, the spread of vaccinations and antibiotics, and other innovations disseminated through the developing world, every
trend pointed toward continued progress on almost every front.
Health officials confidently talked about an "epidemiological transition" as improving health shifted concerns toward chronic diseases, like cancer. That was before AIDS made its appearance,
before new multiple-resistant strains of tuberculosis followed suit,
and before malaria made its great leap forward to become the
world's most widespread mosquito-borne disease. Between 1980
and 1995, the incidence of infectious disease rose 58 percent in

the United States, according to the Centers for Disease Control.

The late epidemiologist Uwe Brinkmann used to say that humanity in this century has benefited from a "honeymoon" from infectious disease, chiefly thanks to the discovery of antibiotics, but that there was no reason to believe that microbes would accept this honeymoon as permanent. Despite rhetoric in the 1950s about winning the war on infectious disease, even then people like Rachel Carson, the award-winning author of *Silent Spring,* recognized such assertions as foolhardy hubris. Now many epidemiologists realize that the relationship between pathogen and host is like an endless cold war that occasionally flashes into full conflict. One side may gain temporary advantage—humans through the invention of antibiotics; bacteria and viruses through some novel way of hiding from or resisting human weapons—but no advantage lasts forever.

Once considered conquered, for instance, tuberculosis is now producing new strains resistant to all but the most elaborate treatment regimens. The resurgent disease is also producing strains that are far more virulent than anything encountered before. In 1994, a new strain of TB swept through a small town in Kentucky. Although it could be treated with standard medications, the emergence of the bacteria alarmed public-health officials in the U.S., because it seemed to proliferate up to a thousand times faster than typical TB germs, and spread to healthy people with great ease. The different strategies of varying strains of TB suggest that nothing in the bacterial rule book says a germ has to stay with one particular plan forever.

Some diseases have gotten so tough from continued human attempts at eradication that prevention is tougher on man and nature than the disease. DDT and other pesticides used to halt the spread of malaria-carrying mosquitoes have destroyed bird and other predator populations that provide a natural control on the spread of anopheles. Meanwhile, the disease itself has become inured to quinine; many expatriates on assignment in infested areas prefer to get the disease and treat it rather than risk the stress on organs that sometimes accompanies long-term use of mefloquine hydrochloride and other new prophylactics. It is only a matter of time before some emergent or resurgent pathogen combines virulence, lethal effects, and resistance to treatment all at once.

Almost all the new improved diseases owe their comebacks to human meddling. A good case study was provided by Rita Colwell, who, with Paul Epstein and Timothy Ford, two epidemiologists from Harvard University's School of Public Health, traced the origins of *Vibrio cholerae* 01, biotype El Tor, a resurgent strain of cholera that first surfaced in the Celebes Islands around 1961. The bug spent three decades expanding its reach through Asia before a series of fortuitous events brought it to South America in early 1991.

Cholera ordinarily makes its home in the human intestinal tract and moves through a population as people come in contact with feces containing the infection. One of El Tor's clever adaptations was its ability to survive by living on algae in the open oceans.

Choosing algae was an astute career move on the part of the cholera germ. Algae prosper in warm waters with an ample supply of nutrients, such as nitrogen and phosphorus. Algae of all types have benefited from a huge range of human impacts on the biosphere, from the destruction of coral reefs to acid rain and global warming.

As human numbers have increased, so too has water pollution, including acid rain, sewage, and agricultural runoff, all of which can help build healthy algae. Even as humans pour more nutrients into the oceans, we have also reduced or damaged the systems designed to filter them out or otherwise control algal growths. Wetlands, which filter nutrients out of water, reducing the amount of fertilizer available for these offshore growths, have been filled in by coastal development and damaged by pollution. Other pollution filters have fared no better. Mangroves are cut for wood, coastal marshes paved over. Coastal development, overfishing, and pollution also reduce the populations of mollusks and shellfish that eat algae, and warming oceans (whether because of a natural cycle or global climate change) create algae-friendly conditions in the open waters. Even ozone depletion in the upper atmosphere may prove helpful for cholera and other diseases. In the open ocean, increased ultraviolet-b radiation hurts the zooplankton more than it hurts phytoplankton, which have chlorophyll to screen harmful radiation. On land, increased UVb radiation may weaken human immune systems, leaving people more susceptible to disease.

The result is that red tides, brown tides, and other algal blooms are appearing off coastlines with increasing frequency over larger expanses of ocean. These blooms harbor a number of diseases harmful to humans, including various types of shellfish poisoning and ciguatera poisoning from fish. And, according to Rita Colwell, algae also offer a hospice to diseases like cholera that were previously thought to be exclusively passed by human-to-human contact.

Colwell and her colleagues hypothesize that the El Tor cholera passed from a human into the fetid waters off Bangladesh, where it entered the bilge of a freighter heading for South America. When the freighter emptied ballast water from its bilges off Chancay, Peru, the microbe found a happy home in algal blooms fed by the untreated runoff from Lima. It quickly spread along the blooms, twelve hundred miles in either direction. From the algae it entered shellfish, and then made its way back to the familiar surroundings of the human intestinal tract, striking three coastal communities within a week in January 1991.

The first victims fell ill after eating ceviche, a popular Latin American dish of marinated uncooked fish. From the coast, the bacteria rapidly fanned out into Brazil, Venezuela, and Bolivia, following river traffic. Freighters brought it to the Gulf of Mexico. As of today, the cholera epidemic has claimed perhaps ten thousand lives and gravely sickened more than a million people.

If cholera were not a highly treatable disease, the death toll would be vastly higher. Countless other microbes, some not nearly so responsive to treatment, also benefit from the increase in human numbers and human impacts on the biosphere. Paul Epstein sums it up: "Microbes flourish in human weakened immune systems. In essence human tampering with ecology has weakened the globe's immune system, fostering conditions favorable for microbes."

Finally, there is a truly frightening possibility. Epstein notes that in recent years variants of measles, the disease that wiped out native populations throughout the Americas and Oceania, recently struck seals in Europe, lions in the Serengeti, and horses in Australia. What, he wonders, is weakening the immune system of such disparate creatures scattered over such huge distances? It may be drought in Africa, pollution in the North Sea, or some other factor in Australia, but the worry is that the conditions for the spread of microbes are becoming universal. Studies with mice have revealed that benign viruses can become virulent in creatures weakened by malnutrition, and then begin ravaging healthy populations. Who knows what microbes are presently biding their time in the weakened immune systems of the malnourished, the HIV-infected, and countless animals and plants under stress from human-wrought changes in their surroundings?

Marine biologists, for instance, are puzzling over a mysterious wasting disease that reduces corals to crumbly white dust; it is devastating coral reefs across a two-thousand-mile expanse of the Caribbean. Some scientists wonder whether the combination of pollution, warming waters, and other stresses have pushed the corals past some tipping point, so that they are no longer able to fend off invading pathogens; others speculate that the disease came to the reefs from land-based sediments. Whatever the cause, these epidemics sweeping natural systems are a disturbing indicator of nature out of balance.

Epstein uses the metaphor of a globe with a weakened immune system. The worst problem facing humanity may not be one epidemic killing millions, but multiple diseases destroying crops, decimating livestock, and otherwise disrupting human societies' life-support systems.

Climate change, whether natural or human-influenced, could give a further boost to plague and pestilence. Heat and unusual weather seem to favor microbes and other opportunistic malefactors while penalizing the creatures that control their numbers. Epidemiologists have had this biological lesson imposed upon them by the unusual weather of the past two decades. Rising temperatures have allowed dengue fever to spread outward from the Pacific coast of Costa Rica, where it had been confined by mountain ranges whose cold temperatures killed the eggs of *Aedes aegypti*, which carry the disease. Recent warming has allowed the mosquito to move ever higher up slopes (on average, the freezing line has risen between 200 and 260 feet around the world since 1970); in 1995, the mosquitoes broached the mountain barrier and spread the disease throughout Costa Rica. Dengue advanced elsewhere in Latin America as well; by September 1995, the microbe had killed 4,000 of the 140,000 people infected.

Dengue fever inspires fear because there is no cure and because it becomes progressively more dangerous with successive infections, but malaria might pose a far bigger problem in a warmer world. Rising temperatures not only expand the range of anopheles mosquitoes, but make them more active biters as well. Epstein notes that a temperature rise of ten degrees Fahrenheit produces a sixfold increase in mosquito metabolism, which makes them feed more often, circulating parasites that much more rapidly. Even today, malaria infects an estimated three to five hundred million of the 2.1 billion people who live in the 45 percent of the globe over which anopheles ranges. The World Health Organization rates it "extremely likely" that climate change will expand that domain, and some models estimate that a five-to-nine-degree warming could lead to a 33-percent increase in the range of malaria and double the number of deaths each year. Should temperatures rise too much above a hundred degrees Fahrenheit, mosquitoes would begin to die off—but, then again, so would people and the crops on which they feed.

Mosquitoes and other pests might benefit from another aspect of climate change: a predicted increase in extreme weather events. These classic R-strategists can rapidly expand their numbers, as happened in Colombia in 1995, when unusually hot weather led to an explosion in the populations of mosquitoes, rodents, and toxic algae. This same strategy enables these pests to adapt quickly as their environment changes.

Humans can adapt quickly too, of course, and for this reason some observers dispute that climate change will be an important factor in future trends in infectious disease. Writing in *Science,* Gary Taubes cites the failure of diseases like cholera, dengue fever, and malaria to penetrate the United States despite climatic similarities to neighboring nations where the diseases exist. The Taubes article also notes that in some parts of Sri Lanka an increase in rainfall might reduce malaria, because some resident species flourish during the dry season, when flowing rivers are reduced to scattered puddles of standing water. On the other hand, as Epstein and others note, the spread of disease nicely matches the warming that has thus far occurred, and the movement of mosquitoes into higher altitudes, where they have not been seen before, offers compelling evidence of how warming might abet their spread.

It is noteworthy that the current resurgence of infectious disease is taking place during a global economic boom. A promising economic global landscape should enable countries to mobilize resources to install sanitation, promote vaccination and health education, and otherwise deliver health benefits to those who need them. Why is this not happening?

Part of the answer is the now dominant free-market economic paradigm. Corporations, blind to their role in fostering the conditions for the spread of disease, build factories in developing countries with no thought to effluents or emissions. Pollution flows into the air and water, fostering the growth of disease-nurturing algal blooms and weakening the immune systems of animals and humans alike. No small increment of the GDP in the poorer nations comes from the cutting of forests and the conversion of wildlands, a process that also favors microbes.

Perhaps the key reason, however, is that the balance between humanity and the biosphere has been altered by the growth in human numbers and the leveraging effects of technology. The recent headlines about mad-cow disease showed how what at first seemed to be an obscure ailment threatening only livestock in the British Isles quickly grew into a potentially much larger problem, as it was discovered that the animal parts carrying the disease were used pervasively in feeds and other products. The threat to the general population from mad-cow disease may turn out to be minimal, but it should not be surprising that microbes find more opportunities in a world in which six billion people are connected by a global network of airplanes than they did at the turn of the century, when one billion people lived in relative isolation. Even if there are more people living healthier lives than ever before, there are also more destitute people with weakened immune systems incubating and spreading contagion than ever before.

The UN's World Health Organization and other institutions still cling to the concept of the epidemiological transition. As late as the fall of 1996 the WHO predicted that rates of infectious disease will fall in the following decades. Such confidence, however, is based on the assumption that governments will take action to deliver the kinds of interventions, such as vaccination and sanitation programs, that have tamed disease in the past. One reason for the resurgence of infectious disease is that governments have not been taking those actions, in part because of the increasing instability both in the developing world and in formerly stable countries like Russia. Instability thus increases the likelihood of the spread of disease, which in turn increases instability and decreases a society's capacity to deal with disease.

Diseases bring about profound change. In an article for the *Journal of Preventive Medicine,* Epstein argued that the first European plague pandemic in 541 A.D., in the disorder following the fall of the Roman Empire, led to a flight from cities and contributed to the development of feudalism. The next pandemic, in 1346, brought about a labor shortage that broke the power of feudal landlords over labor and led to the development of the middle class. What social change will accompany the next round of plagues when they come?

Chapter 9

THE RISE OF THE TRUE BELIEVERS

IN THE EARLY AND mid-1970s, the U.S. was preoccupied with the threat of a leftist revolution in strategically situated Iran. The West developed a deep intelligence network in the country, gave the shah access to sophisticated weaponry, and tolerated, if not encouraged, repressive measures against leftist groups. Obsessed with the Tudeh Party and other leftist organizations, Western analysts and diplomats did not take seriously other groups agitating for change, including a group of Islamic mullahs.

In retrospect, Middle East specialists saw many signals they had missed in the late 1970s as the Ayatollah Khomeini egged on the revolution with tape-recorded speeches smuggled in from Paris. To contain 35-percent inflation, the shah's government had halted huge construction projects, marooning in Tehran thousands of men who had been drawn in by the promises of high wages. Money from Iranian oil freed the shah from seeking support in the bazaars and allowed him to ignore the clergy completely. While clarifying the proximate causes of discontent in the public and grievances that might have galvanized the clerics, none of these explanations account for the religious fervor of the mullahs' supporters. There is far more to Islamic fundamentalism than missteps by the shah and a dip in the Iranian economy.

Given the assumption that Iranians were concerned about issues like freedom, equity, and wages, it is easy to see why the West would ignore a group of anachronistic old firebrands who seemed to have a grudge against the twentieth century. Who would have thought that Iranians would rally around a group that promised austerity, and harsher punishments for lesser crimes than anything meted out under the shah? Who would have thought that Iranians would trade a society in which women were emancipated, had the right to abortion, entrance to professions, and full rights in divorce, for one in which women are believed to be mentally inferior, in which their testimony is worth only half the weight of a man's and their lives, when wrongfully forfeited, are deemed by the courts to be worth only half as much as men's?

The mullahs delivered what they promised. Even before they took power, the clerics directed their violence against symbols of moral corruption such as nightclubs, cinemas, and banks. A woman risked beating, humiliation, or a summons to court if she ventured outside with a lock of hair showing and was spotted by the ubiquitous religious police. Anticapitalist and anticommunist, commerce in Iran since the revolution has been governed to some extent by Sharia, the Islamic code of laws articulated in the Koran. In part as a consequence, Iran's economy shrunk on an average of 1.4 percent a year between 1980 and 1992, impoverishing a once-booming middle class. Iran's economy has surely suffered from a U.S. trade embargo imposed (but ignored by most European nations) because of Iran's support of terrorism and mischief abroad, and from corruption that even Sharia cannot root out, but the economy has also suffered because the theocratic government cares more about the dictates of Islam than it does about building a modern economy. Many in the middle and professional classes are not happy with Iran's economic decline amid a global economic boom, and Iran's leaders periodically have to contend with riots and strikes, but in twenty years no serious counterrevolutionary force has materialized.

How has the rest of Islam reacted to Iran's attempt to return to medieval mores, with its harsh penalties and economic miseries? Millions cannot wait to try the experiment at home. Since it burst upon the world, Islamic fundamentalism has continued to expand its ambit, transforming the politics of Pakistan, Afghanistan, and Sudan, and threatening the established order in Algeria, Egypt, and Turkey among other countries.

The rise of Islamic fundamentalism is a gauntlet thrown directly in the path of the consumer juggernaut. In fact, it is fueled by the stresses imposed on societies by modernity. To the Western mind the shah's attention to women's rights was a sign of progress, but to Persian conservatives it was a direct challenge to Islam and culturally sanctioned male prerogatives. In much of the world, indigenous cultures are dying as the young turn away from their elders, but the surge of Islamic passion has shown itself to be the most effective counterforce to the spread of consumer values that has yet arisen. Perhaps not all traditional cultures are powerless before the West and its images.

To a degree, the religious right in the United States also represents a reaction to modernity, in particular to changes that threaten traditional values and gender roles and thus are perceived as a threat to the community. Witness the meteoric rise of the "Promise Keepers," a moral-rearmament movement for men that regularly convenes hundreds of thousands to dedicate themselves to righteous living according to the tenets of the Bible. Few would argue with the Promise Keepers' mission to become better husbands, but feminists have taken issue with the subtext of this aspect of their mission, which involves taking back leadership of the home and restoring traditional gender roles. As the support mustered by antifeminists like Phyllis Schlafly indicates, a surprising number of women are willing to go along. In an age in which economists take for granted that people equate well-being with consumption, increasing numbers of people seem willing to trade certain freedoms and material comforts for a sense of immutable order and the rapture of faith.

In the 1960s, *Time* magazine ran a cover story entitled "Is ' God Dead?" In a skeptical, rational age in which it is difficult to reconcile the statements of the Bible with the limits imposed by physics and biology, this was a perfectly reasonable question to ask. Religion demanded that people believe in miracles, in reincarnation, in heaven, that God had a Son, that the earth was created in one week, and a host of other phenomena that stretched the credulity of an increasingly literate and educated public. It also demanded adherence to strict moral and sexual mores that were at extreme variance with the laissez-faire attitudes of the counterculture and the sexual revolution.

It turns out that this is OK with a lot of folks. Three decades after His obituary, God in His most literal and traditional form seems to be making a stirring comeback. A *Time* poll in 1996 revealed that 69 percent of a sample of the American public believed in miracles, that the majority of people believed in angels (a demographic noticed by network programmers, who launched the immensely popular television show "Touched by an Angel"). The number of evangelical Christians as well as other sects that take the Bible literally has grown, and the more moderate center of Christianity has withered. Enough men are abandoning high-powered careers in finance and the law and turning to the priesthood in midlife to catch the attention of *The New York Times*. In Latin America, charismatic Christian denominations have also enjoyed a boom, even installing one of their members in the presidency of Guatemala.

The search for higher authority and order extends beyond organized religion. In an astonishing development reported in *The New York Times* in 1997, some college fraternities around the nation are banning alcohol and attempting to reclaim their original mandate to pursue scholarship and the betterment of communities, although it would be prudent to wait before announcing this as a trend. At the other end of the spectrum, amorphous New Age credos continue to grow. Americans have become more open to belief in extraterrestrials and the paranormal.

According to polls, roughly 40 percent of Americans believe that aliens have visited the planet. Sometimes this subculture surfaces in ways that show the lengths to which people will go in service of their beliefs. In March 1997, thirty-nine adherents of the Heaven's Gate cult committed suicide so that they could leave a soon-to-be-destroyed planet earth and join a spaceship that trailed in the shadow of the Hale-Bopp comet. Perhaps as surprising as the event itself was that various opinion polls suggested that substantial numbers of people found the group's actions understandable, if not laudable. Indeed, even before the mass suicide there was a lively debate on the Internet about the alleged spaceship following the comet.

Also on the rise has been a tolerance for nonrational or irrational, not to mention outright lunatic ideas. One such belief, common among members of America's militia movement, is that the UN is amassing a huge armada of black helicopters that will spearhead a takeover of the United States (guided in part by those pieces of tape that can often be seen on the backs of road signs) as part of a plot to impose a New World Order. This conspiracy requires its adherents to believe that the bumbling, fractious, and bureaucratic UN could keep secret and then launch a military operation against the world's only superpower. In a reversal of Santayana's dictum, ideas now seem first to surface as farce (earlier iterations of the staples of the militia movement produced inspired black humor in the Stanley Kubrick film *Dr. Strangelove,* in which an air-force general talked about fluoridated water as a UN/communist plot to sap Americans of their "precious bodily fluids"), and then to repeat themselves as tragedy, such as the bombing of the Murrah Federal Building in Oklahoma City in 1995.

White paranoia is matched step for step by black paranoia in the United States. Breakaway Black Muslim leader Louis Farrakhan and proponent of Afrocentric studies Leonard Jeffries have made careers peddling genocidal conspiracies against blacks. Some of these black conspiracies have gotten a hearing in the U.S. Congress. In 1996, after the *San Jose Mercury News* published a story arguing that the CIA was instrumental in introducing crack cocaine to America's inner cities, Congresswoman Maxine Waters called for an investigation of the theory that the crack epidemic was part of a purposeful plan to weaken the black community. Long after the *Mercury News* retracted the story that originally suggested the CIA/crack connection, the congresswoman continued to refer to the alleged conspiracy. The O. J. Simpson trial revealed that most mainstream black Americans were willing to believe that the former football player was framed by an intricate conspiracy engineered on the spot by more than a dozen different people from several different branches of law enforcement after the discovery of the bodies of Nicole Brown Simpson and Ronald Goldman.

Paranoia is flowering around the world. At a loss to explain the chaos following the collapse of communism, Russians resurrect anti-Semitic conspiracies to account for the nation's troubles. So also do Poles, although almost no Jews remain in Poland after the ravages of the Holocaust more than fifty years ago.

Clearly, there is a world of difference between the faith of an evangelical Christian who believes in the literal truth of the Bible and a militia member's conviction that the UN plans to disarm the United States. The first is an adherent of a two-thousand-year-old religious tradition, whereas the other represents a passing manifestation of the human imagination's hunger for pattern and order. They do, however, both illustrate that, despite a five-hundred-year trend toward secularism, there remains strong movement in the opposite direction, toward the passionate embrace of beliefs that directly contradict the assumptions of science and, in some cases, rational discourse. To hold on to beliefs and ideas, people have no trouble ignoring the evidence of science, what they read, and even the evidence of their senses (if inner-city residents really regarded dealers as stooges for the CIA, solving the drug problem would be a lot easier as neighborhoods would rise up to drive out the subversive agents).

Everybody has his own favorite explanation for the decline of rigorous discourse. Some blame an educational system that fails to prepare students for disciplined argument; others blame multiculturalism, which devalues the Western canon and leaves students adrift; still others blame the rampant relativism of academia and science, which holds that there can be no one truth, only truth in a particular context.

This last is worth considering. When a science like physics becomes unmoored from the notion of certainty, the field becomes wide open for contenders offering absolute answers who suffer no such modesty. Perhaps it is no accident that conservative faiths, charismatic religions, cults, and paranoia are flourishing even as people lose faith in both science and ideology to supply one answer to life's eternal questions. Communism, evocatively described as *The God That Failed* by the late social critic Arthur Koestler, operated under the false belief that materialism could fill the role of religion. So does the consumer society, and so does science.

This touches on a primary source of modern angst since Darwin first articulated his ideas of natural selection. As the philosopher Thomas Kuhn noted, the most troublesome aspect of evolution for intellectuals in the Victorian era was the notion that it was not goal-directed. The idea that humans might have descended from apes was acceptable if natural selection incorporated ideas of progress, so dear to that era. Kuhn wrote that all the pre-Darwinian evolutionary theories of the times, those of Lamarck, Chambers, Spencer, and the German *Naturphilosophers,* had "taken evolution to be a goal-directed process. The 'idea' of man and of contemporary flora and fauna was thought to have been present from the first creation of life, perhaps in the mind of God." By contrast, Darwin offered an existential rather than a teleological vision of the world, a competition for survival whose implications held that no species had any special place in the universe.

Western and other societies still have trouble digesting this idea. It demystifies the glories of the intellect. How could the same blind forces that produced the nematode and the fruit fly produce Leonardo da Vinci and Sir Isaac Newton? Even today, serious physicists continue to fight the implications of evolution. Cosmologists John J. Barrow and Frank Tipler argue in their book, *The Anthropic Cosmological Principle,* that the very constants of nature provide evidence that the universe was designed to evolve a carbon-based intelligent life form that could observe and decode its design.

It is easy to understand why scientists and ordinary people alike find intolerable the notion that life can evolve without getting better. Similarly depressing are the drumbeat of discoveries about the prosaic nature of abilities previously thought to be in the province of consciousness. Prozac seems to alter a person's very soul. Twins, even when separated for a lifetime, display uncanny similarities, right down to specific likes and dislikes, suggesting that biology plays a large role in personality. Ablate one part of the brain and a minister will start cursing like a sailor; damage another and he will speak with a French, German, or Russian accent. Inflict a head injury on a corporate straight-arrow and he turns into a crazed artist. Addiction is the result of chemical imbalance, not character. Every week, science offers some new reductionist explanation for aspects of the human spirit.

Apart from championing relativism and materialism, intellectuals have also contributed in direct ways to the decline in the faith in reason. The disciplines have earned increasing distrust by arrogating to themselves the right to rework the fabric of life, create new organisms, or clone existing ones, with scant heed to the feelings of the community, the potential consequences, or the moral implications of their work; through the creation of horrors such as weapons of mass destruction; and through failures to deliver on promises stated at various times to eliminate disease and deliver free energy and unlimited food.

Science at its most honorable has also undermined confidence in its ability to supply exact answers to life's questions. The mathematician Kurt Gödel proved in 1933 that mathematical truth is of necessity incomplete, which means no mathematics can completely describe reality. Most famously of all, Albert Einstein inadvertently demonstrated that nature can violate the limits imposed by the speed of light, the very foundation of his vision of the universe, and, indeed, of the materialist view of life. This came out of his attempt to prove the absurdity of quantum mechanics, a subfield of physics that deals with the behavior of subatomic particles. He and two colleagues envisioned the following situation: In quantum mechanics, once a pair of photons pass through a filter that gives them a specific polarization (which can be thought of as orientation), they will be correlated by polarization from that point forth. The absurdity Einstein envisioned was that, if the pair were split and sent to the opposite ends of the universe, and then one photon passed through a filter that changed its polarity, quantum mechanics held that the polarity of the other photon would also instantaneously change—a violation of the speed limit imposed by the velocity of light, according to Einstein's theory of special relativity. Unfortunately for Einstein, subsequent physicists found ways to test this hypothesis experimentally, and in each of the dozen or so experiments attempted so far, quantum mechanics has been vindicated at the expense of Einstein's vision of the limits of the universe.

But what does this mean? What would it mean if in fact objects were entangled by forces that ignored the limits of the speed of light? If instantaneous action-at-a-distance were possible? On the one hand, scientists might look at the realm of the paranormal with fresh eyes, finding new avenues through which to investigate whether there was a scientific explanation for phenomena ranging from ESP to the basis of Chinese medicines such as Chi Therapy and acupuncture. In technology, quantum mechanics might supply a new model for the design of the next generation of computers (this is already under study at various labs).

Perhaps most important, however, is that the ascendance of quantum mechanics might ultimately redefine notions of reality, and in so doing spell the end of the so-called stick-and-ball model of reality that has dominated science and everyday life in the West since the days of Sir Isaac Newton. This paradigm shift would entail a tremendous chase to understand what constitutes proof and truth in its brave new probabilistic world. The shift would open the doors both to serious inquiry and to the worst kind of undisciplined charlatanism.

Disciplined argument thus finds itself besieged from all sides. Viewed with deep skepticism by the passionately faithful, perverted by the paranoid, distrusted by the general public, and inadvertently undermined by its most noble practitioners, science approaches the twenty-first century with nowhere near the mandate it had in earlier decades, when all of reality seemed within its grasp, and science was viewed as the key to the future. Many people still enjoy the fruits of technology, but turn away from science as a source of meaning, or when scientists disagree with their own self-interest or beliefs. This stands in stark contrast to the determinist optimism of the Victorian era, or of the 1950s in the U.S., when the average American was intoxicated with both science and materialism. Now society increasingly tends to focus on what science fails to deliver or explain, and more and more people find the promises of materialism empty. Little wonder, then, that a certain percentage of the population will look for some more fulfilling vision of life on earth than what has been offered in the twentieth century. So what if scientists scoff at it, since the limits of science have been proved by scientists themselves. If scientists cannot offer certainty, conservative religions and cults stand ready to reassert absolute truths.

Religion erupts from the deepest part of the human soul, and it is not so easily denied by science or ideology. Like the red-hot mantle in the earth's interior, it lies beneath the surface, and every now and then sends plumes of religious fervor through the rational façade of modern society. The counterculture of the late 1960s might be described as one such eruption; so might Islamic fundamentalism.

In some respects, evangelical and fundamentalist Christian sects represent efforts to unplug wellsprings of rapture that have been capped by reason in the desiccated forms of modern Christianity. These upsurgings also represent a verdict on the sustenance offered by reason when it tries to supplant religion.

This battle between reason and religion offers a window into the next century. At some level, the rise of evangelical faiths, of cults, and of the conspiracies in the U.S., and the rise of Islamic fundamentalism and of other forms of religious extremism elsewhere, are all nourished by the need for meaning and order. This need is only exacerbated by a world where traditions are mocked and everything from gender roles to the nature of civility and manners seems subject to change. Faced with a choice of how to find meaning amid cultural upheaval and change, some turn to established faiths, others rally around charismatic leaders, and still others look for order in conspiracies that coalesce around traditional scapegoats.

The willingness of people to subordinate their critical abilities in the service of faith or paranoia tells us that the ubiquity and availability of information may have less impact on the future than the beliefs people use to filter the evidence collected by their eyes and ears. In a tangle of ironies, the trend toward reason produces ever more powerful eruptions of unreason. The rise of fundamentalist, evangelical, and other passionate forms of faith also tells us that people do not always look forward to a New Age in reaction to the spiritual barrenness of the present.

Does the rise of Islamic fundamentalism represent the first setback in the hitherto inexorable expansion of the consumer society? It is too early to tell, of course. In recent years, the Iranian government has shown signs of softening, as evidenced by its refusal to support the development of a machine that automated the cutting off of fingers. Moreover, it tolerated the election in 1997 of a moderate cleric, Mohammed Khatami, as president. Many voted for Khatami in the hope that he would allow more openness to outside influences, but Khatami is not some Farsi-speaking Jerry Brown. He ran as a cleric, wears a black cap to signify that he is accepted as a descendant of the prophet Mohammed, and has consistently described himself as a supporter of the Islamic revolution. Moreover, the degree to which the clergy in Iran seeks to minimize contact between the sexes and dampen participation in anything remotely resembling fun would be regarded as extreme in any era. The public's desire to enjoy dancing and music does not necessarily mean that they once again want to embrace Mammon. Still, the support for Khatami, who has said that people should be allowed to read what they like in the privacy of their homes, suggests that the competition for the soul between religion and the consumer society is not a battle that is ever completely won.

If the consumer society tears itself apart, however, traditional religions, New Age belief systems, pantheists, technologists, survivalists, and all manner of charismatic leaders will vie to explain humanity's woes. These would-be successors will have a chance to compete to fill the vacuum, just as the woody trees prospered in the aftermath of a sky blackened by some cosmic catastrophe that killed off the cycads that dominated the earth through the Cretaceous period.

Chapter 10

LOOKING FORWARD

NINE CLUES, ALL IN plain sight, but each easily obscured by the background noise of the present. To a degree, it is comforting to see the future in the present, because it makes the future more familiar. Fear of the future tends to focus on unprecedented, alien threats—a nemesis microbe inadvertently brought from the jungle or hatched in the lab, terrorists armed with nuclear weapons, horrible new weapons released on unsuspecting citizens by paranoid dictators, machines that dehumanize the workplace.

Each of these ideas has produced at least one doomsday scenario for the future. But doomsday scenarios, however compelling, very rarely come to pass. More often in history, as in the Mafia, the bullet that gets you comes from a former friend or from something dismissed as inconsequential. We fail to notice that the familiar queen of spades has for some reason become red; we fail to see that the kudzu vine, brought in as the farmer's friend to protect the soil, is slowly taking over the countryside, until it is too late to stop its spread; obsessed with communism, we fail to notice the rise of Islamic fundamentalism until the shah of Iran is swept from his throne; we worry about Ebola, but fail to notice that more and more people are dying of the flu.

The clues cited in the previous chapters are noteworthy not so much because they foretell specific catastrophes as because they are symptomatic of ever-increasing instability or volatility in fundamental aspects of modern life, ranging from the world's financial markets to the systems that run the biosphere. Volatility, the loss of diversity, a narrowing base—these phrases recur in characterizations of the financial system, food production, and ecology.

Nor are the symptoms of the coming chaos developing in isolation from one another. Climate change threatens to exacerbate the problem of epidemics, the loss of biodiversity, and the stability of the world food system. The loss of biodiversity increases the volatility of the food system as well, since geneticists still depend on ancestral forms of crops for the genetic resources to breed into plants resistance to blights and pests. Climate change, volatility in the food system, and instability in the global economy all affect human migration, which in turn affects the stability of nations and regions. Thus the interplay of these symptoms of instability will very likely amplify overall instability in the decades to come.

I make no pretense that the nine clues offered in the first half of this book are exhaustive. Others might argue that the rising influence of mafias and gangs deserves a chapter of its own as a harbinger of instability, or that the end of the Cold War will ultimately produce upheaval as nations vie for position in whatever world order emerges in the years to come, or that future transitions in the world's sources and distribution of energy to fuel homes, industry, and transportation will rescramble the geopolitical map. There are other clues lying in plain sight, and I would encourage readers to take their own survey of the landscape to test my hypothesis: that the forces pushing the world toward instability are ubiquitous, protracted, and, at least for the near term, irreversible. In short, the world is poised to enter an era characterized by ever more extreme events in all aspects of life.

What does all this tell us about the world of 2050? Though the date lies well within a lifetime, it might as well be a thousand years away for today's twentysomethings attempting to envision the world of their dotage. The clues suggest that lying just beyond the edge of the next millennium, befogging our view of the future, are a fateful series of global events, affecting the skies, the earth, and society. Though set in motion by human activities in this century, these events are now largely beyond our control. Like some giant ship, humanity finds itself caught up in accelerating currents at the perimeter of an enormous whirlpool.

It is one thing to grasp the frightening topology that charts humanity as it heads toward this maelstrom. It is quite another to predict what our ship of fools will encounter when it enters the vortex. I have chosen to look ahead to 2050. The fifty-two-year span between this writing and my target time is long enough to encompass events as epochal as the rise and fall of the Iron Curtain, but short enough that it will fall within the expected lifetime of most of the young in school today.

I also choose 2050 because those who live through the next few decades will by then have answers to many of this century's ultimate questions. They will know how both nature and nations respond to the pressures of eight to ten billion in population. They will know whether the cumulative impact of all these stresses on the earth and human political institutions will galvanize human initiative or drive humanity into the darkest period in its two-hundred-thousand-year history. In this sense, the year 2050 will provide a report card on the decisions taken by leaders and ordinary people today. The wise elders of 2050 will know whether *Homo sapiens* deserves its name, or whether humanity is indistinguishable from other creatures whose rise and fall have been driven entirely by biological imperatives.

If the first part of this book is an attempt to reveal the destabilizing forces gathering beneath the apparent stability of the present, the second part is designed to excite the imagination to speculate on how instability will change the way people act and think in the coming decades. I do this through a series of scenarios that examine different aspects of life. Just as the clues overlap and recombine, there is no direct correspondence between any one clue in the first section and any one scenario to follow. No one clue would by itself change the world. Rather, each scenario draws from several different clues and attempts to offer a coherent glimpse of some aspect of life in the middle of the next century.

The first scenario, for instance, looks forward to the financial marketplace of the middle of the next century, and in this respect ties closely to the first of the clues in the previous section. The mood and nature of the marketplace, however, are the product of a host of nonfinancial factors, and the scenario draws from several other clues to show how the interplay of various familiar sources of instability can create a financial landscape utterly different from the one we see today.

Similarly, the scenario set in Oaxaca, Mexico, draws upon the second, third, fourth, and seventh clues, dealing with phenomena as disparate as megacities, migration, water scarcity, and the vulnerabilities of the world food system. Here too the scenario shows how familiar forces in the present can recombine to produce situations that contrast dramatically with the conventional wisdom. I cannot stress too strongly that these scenarios are not meant to be prophecies of any sort, but, rather, plausible responses to an unstable world. I am trying only to dramatize how something as simple as increasing instability can profoundly reorder an otherwise familiar world.

The DNA that rules the future recombines the elements of present-day life. But that does not necessarily mean that the future can be engineered. This is an uncomfortable idea for Americans to digest. It flies in the face of a deeply ingrained can-do spirit to assert that the forces that will shape life in the next century are beyond our reach, that there are threats to our tranquillity that we can identify and understand but still not do anything about.

It is also especially galling to be asked to believe that the application of human ingenuity, which brought about the great advances of this century, will not be able to head off the coming instability. In the coming decades, we will be in the position of watching and understanding events that we cannot control, and that will make the coming instability all the more intolerable.

Many readers who accept that the previous clues point toward instability will balk at the notion that we cannot do anything to head it off.

What, then, will the future bring? Again, there is evidence in the present and past about how people react to instability. I have drawn heavily on that in my attempts to imagine the look and feel of the future.

For instance, when people are threatened by some outside force, they tend to adopt a lifeboat mentality. I recently encountered an example of this in Antarctica, a land of extremes in which blizzards can materialize without warning. The adaptations it has forced on those who choose to defy its storms and cold offer a proleptic glimpse of life when nature turns deadly.

Life in Antarctica is encumbered at every turn by rules and training. Before taking recreational walks outside the main American base, called McMurdo Station, the most civilized part of the continent, a visitor must attend a lecture on safety, and anyone who wants to ski or walk away from the base must do so in pairs, checking in and out. Visitors must even take a course on dealing with waste, since all garbage must be recycled or carried off. Before scientists and other visitors are allowed into the camps deep in the field, they must take survival courses. Before they ride in a helicopter, they must take a helicopter course, the logic being that if one crashes the passenger should know how to work the helicopter and otherwise perform functions of the crew. The National Science Foundation, which has near-absolute power over the community, issues clothing for various regions, lending an egalitarian flavor to life that stands in sharp contrast to the wildly varying displays one encounters in other cold settings, such as ski slopes. Before visiting the Dry Valleys, one of the coldest and driest deserts on earth, people must agree to abide by a set of rules that govern everything from dealing with dishwashing water to how close one can walk to a stream.

It is noteworthy that freedom-loving Americans accept all these infringements on individual liberty without cavil. Most recognize that the rules governing clothing and survival training

serve to protect lives in the harshest environment on earth, and
that the other restrictions serve to protect environments of extraordinary scientific and ecological interest.

It is also interesting to note that in this harsh environment
the support workers enjoy relatively higher status than they
would back in academia, where brains tend to rule the roost. The
basic necessities of life, so taken for granted in the States, are
very much in your face in Antarctica. Much of the day is spent
negotiating around the weather and how it might change, dealing
with the logistics of getting from one place to another, planning
baths and laundry in an area of scarce water. All these activities
bring you into the community and at the same time intrude on
time that might otherwise be given over to investigation, relationships, or recreation. The technology exists to re-create in
Antarctica the heedless life-style characteristic of affluent subur-
bia, but it would be fearfully expensive—and, more to the point,
it would be a dangerous illusion to foster should anyone have to
leave the cocoon.

Antarctica shows us how life changes when nature becomes
unreliable and hostile. I am not saying that the world of the
twenty-first century will be as unforgiving as the Antarctic, but
suggest that as life becomes more volatile people accept greater
intrusions into their lives in the interest of security. As the details
of daily living become a preoccupation, people also pay more attention to how the actions of others affect the welfare of their
group, and become more aware of those who aren't pulling their
weight, or whose actions sap the energy of the community.

In a more general sense, as life becomes more uncertain,
people take out insurance of various sorts. They firm up relationships with their families, their peers, their community. The trade-
off is that these entanglements are a two-way street, acting to limit
the gains and wealth of any one individual. Thus any return of in
stability will likely pit a long-standing drive to maximize security
against a more recent but enormously powerful urge toward max-
imizing individual comfort and material wealth.

In the following scenarios, I try to envision some of the ways in which this collision of basic motives will play out. I have other assumptions that will become clear as I attempt to show how societies might react to the forces described in the clues.

One assumption is that it is difficult to change human nature. After decades of viewing people as infinitely plastic, a legacy that B. F. Skinner and behaviorism laid upon the social sciences, a welcome counteraction has emerged in such fields as ethology and evolutionary psychology, which recognizes that millions of years of evolution imbued humans with needs and proclivities that are difficult to change, period, if not impossible to change on a generational time scale, regardless of whether technology has changed the nature of work and gender roles.

Any vision of the future that either expects or demands a new human, a higher consciousness, or some other transformation of human nature should be automatically suspect. It's unlikely, for instance, that people will be better Christians in the future than they have been for two thousand years. People will look for angles and tend to overdo things in 2050 no less than they do today. That said, human behavior does vary tremendously with values, as the executives of Kentucky Fried Chicken found out when their efforts to introduce the fast food to India were met in 1996 by mobs of stone-throwing vegetarians.

As a basic condition of life, instability can have a profound effect on values. One of the byproducts of ecological or climatic instability is the reminder that there are forces larger than humanity at work in the world. These reminders can have a profound effect on a culture.

Take, for instance, the ten plagues visited on Egypt described in the Old Testament. In an entertaining reinterpretation of sacred texts, Dr. John Marr, a historian of medicine, argues that the plagues were the result of ecological disruption. Poor sanitation and/or climate change produced red algal blooms in rivers and ponds. The loss of oxygen during eutrophication forced frogs (or toads) out of the water and into palaces, as described in the Bible. This set in motion a cascade of catastrophes as disease-spreading insects fed on dead fish and amphibians. The Egyptian bad luck continued when crops ruined by hail festered, producing airborne mycotoxins which felled the first people—presumably a perk accorded to favored first sons—who entered granaries after sandstorms produced three days of darkness.

Fanciful or not, Marr's argument draws on a well-explored phenomenon, as cultures encode in myth the lessons of history, either reaffirming, altering, or creating a world view in the process. It is easy to imagine how the world might have been different had these ancient Semitic tribes interpreted the plagues as God's wrath for the abuse of the earth, rather than His smiting down the oppressor of a favored people.

We can see the beginnings of just this type of adjustment today, as religions attempt to grapple with the looming environmental crises. This process too provides a window into the way in which instability forces cultural adaptation. Various Christian thinkers, for instance, are grappling with the question "Is the Creation sacred," an issue that goes to the heart of the Christian view of humanity's rights in nature. For many hundreds of years, mainstream Christianity has taken the view implied in the Book of Genesis: that earth and its creatures are there for mankind's enjoyment and betterment. Now, with many of earth's ecosystems obviously in decline, even conservative evangelical Christians have begun to adjust to the view that "only the Creator has the right to destroy His creation," as Calvin DeWitt, a leading American evangelical environmentalist, put it. These shifting tides led to an extraordinary scene in February 1996, when a group of evangelical Christians lobbied conservative Republican lawmakers, normally a group that counts on unqualified support from religious conservatives, not to weaken the Endangered Species Act, which this Christian group called in a news conference "The Noah's Ark of our day."

Unstable times have a profoundly different impact on values from stable times. In stable times, it is easy to fall into what the University of Maryland economist Robert Costanza calls "social traps," situations in which a destructive path is pursued, whether the behavior be smoking cigarettes or deforestation, because the

gains are immediate and the penalties far off in the future. In unstable times, consequences are very much on people's minds.
Some, like the looters running amok in anarchic Albania in 1997,
assume they are temporarily released from all moral restraints, but
many seek a new order that makes sense of the times. The ways
in which this process of adaptation might continue surface repeatedly in the coming pages, as a leitmotif that informs several of the
scenarios I offer.

These, then, are the assumptions upon which this thought experiment proceeds: First and foremost is that humanity is poised
to enter a period of increasing instability. Second is that the increase in human numbers and global reach of the consumer society have changed the stakes for any return to instability. Third is
that it helps to look at how people and cultures have reacted to
instability in the past and present in any attempt to envision how
they will react in the future.

Underlying all of these assumptions is an assumption about
the role of technology: namely, that, despite the huge role technology plays in the survival of humanity and the details of day-to-
day living, our inventions have not appreciably changed human
nature and will not do so in the future. I realize that this is a
provocative assertion in an era giddy with the supposed transfor-
mational potential of technological developments ranging from the
Internet, to cloning, to Prozac. But at the end of the nineteenth
century, the last great period of technological innovation, patterns
and proclivities embedded in humans by hundreds of thousands of
years of evolution were not overruled, even if the era's revolutions
in transportation, communication, and lighting had a profound effect on daily life. It is indisputable that technological changes will
occur in the next fifty years that will have great effect on daily life
as well. Rather than predict what will come out of fifty-two years of
unpredictable interactions between science, development, com-
mercialization, economic circumstances, and human tastes, I will
suggest (for reasons that will be explored in the final chapter of
this book) that no innovations, no matter how wondrous, will be
able to stave off the coming instability.

As in the case of the clues, the following eight scenarios are not meant to be comprehensive so much as suggestive. The world is large and complex, and no doubt there will be places fifty-two years from now, in both the developed world and remote plateaux and jungles, where people lead lives very similar to the way we live today. And it is all but certain that some people will react to change in utterly unpredictable and alien ways. With these disclaimers in mind, let us look forward and, in a playful and speculative spirit, attempt to envision what the wise elders of 2050 will know.

PART II

SCENES
FROM 2050

Chapter 11

LONDON:
THE VICARS OF FINANCE

Of all the major world capitals, London in 2050 would be the most familiar to those peering into the future from the vantage point of the late twentieth century. Its greenbelts and parks are not so green, browned by hotter, sunnier summers and otherwise chaotic weather, but, as had been the pattern down through the centuries, the look and feel of London's districts have only stiffly and slowly adapted to changing times as they were built and re-built. In dress and manner, many of London's citizens would also look familiar to the time traveler from the twentieth century. Such sartorial links to the past stand in stark contrast to fashion in many capitals. The British wore suits in the tropics during their colonial heyday (dying like flies as a result), and they continue to wear suits into the twenty-first century.

Those practitioners of the arcane arts of banking and trading still scurry to and from offices in the City, as the financial district continues to be called. Cosmetic ties to earlier eras, however, conceal profound change, particularly in finance. A typical investment banker would be unrecognizable to anyone who followed markets in the late twentieth century. He has more in common with a vicar than with Larry the Liquidator, Gordon Gekko, or any other stereotype of the aggressive, amoral, workaholic deal-maker.

Investment banking in 2050 draws upon a different reservoir

of talent from fifty years earlier. Whereas, at the end of the previous century, great numbers of academics, lawyers, and scientists abandoned their fields in search of riches on Wall Street, the tide has now turned. The so-called Quants and Rocket Scientists, who had spent their days devising ways to slice up and repackage bonds, create options on securities, and otherwise devise new financial instruments, now have nowhere near the influence they formerly exercised. Because of its diminished status and reduced opportunities, fewer mathematicians and scientists have gravitated toward the field. By the middle of the twenty-first century, the best and brightest once again pursue truth and beauty, and bask in the respect conferred on those who forsake Mammon for higher things. Those who enter investment banking now tend to be a priggish bunch, selected for their character as much as for their facility with numbers.

Family connections still draw new talent into the field, and finance remains a skill largely acquired through apprenticeship. Now, however, much of what passes from mentors to novices involves cautionary tales drawn from the events that led to depression and civil unrest earlier in the century. These sessions have the flavor of arguments over scriptures or the Talmud, though their purpose is to familiarize would-be financiers with the subtleties of investing in this highly scrutinized and suspicious world. Such conversations are the mirror image of the type of discussions that characterized the dawn of capitalism six hundred years earlier, when merchants in Antwerp would seek Church approval to collect interest. Back in the fifteenth century, commerce was just breaking out of the straitjacket imposed by religion, but now religious and cultural values are reasserting their supremacy over business. Traders enter the pits with the fear of God in their minds.

How did this happen? Capitalism did not suddenly develop a conscience. Rather, the world changed, and financiers, those most agile creatures, have been forced to adapt.

The lessons of a time when the world came apart are emblazoned in the consciousness of every soul who entered finance or the markets. By 2050, every fund manager is familiar with tales of the early part of the century, when a series of financial panics and crises spiraled out of control, plunging the world into more than a decade of depression. Every trader knows horror stories of days when all the fail-safe mechanisms and circuit breakers proved illusory and the financial community stared into a bottomless pit.

As the economist Herbert Stein once quipped, "If something cannot go on forever, it won't." These sentiments exactly describe the perils of the global monetary system as the twentieth century drew to a close. Like the apocryphal hurricane started by a beat of a butterfly's wing in tropical air, a meltdown was ripe to happen. And like the U.S. Forest Service, which for a century suppressed forest fires before it discovered that all they were doing was setting the stage for a mammoth conflagration when the inevitable fire occurred, the feints of the financial community in dealing with local crises did little more than raise the stakes of the coming collapse. With the passing of each year without calamity, the "event risks" of a teetering global financial system became so great that every inconsequential event threatened to become consequential. Something as minor, for instance, as the midterm elections that swept populists into power in the U.S. in, say, 2006 had the potential to trigger a global financial meltdown that ultimately reshaped finance in market capitals around the world. Here's how:

Populist sentiment arose in the first decade of the new millennium in response to the steadily widening gap between the vast middle class and the favored elite of executives and successful entrepreneurs. Having watched their incomes stagnate or erode for decades at the same time that corporations cut back on benefits and job security, people were less and less willing to buy the argument that America had to be lean and mean to compete in the global economy. Tired and demoralized Americans became ever more primed for conspiratorial explanations of their plight, and ever more willing customers for those demagogues who promised simple solutions.

Recognizing their own market opportunity, demagogues began winning elections with promises to save American jobs and

guarantee incomes. From the point of view of the financial markets, the problem was that these promises all contained fiscal time
bombs: a new social net for the poor, for example; punitive taxes
that were supposedly targeted on the wealthy, but which burdened the middle class in direct and indirect ways; protectionist
tariffs on imported goods; low-cost federally guaranteed loans for
housing; a suite of new corporate taxes; and so on.

With the U.S. contending with a multitrillion-dollar national
debt in the first decade of the twenty-first century, these deficit-
increasing policies would lead to inflation. The prospect of renewed
domestic inflation scared investors, because of the exquisitely delicate balance of the world's monetary system. Specifically, inflation
threatened the value of foreign holdings of U.S. Treasury notes.
Even before the turn of the millennium, these notes had become
like a store of plutonium, which, as it grew, became ever more
likely to go critical.

The Treasury notes held by foreign central banks are analogous to IOUs which the banks accept as payment for selling exports, in lieu of converting dollars into their own currency. It is in
the interest of exporting countries to hold these notes for redemption at a future date: the exporting nations have little to gain
from converting trade surpluses to local currency, which would
drive down the dollar, and thereby making their own products
uncompetitive, or spending the dollars on foreign imports, which
would weaken their own industries.

For the U.S., this arrangement was one of the perks of the
dollar's role as the world's reserve currency, since foreign demand
for U.S. debt obligations helped keep interest rates down. Even
the simple desire of foreigners to hold $100 bills saved the U.S.
Treasury $15 billion a year in interest in the 1990s. But it could
only work as long as foreign holders had the expectation that they
would be able to redeem these notes at full value at some point in
the future. In other words, the global monetary system rested on
the faith that U.S. politicians would reduce their government
deficit while the Federal Reserve Board chairman held inflation in
check and otherwise defended the value of the dollar. As it turned

out, this was a shaky foundation indeed for the world's reserve currency.

By 2006, so many of these notes—more than $1.5 trillion— were in the hands of foreign central banks that the U.S. and the rich exporting nations each held the financial weapons of mutual assured destruction. In effect, the U.S. had all but ceded control of its fiscal policy to foreign masters. In turn, the dollar-rich nations had trusted the U.S. to safeguard the value of a good portion of their export earnings and assets.

America's complicity in this ever-growing overhang of foreign-held Treasury bonds was akin to borrowing blood from a vampire—the foreign-held debt might keep you alive temporarily, but the vampire was going to need it someday and take it back. Should foreign governments attempt to sell these notes and buy U.S. goods or assets, U.S. consumers would find themselves priced out of much of their own market, and a substantial portion of the nation's production and wealth would end up in foreign hands. It would bode equally ill for the U.S. if foreign governments converted these holdings into their own currencies for their own domestic purposes.

Thus, with every passing year at the turn of the millennium, the nations of the world walked an ever more treacherous path. Banks, mutual funds, and nations alike found themselves in the prisoner's dilemma described in chapter 1. In this case, the foreign banks had an interest in maintaining the value of the dollar to protect their exports, but they also had a powerful motivation to be the first on their block to sell their dollar holdings, because of the increasing likelihood that some event would precipitously wipe out the value of years of export earnings tied up in Treasury notes and simultaneously devalue their dollar-denominated assets. In the years before 2006, financial-policy makers were aware that the U.S. needed somehow to reduce this debt burden, but inflation or currency depreciation (the favored means of stealth debt repudiation among nations) would also inflict severe pain on Americans.

One way to reduce painlessly the explosive pressures of this mountain of foreign-held U.S. debt was through American exports, and the best hope for that lay in renewed spending for capital goods at a point when economic growth outran industrial capacity, or as change in manufacturing or energy precipitated a new round of investment in next-generation technologies. Unfortunately, when both these moments came, the U.S. garnered only a meager portion of the rewards.

The U.S. maintained its lead in supplying the world with chips to drive the information revolution, but the export boom in capital goods never really materialized, as companies like Intel exported much of their production capacity to low-cost labor markets. The U.S. also paid the price for its political and economic addiction to fossil fuels, allowing countries with high gas prices to steal a march on the development of alternative-energy industries. When worries about climate change finally began expressing themselves politically around the world, just after the turn of the millennium, European and Asian companies cleaned up financially, because earlier they had cleaned up their industries. The one exception was the chemical industry, where U.S. companies began integrating environmental concerns into their strategic thinking before their European and Japanese competitors.

The buildup of foreign-held Treasury notes caused other nations to pay ever-closer attention to the rivets popping out of the aging monetary system as pressures built up on the dollar. Everybody knew that change was overdue, and the vulnerability of the system became increasingly apparent as the looming overhang of Treasury notes made economies around the world hostage to the common sense of the U.S. Congress and the chairman of the Federal Reserve Board.

Foreign bankers knew all too well that the average life of a monetary system was little more than a generation. Most of the monetary systems since gold replaced the British pound in the 1880s lasted twenty-five years or less. At the end of the twentieth century, the European countries planned to unite behind a common currency called the euro, but the stresses of internal politics and the different agendas of the nations involved so weakened the euro that it ended up being the monetary equivalent of Esperanto, the now forgotten universal language once pushed by the UN.

Indeed, the advent of the EMU temporarily strengthened the dollar, since Germans who had their investments in marks were more willing to trust their life savings to the devil they knew than they were to trust some new shadowy organization of faceless foreign bureaucrats. Still, by 2006, the dollar had been the reserve currency for thirty-five years. Everybody knew that the end of the reign of the dollar was near.

Various bankers, analysts, and government officials proposed solutions, such as establishing a supranational institution that would exchange long-term notes for U.S. debt. But even if the U.S. was willing to cede sovereignty to some new institution (which it wasn't), and even if governments trusted each other to hold by the deal (which they did not), giant holders of dollars like China faced internal stresses and civil upheavals that made them anxious to have ready access to their troves of T-notes.

While the world monetary system became more tenuous, the giant equity markets continued to swell. Buoyed by the growth of trade with the former communist countries and the development of Asian and Latin American markets, the unprecedented bull market in the U.S. that began in 1982 became even more unprecedented. From $8 trillion in 1997, the market capitalization of the U.S. stock markets swelled to $20 trillion by 2006. True, there was the occasional sharp, if temporary, correction, such as the market turmoil that followed the financial contagion that spread from Asia beginning in 1997, but after surviving these and other shocks, the equity markets continued to grow in some measure simply because they did not fall. Investors recognized that this situation was much like the Japanese "bubble economy" of the 1980s, which ballooned because of an inflated real-estate market and then burst in 1989. But as the market continued to confound predictions of its imminent demise, even famous bears like James Grant threw in the towel and gave up predicting when their day would come.

By 2006, investors also faced a critical dilemma. During the prior twenty-five years, they had poured an enormous amount of money into the markets—$20 billion a month in the U.S. alone at times in the 1990s—as twentieth-century baby boomers took control of their retirement accounts and invested the astonishing amounts (the greatest transfer of wealth in history from one generation to another) they had inherited from their parents. Now they were starting to spend their savings, and they were nervous about a stock market that had not suffered a prolonged downturn since the early 1980s. Moreover, most investors and retirees now had greater control over their stocks and bonds, having moved massive amounts of money from pension funds to self-directed funds. Though a multibillion-dollar pension fund cannot decide in one day to move from stocks to cash, individuals can, and this trend toward "disintermediation," as it was called, introduced a further element of volatility into the market.

Nor was it just Americans who were shifting from investment to liquidation of portfolios. Japan, with its xenophobic attitudes toward immigration, was one of the first countries to discover that, just as its crowded islands could not absorb more population growth, its economy could not live without it. By 2006, more than a fifth of the population was over sixty-five. Top-heavy with pensioners, Japan shifted from a society of savers to a nation of spenders. This put pressure on both the dollar and the world's equity markets.

In the end, it became clear that the integrated global market was at its base an elaborate pyramid-sales scheme. It needed population growth to supply cheap labor and a constant source of new consumers. As population growth slowed in industrial countries, more fault lines in the system began to appear.

Growth stagnated in the developed countries as consumer spending stalled and capital spending slowed. The fossil-fuel lobby had successfully stalled the adoption of alternative energy in the industrial nations, inadvertently spurring the economies of developing nations, who eagerly embraced solar, wind, and fuel-cell technologies as a low-cost alternative to massive infrastructure investments for centralized power generation. The maturing of information technologies around the world had the effect of further undermining the economies of industrial nations, as multi-nationals farmed out back-office functions to modem-accessible workers in the developing world and used knowledge-based software to replace experts at home.

Though the emerging economies at first benefited as the industrial nations faltered, they had their own problems. Repeated weather-related crop failures around the world contributed to extreme volatility in the global grain markets that in turn spurred migration and political instability in dozens of nations. Investment capital shied away from politically unstable regions, which, naturally enough, contributed to more economic hardship and instability.

And so it happened. The end of the integrated global economy came not with a bang but a whimper. The bangs came later. A week before the midterm election of 2006, as it became obvious that the populists might take control of Congress, a number of pensioners and investors decided that it would be prudent to move out of stocks and mutual funds. Engineers, doctors, lawyers, entrepreneurs, and coupon clippers began logging on to the Internet and put in orders to sell equities. As this virtual mob began trying to execute their trades, it became clear that something was wrong. People would hit the "enter" key and find that nothing happened. Across America, thousands of people stared in perplexity at their screens; first in a trickle, then a flood, they began calling hot lines and using e-mail to try in vain to find out what was wrong.

The problem was very simple: everybody was selling; nobody was buying. All over the country, investors began to panic. Faced with an avalanche of sell orders in a collapsing market, mutual funds could not find buyers for the tens of billions of dollars in stock they needed to sell to honor their commitments. Such selling as they did drove prices down further. The markets imposed trading controls, but investors vainly tried to unload shares in secondary markets, off-line, any way they could.

By itself, the market free-fall might have been manageable, but Americans were not the only ones watching the midterm elections closely. The populist surge also deepened concern among the major holders of U.S. Treasury notes in Asia. The Bank of Japan at first tried to sop up the flood of dollars, but was soon overwhelmed, as Singapore, Saudi Arabia, and China joined in the flight.

Following the advice of his political consultants, the U.S. president, along with his Treasury secretary and the chairman of the Federal Reserve, flew to California and met with the most strident of the demagogues, who was calling for bans on imports and a moratorium on Treasury-note redemptions. The idea was to bring the full weight of the presidency to bear on the California populist in order to convince the man that the global economy was at risk if the U.S. embarked on a protectionist path. Through threats and cajolery, the three men tried to get the actor-turned-political-messiah to declare publicly that he would not pursue policies detrimental to the dollar. The messianic antipolitician, who had but a minimal grasp of markets, instead took the opportunity to humiliate the president by saying that he ought to be thanked for helping relieve the U.S. of an unfair burden imposed by foreign countries whose unfair trade practices had beggared the nation for decades.

Words like these were the beginning of the end for the dollar in its role as the world's reserve currency. Spasms of liquidation wracked the world's markets for months. The breakdown also marked the end of the so-called Paradigm, the nickname given to a model of open markets and fiscal restraint that was demanded of emerging and developing nations if they were to have access to capital. Nations imposed protective tariffs and controls on currency movements, in desperate attempts to carve out some stability amid the wild gyrations of the financial markets, but these only served to deepen and prolong the crisis.

The tipping point came when, some weeks into the crisis, terrorists exploded a crude, home-made fifteen-kiloton nuclear device on the outskirts of Las Vegas, Nevada, killing eight thousand people (the bomb was sufficiently far from the center of the city so that it did not kill the hundreds of thousands it might have).

The blast leveled homes and businesses in a sparsely populated region of four square miles and severely damaged buildings in a twelve-square-mile, more densely populated area. No group claimed responsibility, although the most massive investigation ever launched in the United States eventually traced the act to a tiny millenarian cult that saw Las Vegas as a twenty-first-century Sodom.

The surprise was not that a nuclear device had been used for the first time since World War II but, rather, that it had not happened sooner. The collapse of communism, the rise of mafias in Russia, and the haphazard security of Russian nuclear materials made it inevitable that highly enriched uranium (HEU) would make it onto the black market. Indeed, as early as 1997, former Russian National Security Adviser Alexander Lebed claimed on "60 Minutes" that an unfinished nuclear inventory he initiated had discovered that eighty-four suitcase-size one-kiloton devices were missing. These weapons could be activated by one person in twenty or thirty minutes.

The millenarian cult that planted the bomb outside Las Vegas did not have a suitcase bomb, but they did obtain a grapefruit-size lump of HEU. Then all they needed was a few hundred thousand dollars, a month or two, and expertise they could tap on the Internet, in order to build a bomb that could easily fit inside the types of vans used in the bombing of the World Trade Center in 1993, and the Oklahoma City Murrah Federal Building in 1995. Graham Allison, an expert on nuclear anarchy, had warned of just such an eventuality in the 1990s, when he monitored "loose nukes" in the Defense Department and later in academia. With a triumphant U.S. enjoying a Pax Americana, however, neither he nor anyone else could raise the profile of the issue sufficiently to divert resources from tight defense budgets to ward off a hypothetical threat.

The HEU used in the Las Vegas bomb originated at the Russian nuclear facility in Sverdlovsk and was stolen by a disgruntled guard from a storage facility in the closed city of Chelyabinsk, a thousand miles from Moscow. From there it made its way east to

Mafia-controlled ships in the Pacific trawler fleet, and then onto a Mexican tuna boat owned by a major *narcotrafficante*. The drug lord, who carried a deep grudge against the U.S. for time he had spent in an American prison, sold the HEU through middlemen to the Texas-based messianic group, and shipped the material in a special compartment attached to the undercarriage of a natural-gas tanker truck he regularly used for drug deliveries. The truck crossed the U.S. border through a "safe" customs post where he had bought off the agents. Once they had the HEU, the cult members used a bomb "recipe" they took off the Internet, with little worry about getting caught before the act.

The U.S. economy could easily absorb the immediate economic impact of the attack, but the cult members had unwittingly hit a critically important underpinning of the entire global financial system. Occurring during a global economic crisis, the attack further cracked the sense of impregnability and entitlement that had emerged during the unprecedented bull market. It was the worst possible time for America to look vulnerable. Perception and mood play such an important role in the life of markets that the bomb's second-order impacts were almost incalculable.

Social upheaval following the attack heightened the image of a nation on the point of unraveling. Americans did not know that the culprits were home-grown, and the country was swept by a tide of xenophobia. Politicians who a day earlier had sought to calm the markets were suddenly calling for America to bar the gates to anything foreign, whether products or people. Foreign-looking residents of American cities went for days without leaving their apartments, out of fear of the vengeful mood that had settled over the country.

The bombing in 2006 provided the world with a vivid demonstration of the meaning of the phrase "event risk." It was a turning point, but even if the bombing had not occurred, another event would have served the same purpose. The issue was perception, and people were looking for a symbol that embodied the darkening mood. One event cannot bring down the global economy, but, as the Mexican peso crisis of 1994 demonstrated, something as intangible as a mood change can set in motion actions that can create a self-fulfilling prophecy. By 2006, so many cross-currents of volatility were sloshing around the financial ocean that it was inevitable that at some point some of those currents would combine into a gigantic rogue wave.

As the global economy shuddered, it was hit by a severe secondary shock in the form of a banking crisis. For years, this unfolding crisis had been concealed by lax scrutiny and by the booming global economy, which allowed shaky banks to pretend that non-performing assets on their books had some future value. In 1997, the International Monetary Fund published figures revealing that 133 of its 181 member countries had significant banking problems. These countries ranged from the industrial powerhouse Japan to shaky democracies like India and Turkey. In over fifty developing countries, the banking system was operating essentially without capital, which meant that any disruption of credit flows could bring the whole system down. Other countries required only minimal set-asides for loan losses, further increasing the potential for instability.

Even before the debacle of 2006, the world had a vivid preview of the costs and consequences of bank failures. In Bulgaria, a quarter of the nation's banks collapsed in the mid-1990s, bringing the economy down with them. The collapse of the Mexican peso was followed by a banking crisis as consumers reneged on loans and found they could borrow only at extortionate rates. The collapse of the savings-and-loan industry in the United States cost taxpayers roughly 3 percent of GDP, but in a number of emerging nations banking collapses cost as much as 20 percent of GDP, burdening economies with years of recession.

When it came, in the years following 2006, the banking crisis also exposed the true costs that corruption imposed on an economy. Corruption had soared throughout the developing world following the collapse of communism, and many of the countries with the most fragile banks were also the most corrupt. A correlation of bank ratings and business practices in 1997 revealed that the most corrupt nations, including Indonesia, India, and China, also had the weakest banking systems.

This was more than coincidence. Nations like Indonesia and Mexico courted an image as economies on the verge of entering the ranks of industrial powers, but in reality they functioned as banana republics, where a favored elite could insist on a piece of lucrative deals and also control the flow of lending at banks. With credit channeled toward favored projects regardless of their worth, and with money-generating enterprises bled by a class of politically connected leeches, banks found themselves saddled with underperforming, nonperforming, and occasionally nonexistent assets. *The Wall Street Journal,* for instance, reported on the failure of Brazil's Banco Nacional SA, which, after years of directing money to politically connected borrowers, had a $7-billion negative net worth when it collapsed in 1995.

The currency and markets collapses of 1997 in Southeast Asia also exposed the ways in which corruption and cronyism hemmed in policy makers once a financial crisis was under way. When Thailand was confronted with the prospect of a liquidity crisis in early 1997, resulting from weakening export earnings and increased consumption, it found its policy options limited by the very cronyism that put the nation in a vulnerable position in the first place. To restore the confidence of the international markets, Thailand should have pre-emptively devalued its currency, the baht. Thai officials did not take this course in part because a devaluation would have hurt the elite, who would have found themselves paying more to service dollar-denominated loans and more to pay for imported goods. Alternatively, the Thais could have raised interest rates to dampen speculation and attract foreign capital, but this would have forced a cohort of politically connected real-estate developers into insolvency, bringing down a banking system that tolerant bank supervisors had permitted to remain undercapitalized for years. Stymied from taking reasonable actions, the Thais tried to brazen out the crisis, and as a consequence suffered a currency-and-market collapse that cost the nation over $50 billion and led to political unrest.

Even before the events of 2006, numerous banks collapsed simply as a result of the increased volatility in the international credit markets. An election in Turkey in 2002 that gave power to the most radical factions of Islamic fundamentalists scared the capital markets, and left four major banks insolvent as money fled the country and interest rates soared. The World Bank stepped in where it could with loans and guarantees, but even its resources were dwarfed as bank failures hit Thailand, the Philippines, Russia, Pakistan, and Egypt, not to mention Korea, Japan, India, and China. Frantic depositors saw their life savings vanish in country after country, and irate people took to the streets and governments tumbled in a number of emerging nations. As the dominoes fell in the global economy in the first decade of the new millennium, more than one developing nation descended into anarchy not unlike the chaos that tore apart Albania in 1997.

And so the dollar lost its position as the world's reserve currency. In the chaos that followed, many people and some nations turned to gold and other precious metals for security. Thanks to high-tech legerdemain, however, a new multifaceted international financial system emerged. Countries with prudent fiscal policies and highly transparent accounts still had the luxury of settling accounts in currency backed only by the good faith and stability of the government. Many others pegged their currency to either precious metals or other commodities in a hybrid arrangement. Thus ended the world's experiment with a monetary system based entirely upon something as intangible as confidence in the prudence of America's elected officials.

Financial shocks continued to reverberate through the financial markets for years after 2006 as governments, major corporations, and bankers desperately sought measures to reduce risk and restore investor confidence. The meltdown ruined many former masters of the universe, and drove others to despair if not outright hiding. The decline fed paranoid sentiment, and politicians around the world responded with ever more confiscatory policies and taxes. Guerrilla wars and terrorist movements spread anarchy in nations like Indonesia, China, Russia, and India. Poor nations in Africa returned to barter and subsistence economies. Sophisticated international gangs gained power as the strong and the ruthless banded together to profit from the spreading chaos. Given changes in climate and the collapse of services in the cities, infectious disease spread rapidly, killing millions and further fueling xenophobia and isolationism.

The plague and chaos spurred a burgeoning religious revival as people sought to understand their plight. Increasingly, ordinary people turned to nonmaterial satisfaction, a trend that was driven in part by the practical circumstances of living in an age of diminished material prospects. The more spiritual and moralistic mood turned the public against the corrupt and lawless elements in society. By the beginning of the third decade of the new millennium, intolerance and vigilantism had risen to the point where authorities found the backbone to tame the gangs. In some parts of the world, democracy gave way to authoritarian regimes, as scared and angry people accepted dictatorships and military regimes, believing them to be the price of restored order. The religious revival that had begun in the twentieth century continued to gather strength with every passing year. Conservative forms of Christianity and Islam gained new adherents at the same time that pantheistic and syncretic cults flourished.

Even in this climate, there were still fortunes to be made, but banking became a very dangerous game. The public was quick to blame the financial community for the misery caused by the depression. For the financial community, the most urgent issue was to regain the trust of ordinary citizens, and so bankers and traders alike devoted considerable efforts to building a reputation for rectitude. Gunslingers had long since slunk away, to be replaced by pillars of the establishment, who paid attention to social, cultural, religious, and community values as well as financial return. In this sense, the financial managers of 2050, whether in London, New York, or Frankfurt, superficially resemble the staid establishment that periodically dominated the financial markets in the late nineteenth and early twentieth centuries.

Though immersed in political and economic chaos for over a decade after 2006, the U.S. had powerful tools of recovery because of its long-standing tradition of respect for law; sound, if tattered, market structures; and great reservoirs of technical, legal, banking, and managerial talent. The process of sorting through the wreckage called upon all these abilities. Unfortunately, the U.S. was not as well positioned to recover from this depression as it had been in the 1930s. Back then the country still had a relatively small population and tremendous reserves of natural resources to fuel its growth. Now the nation had over three hundred million people and had exhausted much of its patrimony.

Great Britain and France also faced recovery with the advantage of a history of laws and market structures and the disadvantage of an impoverished resource base. To address this second problem, both nations took the expedient approach of bolstering ties with their former colonies in Africa, now weak federations of tribes desperately in need of technical assistance. The French went further and established relationships with some of the international gangs that dominated trade in parts of Latin America and Asia.

In order to rebuild markets, governments around the world imposed a number of new regulations on both stock and bond markets starting in the years immediately following the meltdown. Among these restrictions were extraordinarily high requirements on margin accounts, instantaneous settlement of trades, and transparency provisions that allowed brokers and traders to reassure themselves at any time of the solvency of their customers and partner institutions. These regulations, bolstered by acute consciousness of the risks of failure, had the effect of retarding the pace of investment. Investment and trade slowed even further as investors shied away from anything perceived as risky, and consumers hoarded their scant savings.

Finance thus entered a schizophrenic period, during which technology permitted an integrated global, light-speed economy, but caution, xenophobia, and regulation imposed a stately pace and parochial outlook on finance.

*   *   *

If any group in 2050 has retained some of the flavor of capitalism of the 1980s and 1990s, it is those so-called vulture capitalists who invested in distressed securities. The field had emerged in the latter part of the twentieth century, as the markets tried to recycle bankrupt railroads, steel mills, and other heavy industries as the American economy shifted toward information and services. Investors tend to react emotionally to news of a default or bankruptcy, quite often driving prices of stocks and bonds well below their real value when the company's parts are sold off. In these circumstances, distressed-market players step up, providing vital liquidity and reaping solid profits in return.

By the end of the twentieth century, there were so many vulture wannabes chasing distressed securities that even these markets became overbought. With the series of global financial crises in the early years of the twenty-first century, however, the distressed-securities players flourished again, although they faced a far more difficult financial landscape than they had previously encountered. To be sure, there was no shortage of corporate body parts to sort through in search of discarded treasure, but the rapid value change that accompanied the financial panics of these years made a lot of businesses irrelevant.

In 2050, these undertaker beetles are still recycling the wreckage of the century's financial upheavals, although by this time what is left to process consists of odds and ends. Some of these companies would seem surpassingly strange to the financiers of the day. What, for instance, would a young London analyst steeped in the values of 2050 make of the remains of some of the more flamboyant businesses of the twentieth century?

Consider the case of one such analyst. This young distressed-market player, second son of a minister by the name of Purdy, one day finds himself looking for opportunities in a box of documents relating to a company called Calvin Klein. Puzzled, he ponders the cracked and fading old publicity kit of the company, whose ads were once ubiquitous on buses and billboards throughout the first world. Photos depicted plain and gaunt young men and women dressed in underwear staring at each other sullenly. Was this the "before" picture, and would something the company was selling—prescription drugs? clothes? exercise devices? therapy?—transform these poor souls into healthy, well-dressed, fulfilled people? Purdy scans the rest of the folder looking in vain for the "after," and quickly loses interest, because the company had no remaining assets beyond the trademark rights to the name of its founder.

The dustbin of dead corporations which the young analyst is sorting through also includes a casino company that still holds title to now vacant properties in Atlantic City and Las Vegas. The analyst is intrigued because the terrorist bombing made Las Vegas the symbol of a turning point in world history akin to Dunkirk or the assassination of Archduke Ferdinand. Las Vegas suffered from the aforementioned terrorist attack, of course, but even after decontamination, its gambling-based economy was a casualty of resurgent moralism. This explains why properties in Las Vegas and Atlantic City remain in limbo so many years after the crash. Given the taint of gambling which drove real-estate values in those cities down even further than the overall decline of the market, these properties can be picked up for almost nothing.

A young London banker of the day, however, would also be acutely aware of the ever more noticeable impacts of climate change on coastal areas. Purdy knows that Atlantic City was increasingly buffeted by winds, tides, and surf from hurricanes and winter storms. The prudent men who control money would have a jaundiced view of investing in properties so clearly in harm's way.

Las Vegas, however, was a different story. Even before the crash, it had begun diversifying its economy, attracting significant high-tech business. Then, despite some lingering effects of the bombing, a subsequent series of devastating plagues in the 2010s and 2020s lent the idea of living in relatively germ-free desert areas new appeal.

The net result of these conflicting tides was that, even as Las Vegas lost one key component of its economy, many new ventures moved in, somewhat smoothing the city's fall. An empty sixty-year-old casino and hotel, built according to the flimsy building specifications of the previous century? Not on the face of it an attractive proposition, but perhaps the land has some value.

As junior staff ponder the residual value of properties tied to an ethos now very much out of fashion, more senior members of the distress group spend a good deal of their time attempting to evaluate the worth of the detritus of the energy-and-transportation infrastructure of the previous epoch. Utilities, aircraft manufacturers, and automobile makers all suffered greatly during the economic gyrations of the century. Revenues dropped, of course, but the problems of these industrial and energy giants were compounded because the global financial upheavals, in concert with other forces at work on the world scene, radically altered the way people lived.

With central power stations struggling, even in Britain, many more people moved "off the grid," relying on solar or other forms of alternative energy. As climate continued to become more unstable, nations became increasingly alarmed and began taxing fossil fuels more heavily. Neither the energy companies nor the auto manufacturers were prepared for these changes, although they had been predicted for decades. Entrepreneurs were ready to seize the opportunities presented by this fundamental change, but capital was scarce and tightly controlled. Labor was abundant and cheap, however, as was engineering talent and computer power. Result: community, town, and city-based transportation, sanitation, energy, and housing projects flourished.

One unfortunate consequence of the widespread revulsion over the pain inflicted during earlier excesses of capitalism was that good ideas became tainted along with the bad. The privatization of public functions such as energy, transportation, and sanitation ground to a halt, along with the movement to transfer public lands and other assets to private hands.

For libertarians, private ownership meant efficiency, economy, and interest in sustaining business over the long term; many ordinary people, however, thought only of the heedless pain and ruination that had followed the era when capitalism reigned supreme. When given the chance to show that private ownership could better serve the long-term interests of the community, a self-dealing elite all too often proved they were not to be trusted.

In the end, the notion of privatization did not so much disappear as become reified, surfacing in community-based enterprises that, after all, embodied a fundamental postulate of privatization: that those with a stake in the profitability of an enterprise are highly motivated to seek efficiency.

London and the rest of England adjusted to these and other changes more smoothly than many countries. Naturally reserved and respectful of traditions, the British easily adapted to the more priggish temper of the times. As a small island nation with easily patrolled borders, the United Kingdom escaped the tides of migrants that destabilized other European countries.

The nation has had a harder time escaping ocean tides, as rising sea levels and more frequent and intense storm surges have cost them hundreds of square kilometers of low-lying coastal farmland. However, despite these and other effects of climate change, British food security—an important issue in the twenty-first century—has actually increased, thanks in part to declining birthrates. Moreover, whereas manufacturing powers like Japan and Germany suffer from an aging population and shrinking numbers of consumers and workers, Britain, which long ago lost its industrial base to foreign competition, has made a transition toward services, specialty goods, value-added and information-based industries, which depend on skills and knowledge rather than numbers.

During the years of global economic chaos, standards of living declined in the United Kingdom as they did everywhere else, but strong community and family ties somewhat eased the suffering. Luckily, the British had never become quite so addicted to the blandishments of the consumer society as had most industrial nations. Indeed, even in the late twentieth century, the English only reluctantly adopted innovations such as call waiting, for many telephone users found these alleged "advances" rude and intrusive. When the stream of new products associated with modern material culture slowed greatly in the twenty-first century, many British found it easy to live without a number of conveniences they never really wanted that badly in the first place.

The global market of 2050 is but a shadow of its buccaneering antecedent at the end of the twentieth century. Through its excesses, capitalism ultimately created its worst nightmare—a suffocatingly regulated marketplace. It limped along, a wounded bull, still the most powerful tool around for matching money and ideas, but hobbled and prodded at every turn. This is the price to be paid for an earlier obstinate and obsessive fixation on the short term. Now the long term is powerfully represented by government regulation and the suspicions of the community. Finance has adapted to its reduced role in human affairs. Humans tend to overdo things, and, of course, it is open to debate whether the claustrophobic world of finance of 2050 will in the end be any more responsive to human needs and aspirations than have been the unfettered markets of the late twentieth century.

Chapter 12

THE PHILIPPINES:
RUIN, RICE, AND REBIRTH

Nestled in the hills above the International Rice Institute in Los Baños on the Philippine island of Luzon is a small arboretum. In the year 2050, the park is laced with paths running down to a river that flows from the surrounding mountains, just as it was at the end of the twentieth century. The park's paths are still bordered by faded markers which describe the botanical wonders collected by generations of curators: *bagtikan,* a member of the dipterocarp family, used to make veneer, cabinets, and plywood; *tuai,* a rusty, papery-barked tree found in drier places, used in pulp and paper; *antipolo,* whose wood is used to make musical instruments; *santol,* coveted for its roots, which help prevent infection after childbirth. On and on go the markers, describing the bounty of the tropical forest.

The infrequent visitors who stumble upon these descriptions, however, must visualize the trees they describe, since the markers stand before stumps. What was once a graceful park where schoolchildren and scouts would go to learn about the surrounding rain forest is now barren scrubland, having been picked over by timber thieves during years of civil strife earlier in the twenty-first century. For the better part of half a century, the park has been shrouded in silence. The surrounding national forests are almost all gone as well, cut by farmers and pirate timber operators.

The markers themselves indirectly point to one reason for the destruction: the utilitarian descriptions imply that trees evolved on this planet solely to become furniture or construction forms or otherwise be of direct use to humans. Beginning in the latter part of the twentieth century, the Philippines implemented this philosophy with a vengeance. They began paying the price almost immediately. Through the folly of its actions in the twentieth century, the Philippines provided the world with a case study of the dramatic real-life consequences of economic theory gone awry.

One of the easily missed side shows of the close of the twentieth century was an emergent rift among economists about how best to tabulate the prospects of a nation. When making their assessments about the economic prospects of a country, traditional economists tended to focus on such things as tax and monetary policies, the freedom and health of markets, the education of the workforce, the burden of regulation, access to capital, and other factors that might impede or smooth the way for manufacturing and trade. If environmental considerations showed up at all, they did as an "externality" that would be addressed in the natural course of development as a country became more affluent.

A favorite indicator of economic health was a nation's Gross Domestic Product, or GDP, which measured the aggregate annual amount of money changing hands. This measurement, however, took no account of whether the nature of an activity was helpful or harmful. Clear-cutting forests, for instance, showed up as a positive in national accounts, even if it led to the loss of fisheries as silt choked rivers and lagoons. If mudslides wiped out homes after clear-cutting, then reconstruction showed up as a positive in national accounts as well.

Most people intuitively recognize that humans need a livable planet, but classical economists needed a little help. During the last two decades of the twentieth century, a new group of economists began to argue that such forms of environmental degradation as pollution, deforestation, and desertification were central to the future well-being of societies. Thinkers like Herman Daly of the World Bank warned of the consequences of a national accounting system that treated the earth like a business in liquidation. What did it say about the assumptions behind measures of well-being, asked these critics, that current measures of GDP made an economic hero out of a business that stripped the seas of fish, and the land of trees, and poisoned lakes and land with toxins? One dissident economist sarcastically noted that from the point of view of GDP the most valuable member of society is a terminal cancer patient simultaneously going through a divorce.

To redress this absurdity, economists and conservation biologists got together to try to put together rough estimates of the worth of "ecosystem services" that were customarily deemed irrelevant in economic calculations affecting land use and development. Looking at flood control, watershed protection, prevention of erosion, waste recycling, pollination, and nutrient cycling, among other factors, one group of ecologists, economists, and geographers, led by Stanford University's Gretchen Daily, published an article in the journal *Nature* in 1997 in which they attempted to quantify the cost of replacing ecosystem services with human-devised prosthetics. The group estimated that such services would cost the world's nations as much as $54 trillion, or more than three times the turnover of the $18-trillion global economy, if nature did not provide them for free.

There is a big difference between "free" and $54 trillion. This rift in the way economists looked at reality lent a trompe-l'oeil quality to predictions of a nation's future prospects. A number of nations that looked like emerging giants from an economic standpoint appeared to be on the road to ruin from an ecological perspective.

This was the case with the Philippines. Perhaps no twentieth-century nation better exemplified the rift over the role of environmental factors in national accounts and economic prospects. As the twenty first century unfolded, this dispute played out on the face of the land. By 2050, it has become painfully clear which school of thought best reflects reality.

Despite the impacts of four hundred years of European contact and exploitation, it was the twentieth century that had the most profound effects on the face of the Philippines. At the beginning of that century, this nation of seven thousand islands still had 94 percent of its forests and was inhabited by seven million people. By the end of the century, population had swollen by a factor of ten, and, in neat symmetry, forest cover had been reduced by a factor of ten. The nation's more than seventy million people were crammed into a nation with less land area than the United Kingdom. Even as logging and agricultural activities were destroying terrestrial watersheds, overfishing and pollution were killing its freshwater and marine resources. With few exceptions, lakes and lagoons became fouled by pollution. By the end of that century, more than 70 percent of the island nation's reefs had been destroyed or damaged, as fishermen used dynamite and coral-killing cyanide to collect delicacies such as the slow-growing, jade-colored humphead wrasse, that would then be exported to Asian markets.

The nation entered the new millennium with a swollen population still growing by 2.3 percent a year, and its life-support systems in tatters: a perfect script for tragedy. Some estimates held that environmental degradation alone discounted growth by 4 percent a year in the early 1990s. The costs imposed by this decline surfaced in both direct and subtle ways. Although the Philippines is blessed with an abundance of natural rainfall, it began to suffer water problems as deforestation destroyed watersheds and filled reservoirs and rivers with silt. Overpumping of aquifers allowed salt water to seep in, poisoning wells in provinces like Cebu. Indeed, once the saltwater intrusion reached the foothills in Cebu and other provinces, millions of Filipinos were cut off from all groundwater supplies; fresh water flowing down from recharge zones in the mountains was befouled as soon as it reached the aquifer. Whole provinces found themselves forced to rely on the uncertainties of rainwater, which imposed limits on both agriculture and industry.

Hard-nosed classical economists who looked at the Philippines in the twentieth century, however, tended to dismiss the importance of these constraints. They would point out, reasonably enough, that the United Kingdom, Japan, and Korea are among the nations that have prospered despite suffering vast deforestation. If this is the result of environmental degradation, said the finance ministers of many a poor nation, let us have more of it. (Of course, the simplistic linkage of environmental harm and growth does not hold either. Otherwise, the Russia of 1997 would have had the highest standard of living on earth.)

In fact, from the limited perspective of crude economic indicators, it looked in the 1990s as though the Philippines were heading for an economic boom that would place it among the Asian "tigers," such as Korea and Taiwan. In 1995, its GDP grew at roughly 7 percent (although per-capita income had not yet regained the levels prevailing before a revolution toppled the Marcos regime in 1986). The Philippines felt the reverberations of the dominolike collapse of Southeast Asian currencies and markets in the summer of 1997, but with low wages, high education levels, and many English speakers among its population, the country still sold itself as a low-cost producer of watches and other labor-intensive products. Life expectancy was increasing, as was per-capita income, and it looked as though the nation was poised to get rich off the expanding Asian market. One international economic-consulting group picked it to be one of the top economic stars of the first decades of the new millennium.

This position was by no means indefensible. If, through conquest or trade, a nation has access to resources elsewhere; if it has honest courts, police, and healthy markets; and if its people are hardworking and value education, then it is possible to "decouple" an economy from resource limitations. But the process is not algorithmic. Though the Philippines had some of the elements necessary to escape its limitations, its thrust toward development could not overcome the drag imposed by its earlier profligacy and events in the rest of the world.

Intimately involved in the nation's desperate efforts to overcome this drag, and witness to its failure, were the researchers and staff of the International Rice Research Institute. Amid the desolation around Los Baños, its campuslike facilities remained an oasis of green well into the twenty-first century. IRRI, as the institute was called, had survived insurrection and anarchy because every Philippine government, democratic or dictatorial, recognized that its work was essential to the national security of the country. Founded in 1962 as an addition to a network of institutes devoted to the improvement and protection of the world's staple crops, IRRI played a huge role in the economic progress of Asia in the latter half of the twentieth century.

As noted in chapter 7, rice is the food of most of the world's poor. If IRRI could help world rice growers to increase production by more than 2 percent a year, rice production could keep pace with population growth, but if production failed to match population growth, tragedy lurked. The people who depend on rice have nowhere else to turn. The IRRI researchers did their best.

In the early years of the Green Revolution, the gains came easily, because land and water were relatively plentiful and traditional methods produced yields that were a fraction of newly engineered crops. High-yielding variants of rice developed at IRRI enabled farmers to increase world production of rice by 150 million tons per year between the 1950s and the 1990s. This new bounty more than kept pace with population growth, forcing prices to drop by 40 percent in real terms over the decades. This in turn allowed some of the poor to spend a lower proportion of their income on food, and improve their housing, health, and education.

Giddy with technological optimism, both scientists and policy makers decided that the food problem had been solved. But Nobel Laureate Norman Borlaug and the other progenitors of the Green Revolution knew well that all they had bought was time: time to develop the nonfarm economy, time to bring down population growth. If governments simply used the magic of high-yielding crops to feed their booming populations without accompanying efforts to bring down birthrates, then the Green Revolution would be remembered more for increasing the stakes of future disasters than for improving the lot of humankind.

As it turned out, the results of the Green Revolution were mixed. India, for instance, moved hundreds of millions of people out of poverty, but its population also doubled, so that, as the Green Revolution began to sputter in the 1990s, India still had as many people in absolute poverty as it had had before the previous surge in food production. Even as agricultural gains began to falter, however, India somehow held together. In its favor were strong democratic traditions, albeit ones that often produced political paralysis and a suffocating bureaucracy. The nation also had a vibrant and free press, which publicized periodic famines and disasters and helped mobilize resources when a crisis occurred. Still, India entered the new millennium adding eleven million people each year, and facing another doubling of its population in the next century, with vastly reduced wildlands, decreasing acreage under irrigation, and increasing problems with desertification of its most productive lands.

The situation was even more dramatic in the Philippines. There it did not take long for water problems, deforestation, and other symptoms of environmental degradation to begin to impose constraints on development. At the end of the twentieth century, more than half the Philippines' population still depended on natural resources for their livelihoods, and twenty-three million Filipinos depended on rice as their primary source of nourishment. As elsewhere in the developing world, the government made a strategic decision to subsidize production in order to maintain supplies and moderate prices. This was a political decision designed to prevent unrest among the poor, but the subsidies weakened both agriculture and the economy in general.

At the century's end, rice production began to slip behind population growth as farmlands went out of production or were lost to urban and industrial sprawl. By the second decade of the twenty-first century, cereal and other food imports were becoming a significant drag on the economy; purchases of the staples consumed export earnings that might otherwise have been invested in the development of the country.

The money spent on food imports also weakened the Philippine peso. Although a cheap peso would seem to make Philippine exports more competitive, the weakening peso actually further slowed the pace of development, by raising the price of imported equipment needed for industrialization. Worst of all, however, was that worldwide grain production only erratically kept pace with demand. Beginning in 2015, at crucial times the Philippines found itself unable to afford the price of imported rice.

Scientists at IRRI were not to blame. By the first decade of the twenty-first century, they had developed a new "super rice" which increased potential yields by 25 percent. The key to the new rice was its ability to carry 25 percent more seeds than other high-yielding varieties. It grew out of experiments testing two thousand different rice variants to select those with the strongest stems and the longest panicles, or seed carriers.

The IRRI scientists did not stop there. They used biotechnology techniques to tackle the problem of crop losses to pests, transferring genes to high-yielding strains that enabled the plants to resist the yellow stem borer, a pest that by itself ate 5 percent of the world's rice crop each year. The tireless crew at IRRI also found ways to use water more efficiently, so farmers could continue to maximize yields even as water available for irrigation was reduced. They developed salt-tolerant strains, so that farmers could continue to get production out of soils damaged by overirrigation or saltwater intrusion. When it was discovered that rice production was contributing to the atmosphere significant amounts of greenhouse gases such as methane, IRRI researchers found ways to reduce these emissions from rice fields without hurting yields. Panicked by the prospect of instability as supplies continued to tighten, other institutions, such as the World Bank, attacked the problem of losses due to shipping and storage as well as other infrastructure problems that held down production.

The success or failure of these international efforts rested on the degree to which they helped the lives of small farmers. Ramón Rojas came of age in the first decade of the twenty-first century, just as the world around him was falling apart. An enlightened peasant farmer who worked a two-hectare holding, Rojas became a favorite of the agronomists and plant breeders at IRRI because of his willingness to try innovations worked out by the researchers. In 2005, when, at the age of nineteen, he took over his parents' farm, he began using the super rice. Later he adopted new water-management schemes, biological controls on pests, biotech fertilizers, and other developments coming out of the institute. These techniques worked, up to a point. Other forces, however, frustrated his bootstrapping efforts, as well as those of millions of other farmers in Asia and around the world.

As an upland farmer, Rojas was safe from the continuing sea-level rise, which ate up some of the world's most fertile rice lands in river deltas in Bangladesh, China, Indonesia, and Burma. But he was not immune to the losses caused by a longer, more vigorous typhoon season which randomly assaulted the rice belt. Relative to other crops, rice is well adapted to storms, but the grain is vulnerable just before harvest, when the plant's spikelets are fully developed. With an increase in storms and extreme rainfalls, flooding-related crop losses inexorably increased. Uttar Pradesh, in India, would lose its crop one year, parts of Thailand the next, and so on. Over fifteen years, Rojas lost his entire crop six times, or about 13 percent of his total plantings.

Elsewhere in the Philippines and Asia, heat stress lowered yields for upland farmers, as scorching heat waves caused rice plants to flower early, spontaneously abort their seeds, and otherwise wither. Warmer temperatures also had the effects of emboldening pests and lowering the crop's resistance to disease. This set the stage for a series of devastating blights that further undermined efforts to increase the world crop.

Rojas and other Asian farmers found themselves whipsawed by the same conflicting tides of nature and market forces that buffeted their counterparts around the world—although the Asian farmers were more vulnerable to being buffeted by the needs of the desperate poor. In an era of good grain and vegetable prices, many tried to switch to higher-value crops, only to find themselves stymied by government officials worried about the prospects of food riots and civil unrest.

Successive governments tried to sweeten the pot for farmers with additional credits and direct subsidies. Government-owned trading groups entered the markets and acted as the principal buyer of rice, so that they could control prices paid by the poor. These efforts temporarily dampened unrest, but led to longer-term problems as the peso continued to weaken and food imports rose in price.

Stuck in the treadmill of growing rice, Rojas began planting three crops a year to try to make ends meet. This strategy did not work either, even though he faithfully followed IRRI's recommendations on water use. Yields seemed to decline the more intensively he farmed. Rojas became uncertain of what crops to plant and, as weather patterns varied, when to plant them. Technology can only do so much.

Demoralized and bankrupt by 2020, he packed up his wife and fourteen-year-old daughter and joined the legions of discontented migrants roaming the nation. Some were farmers like Rojas; others came from elsewhere on Luzon, where a volcanic eruption killed thousands and ruined tens of thousands of hectares of forest and rice land. Others joined the floating population simply because there were no prospects in their overcrowded villages. Manila by this time had twenty million people. Many of them came to the city looking for a staging area for moves elsewhere, only to find, once they got to Manila, that there was nowhere else to go. Interpreting a lukewarm greeting from his brother as an invitation to move in, a desperate Rojas installed his family in his brother's tiny apartment.

In Manila, Rojas discovered that he did not have the resources to overcome the barriers that neighboring nations had erected to discourage illegal migrants. Horrified by stories of xenophobia and hostility in the outside world, he abandoned hope of homesteading elsewhere in Asia. He resigned himself to a life as a mechanic, assisting his older brother, who owned a hole-in-the-wall shop where he repaired the gaudy, chromed-up "jeepney" taxis that had long served as a flamboyant symbol of the peasants' material aspirations. When his brother and his brother's wife were killed in the crossfire of a gang war, Ramón took over the apartment, the "jeepney" business, and the care of their aged parents.

The urban disorder itself was a product of the rice crisis. During the early part of the century, peasant uprisings and tides of internal migration had brought down successive democratically elected governments. Then, in 2018, a clique of generals financed by industrialists and large landowners staged a coup. Their grip on the countryside, however, was uncertain, and large parts of the cities remained contested ground. Guerrilla groups competed with ruthless and corrupt police and army gangs for control of the shantytowns and sprawling slums. For a decade, Manila descended into a Karachi-like anarchy. Ramón and his family managed to survive only by keeping their heads down, dutifully switching allegiance and redirecting payoffs whenever a new group took control of their district.

By 2030, the country was in the middle of a full-scale demographic collapse reminiscent of the population bust that hit Russia at the end of the twentieth century. Strife, disease, and, most important, a sudden and extreme drop in the birthrate slowed the Filipino population explosion. With limited prospects for either work or migration, with housing and food expensive and health care uncertain, and faced with an ever more dour future, couples simply stopped having children. By 2035, the situation had begun to improve, as the effects of events of the previous decades began to make themselves felt. By 2040, the population was sixty-five million people, below its levels in the 1990s. By 2050, it had dropped below fifty-five million.

The number is still high, given the country's gravely wounded landscape, but with a consolidation of land holdings and the continued intensification of agriculture, some of the Philippines' beleaguered ecosystems have had a chance to stabilize. Rain forest, a robust system as long as some pieces remain intact, has begun to reclaim some abandoned hillside plots, but the reforestation has been haphazard and incomplete; in many exposed areas, the soil had hardened into concrete, and many of the seed-distributing birds and animals had been wiped out. With the help of zealous environmental scouts, some of the poisoned lakes are beginning the slow process of cleansing themselves. Now completely protected, mangroves are coming back along the ravaged coastline, restoring a vital nursery and buffer against storms.

Still, much of the country is damaged beyond repair. Just as the Roman hunger for trees to fuel the smelters at the Rio Tinto silver mine permanently altered the face of Spain, the earlier excesses of the Philippines and the global forces unleashed by humanity have left an indelible imprint on the land. Hundreds of thousands of hectares of once-prime forest and agricultural land now only support salt-tolerant grasses. Most of the reefs and many of the lagoons are dead, their fisheries gone, victims of silt, pollutants, dynamite, and cyanide.

The nation once boasted one of the most diverse arrays of plants and animals on earth, because of its position bestriding the two major biogeographical regions of tropical Asia and the Pacific. By 2050, it has lost over 70 percent of its original complement of life forms. The Philippines' human suffering has been more than matched by its ecological catastrophe.

The Philippines of 2050, however, is not without hope. Its citizens have learned the harsh lesson that you can neither ignore nor negotiate with nature. Now, humbled but toughened by the harsh lessons of the previous decades, they are picking up the pieces, and treating what remains of the nation's formerly rich patrimony as a precious treasure. Moreover, after fifty years of argument and experimentation, the discipline of economics has changed its assumptions about the nature of economic well-being, integrating social and environmental consequences into the tabulation of national accounts. Economists and ordinary people alike now recognize that, though nature is readily convertible into capital, the reverse is not the case. The next fifty years will be better.

Chapter 13

CALIFORNIA:
THE FOG LIFTS

WHAT CAN BE WRONG with a series of beautiful summers on the California coast? This question first came up at the end of the twentieth century, when people living along the northern coast began noticing an inordinate number of bright, cloudless days. Only a killjoy could take issue with whatever forces released California from the fogs that had entombed its coastline down through the ages. Still, although people might enjoy sunny days, anyone who has spent time on the northern-California coast knows that this is not the way it is supposed to be. The ubiquity of fog was noted most famously by Mark Twain, who, in the nineteenth century, quipped that he spent "the coldest winter of my life in San Francisco—in August." This remark might have been made at any point going back millions of years, had there been sentient beings around to remark on the weather. A soggy belt of fog had moved up and down the coast a bit over the millennium, as climate had changed, but for millions of years mist has seasonally enshrouded the area between Big Sur and the border of Oregon.

One of nature's most evanescent and insubstantial creations, fog may be the most durable feature of coastal North America. Sea level has risen and fallen by hundreds of feet during the millions of years since the fogs began, driven by huge geological and climatic changes. The Cascades surged upward ten million years ago, changing the climate to the west of the mountains. The Isthmus of Panama completed its emergence from the ocean 2.6 million years ago, interrupting vast circumequatorial currents, contributing to a cycle of ice ages and climate change in the Northern Hemisphere that in turn led to the extinction of countless life forms and spurred the evolution of many new ones, including humanity's direct antecedents. Throughout these epochal events, however, one segment of the California coast remained foggy during the summer.

The recipe for California's fogs was written by the fundamental systems that govern climate on the planet. The ingredients are simple: the coast of a continent and an ocean. Then all you need are trade winds that pick up moisture and drive water toward the coast, over the open ocean. This causes an upwelling of cold water to replace the wind-driven surface waters, and it is one crucial part of the recipe where fog chefs can go awry.

In the case of California, this wind-driven water hits the coast near southern Oregon and splits into two currents—one stream of water heading north, and the California current, which heads south along the coast. The current is held near the coast by the seasonal northwesterly winds created as air piled up by the Pacific High flows toward the lower pressure over the North American continent that accompanies the summer heating of the land.

As the current moves southward, it draws up cold water from the ocean depths, and this in turn cools the air. Since colder air can hold less moisture, the water picked up by the winds condenses as fog as the air cools. Drawn toward the coast and through gaps in the coastal range by the heating over the Central Valley, the fog rolls in regular cycles; depending on conditions, it might be dripping wet or relatively dry, close to the ground or higher and more cloudlike. In parts of the San Francisco Bay area, for instance, the summer fogs in the twentieth century would deliver as much as the equivalent of ten inches of rain, sufficient moisture to support a vast array of flora and fauna that otherwise could not live in this region, which has virtually no precipitation between April and November.

So it was, with few interruptions, since the seasonal high-pressure system that governs the summer trade winds first took shape in the Western Pacific just north of the equator—a period that extends back perhaps as much as fifteen million years. The moderating influence of the oceans protected the coast from extremes of climate as well. Even when the Laurentian and Cordilleran ice sheets covered a two-thousand-mile-wide stretch of North America with ice a mile thick, twelve thousand years ago, the narrow stretch of California between the coastal ranges and the Pacific still enjoyed frost-free winters. In sum, fog and the California coast go way back.

Consequently, scientists took notice when the fog regime became more uncertain in the 1990s. Botanists, geophysicists, oceanographers, and others concerned with changes in the biosphere began to wonder if a succession of fogless summers was just an enjoyable but temporary respite from normalcy, or, rather, a signal of some more profound change. The northern-California coast is not supposed to have sunny summers, and this stretch of coast had been foggy for so long that myriad life forms had evolved dependent on its sheltering moistness. What would happen to these damp-loving things if the fogs disappeared?

As the beautiful summers continued in the late 1990s, broken occasionally by the return of the fogs, a consortium of scientists formed to monitor these and other changes around the world over time. In the year 2000, the consortium launched a pilotless aircraft, towing the drone aloft and starting its solar/fuel-cell-powered electric engines (the drone needed an initial tow because the propellers, designed to perform sixteen miles up, where the atmosphere is a twentieth of the density at sea level, are too cumbersome to get the aircraft off the ground).

Year after year the mission continued. As the summer of 2050 approached—the fiftieth anniversary of the pilotless vehicle's silent monitoring of the land and atmosphere—its overseers decided to replay its original mission up the coast of California. The idea was to monitor the transformations wrought by the disappearance of the fogs.

Of particular interest in this mission is the fate of one of nature's most extraordinary creations: the California redwood, whose history as a species was deeply entwined with the misty coast. Indeed, the coast's combination of fogs, wet summers, and security from frosts had created a safe house for the giant trees, even as their habitat disappeared throughout the rest of the continent.

Once certain basic conditions are satisfied, the California coastal redwood is as close to immortal as any living thing today. The trees themselves live as much as twenty-two hundred years, growing to be over three hundred feet tall. Even if these two-thousand-ton monsters should fall, the root system will sprout new trees, so that it is possible to find a circle of giant trees that have grown out of the roots of long-since-fallen trees in a lineage of clones that may extend back to the last ice age—a living thing whose life span encompasses the breadth of civilization since well before the dawn of agriculture. The redwood's bark is fire-resistant and pest-resistant. The tree's strategy, perfected over millions of years, is to grow as tall as possible as fast as possible, stealing sunlight from competitors. To do that, the redwood has to make wood rapidly; the basic ingredients for this are carbon dioxide and water.

The trade-off is that the fast-growing trees are poor pumpers of water to the upper branches. During the winter, the upper part of the tree gets its water from plentiful rains. Millions of years ago, when the North American climate was much warmer and wetter, redwoods grew throughout much of the West. As the West dried out, however, redwoods retreated to their present coastal refuge. Despite California's parched summers, the redwoods still find plenty of moisture in the form of fog, which bathes the tree's leaves with water droplets. The giant tree has even developed different needles in adaptation to the different climates at its top and bottom. In the upper reaches of the tree, the needles are short and bunched close to the stem, to minimize water loss; the lower needles are larger and arrayed in double ranks, to take maximum advantage of the sun.

For at least eight million years, redwoods prospered in a sliver of coastline where it never freezes in winter and where fog cloaks the glades in summer. Indeed, the past hovers close upon the present in this emerald haven. Seven miles southwest of Mount St. Helena, in Sonoma County, lie the petrified remains of massive redwoods that were blown down and buried by ash and mud during a volcanic eruption three and a half million years ago—trees so perfectly replicated in stone that at first glance they might be mistaken for the result of recent logging.

Like some magic kingdom that lives in the thrall of a dragon's breath, the foggy world of the redwoods has not been fixed to one locale but, rather, has migrated according to the vagaries of climate. When the coast warmed, the redwoods followed the fog north up the coastline; when it cooled, the forests marched south; but always the trees flourished within their protective layer of fog. If ever there could be security in an ecological niche, these durable monsters seemed to have found it, since their refuge was the result of the structure of the earth and oceans as well as atmospheric features that had been stable for many millions of years.

The redwoods, of course, could not know that in the most recent ten thousand years of their history—the merest blink of an eyelash in their long tenure on the coast—a new mammal would arrive in North America. Nor could they know that this biped would proliferate until it would emerge, in the words of biologist E. O. Wilson, as the first species to become a geophysical force. By the end of the twentieth century, humanity had unwittingly begun to affect the giant global systems that produced the redwood's nurturing fog, as well as much of the world's climate. Also by that time, humans had begun to be alarmed by their impact on the home planet.

Following the programmed instructions that have re-created its earlier flight path, on August 23, 2050, the drone heads inland over Muir Beach, which lies in one of the few gaps in the rampart of coastal ranges that runs for hundreds of miles at the edge of the continent. Formed of greenstone, sedimentary rock, and sandstone, the headlands north of the Golden Gate date back a hundred million years, to the days when dinosaurs ruled North America. As the drone flies over the beach, scientists watch its journey on a split screen. One side replays footage recorded in the year 2000; the other, real-time images from this commemorative flight in 2050. The split screen shows scenes that have changed little over the decades. On both screens, people sport on the beach. In the year 2000, a girl and her dog played with a Frisbee; in 2050, children throw a variety of airfoils to each other and their pets. If there is a difference, it is that the beachgoers of 2050 are far more covered—not out of modesty, but in fear of the sun.

The drone flies slowly over the Pelican Inn, the half-timbered Norman-style anomaly that still serves publike food, as it did in the twentieth century, and then up Muir Woods Road. It wafts over the chaparral-, shrub-, and grass-covered hills of Gateway National Park. The images of the protected area displayed side by side look remarkably similar, despite the passage of the decades.

The drone begins to enter the glades and valleys of Muir Woods, its immediate objective, and here its cameras begin to beam back images very different from those captured fifty years earlier. Muir Woods now looks like a sylvan stonehenge—the ruin of a once-magnificent structure. Many of the giant redwoods, among the largest and oldest living things on earth, are dead or dying. Some are browning at their lofty tops, others have been toppled by storms, others are dead in place, still others show signs of beetle infestation. Some trees in the deeper, more protected glades are still healthy. As with everything on the redwoods' time scale, change is happening slowly (one tree that began leaning in the 1500s, when the Spanish first came to California, finally toppled over in a storm only in 1993), but clearly something terrible is happening. This redwood forest has been protected from direct human destruction since 1908. It was then that President Theodore Roosevelt dedicated Muir Woods as the nation's seventh national monument, acceding to the wishes of Congressman William Kent, who with his wife had donated the land to the government.

As the drone's remote sensing instruments probe deeper toward the forest floor, images from its first trip show a moist green world of lady ferns, bay laurel, redwood sorrel, and other moisture-loving understory plants and fungi. A California polypody, a fern whose roots were used in antiquity by Amerindians to make a treatment for sore eyes, conceals a huge and gaudy yellow banana slug oiling its way across the forest floor. The camera also picked up a giant Pacific salamander, as long as a man's foot, the largest amphibian in western North America.

With its sensors programmed to seek the chemical and color signatures of the fauna and flora recorded in the year 2000, the drone scans the forest, but the ferns, the banana slugs, the giant Pacific salamanders, and the other denizens of the moist understory have disappeared. Instead, sword ferns, habituated to the drier hillsides, have invaded, along with other species from more arid areas. It looks as if somebody took a hair drier to the area.

Ironically, the spotted owls, endangered earlier by the cutting of the redwoods, are doing fine, at least for the time being. The number of dying trees created a wealth of snags the birds use for nesting places. Populations of vole and other small mammals are still healthy. Red-tailed hawk, gray fox, and bobcat still roam the area, feeding on vole, chipmunk, squirrel, and jackrabbit; turkey vultures find plenty of carrion and road kill.

In the late 1990s, scientists looked for a culprit for the dry, fogless summers in a periodic event called El Niño, a cyclical shift in ocean temperatures and atmospheric patterns in the Pacific that raised havoc with normal climate patterns. Despite its sweet name (which means "The Christ Child," a nickname the event acquired because it first became noticed off the coast of Peru around Christmas), "El Niño" refers to enormous changes in the oceans and atmosphere that spanned the Pacific and which in turn left their imprint around the globe.

Every three to five years, temperatures would begin to rise in a continent-sized part of the Western Pacific. Coincident with these rising temperatures, the North Pacific High would fail to develop, and instead the region would become dominated by a seasonal low-pressure system that ordinarily sits off the coast of Australia. Trade winds which blew across the North Pacific were produced by the difference in air pressure between the North Pacific High and a low-pressure system that hovered near the Aleutian Islands. Without the high to spill off air, however, during an El Niño, the trade winds die, and without the trade winds piling water off the coast of Oregon, the California current weakens, and waters as warm as the Pacific off San Diego replace the cold upwelling off the redwood coast. Warm-water fish like marlin and mahimahi would follow the El Niño waters as far north as Washington State. Without sufficient contrast between cold Pacific waters and the warm air over the continent, the fog fails to develop. Without the fog and the current to cool the air, temperatures on the coast regularly rise into the nineties on cloudless summer days.

Redwoods had survived El Niños for millions of years, of course, but in the early 1990s, these ordinarily cyclical events started returning with startling regularity—three in the four years between 1991 and 1994. The trees would get plenty of moisture during the winter, because the area was also hit with unprecedented rainstorms accompanied by extremely high winds, which blew over the more exposed giants.

Some geophysicists suspected that global warming was influencing El Niño, but then nature threw another new twist at the California coast. Beginning in the early twenty-first century, the coast began experiencing fogless summers even without the occurrence of El Niño. Satellite imagery quickly pinpointed the cause, if not the explanation. In non–El Niño years the North Pacific High was forming, but with each passing year it was centered farther north. Similarly, the Pacific High's summer companions, the Aleutian Low and the North American High, also seemed to be edging northward. The effect of this repositioning of vast atmospheric systems was to change the geometry of the trade winds and ocean currents over the North Pacific. Instead of northerlies, the prevailing summer winds off the coast of California shifted more westerly, dampening the California current.

It did not take long for theory to catch up with reality. Though scientific debate over what was driving climate change continued, most climate specialists agreed that increased heating due to the buildup of greenhouse gases had led to increased convection, the rise of hot air, near the equator. This in turn pushed the area where this giant flow of heated air subsided farther to the north. These massive changes in the invisible systems that govern climate profoundly altered life on the California coast.

Keeping within the narrow ten-kilometer sliver of what had once been the fog belt, the drone turns northward, leaving Muir Woods and heading toward Mendocino. Here too the images are vastly different. Redwood stands are few and far between, and all are in sad shape. Douglas fir, however, seems to be thriving. All of the forests have been compressed to fragments by an enormous increase in the human presence in the three-hundred-mile stretch between Stinson Beach and the Lost Coast. In the late twentieth century, the northern-California coast remained sparsely populated, in part because its foggy damp summers had limited appeal for vacationers. Now, even as the region's signature species has declined, the weather has improved, subtly altering the complex calculus that determines California's settlement patterns.

If there are more communities, however, they are also farther inland. As the drone moves up the coast, it is as though some giant hand has pushed the houses and buildings away from the coast. In fact, this is exactly what did happen: the invisible hand of the marketplace has been at work. An endless series of coastal storms that began in the 1990s inexorably raised the price of living by the Pacific. Disaster-insurance rates rose to tens of thousands of dollars a year, and banks became reluctant to lend mortgage money in areas vulnerable to storm damage. Even the federal government eventually realized that it was absurd to offer a safety net in federal disaster insurance that effectively encouraged people to put themselves in harm's way.

Redwoods are not the only life forms to seek refuge in the mists of the California coasts. As the drone enters the rugged terrain of California's Lost Coast, between Mendocino and Arcata, the images reveal numerous settlements scattered through the woods, many of which have what look to be altars situated in their center.

It would not be surprising to the visitor from the twentieth century that the northern coasts still shelter survivalists and adherents of fringe cults. The pantheistic cults, however, are no longer the fringe. Many have moved to the center as part of the world-wide religious efflorescence. Traditional and nontraditional faiths all draw new adherents. Conservative sects have grown, but so have new forms of Christianity, as the various churches attempt to adapt to emergent pantheistic sentiment around the world. Druid and Goddess cults also flourish, mostly centered around charismatic leaders, not all of whom are charlatans.

Perhaps more noteworthy is that the scientists studying the California coast for clues to global change do not scoff at those beliefs. The geographer or geophysicist knows that something as local as the disappearance of fogs in coastal California is connected to faraway global events like changes in ocean currents in the seas off Antarctica or alteration of wind patterns in the Arctic North Atlantic. But the scientists now also know that what they do not know is dangerous. One can never be sure whether human activity is harmless or hurting crucial integuments of the biosphere. And so scientists too now look for answers beyond the realm of reason.

Driving all of this introspection is the changed world of 2050. In response to human numbers and impacts, nature has thrown a bewildering series of riddles at humanity—the disappearance of fogs, the disappearance of frogs, the resurgence of disease, ever more frequent superstorms, droughts in the wettest places on earth, and floods in some of the driest. What is going on; how is this irate god to be propitiated? Religion and science now have common cause. Long before 2050, humanity remembered a lesson learned by countless generations, but then forgotten through most of Western history—humans act, nature reacts.

Chapter 14

OAXACA, MEXICO:
THE POOREST FIND A WAY

NESTLED IN THE HILLS of the Baja Mixtec, a remote mountainous territory in the Mexican state of Oaxaca, lies the tiny native village of Almoltepec. Even in 2050, the village remains isolated from the outside world. It can be reached only on foot, or by air if the pilot is brave enough to risk an approach into a treacherous, short airstrip cut into the mountainside. The government has long promised to build a road, but ancient and ongoing conflicts between the Mixtec Indians of Almoltepec and the surrounding Zapotec, Chatino, and Mestino Indians stymied the project for decades. Now the federal government has withdrawn from Oaxaca, and it is likely that the road will never be built. In other respects too, the outward life of the village retains the flavor of a timeless native village. People still farm corn and beans on the steep slopes, and gather in the dusty village square to discuss the affairs of the day.

In significant ways, life has improved for those who live in the remote settlement. Information technologies allow the Mixtec access to the collective knowledge and expertise of humanity. The village now has some electricity and refrigeration, thanks to solar-power and fuel-cell technology, and farmers use sophisticated catchments and antierosion techniques on their tiny plots when they plant the traditional mixed crop of corn and beans called *milpa*. The community has reforested a number of slopes denuded in earlier years, and deer, boar, and other game animals have returned to the dry semitropical forests after nearly a century of absence. Crime is low, elders are respected, and families are now strong and devout. Most of the improvements in Almoltepec are the result of efforts sponsored by the natives themselves, who began banding together early in the twenty-first century, as the federal government retreated from its role as patron of the poor.

Why, then, do the residents of Almoltepec look hunted and exhausted? Why are so many conversations whispered and short? Why do so many of the men have the hollow look of people who have witnessed things they would rather not remember? Descriptions of Almoltepec's material improvements do not begin to encompass the stresses buffeting its residents. Poking through the veneer of progress are telltale signs that the village has endured cataclysms, and that the winds of chaos are still loose in the world beyond the village. Most of those who live in Almoltepec in 2050 accept the limitations of village life more out of fear of the outside world than out of enthusiasm for the traditional Mixtec way of life.

In the twentieth century, as each new generation subdivided their holdings, those squeezed off the land would seek seasonal farm labor in Sinaloa, or migrate to Mexico City, or make the dangerous trek to the United States. Long before 2050, however, all of Mexico's labor markets were saturated, as were its cities. The increasingly fortified border and increasingly hostile American public had also long since reduced illegal immigration to the U.S. to a trickle. Nor did the rest of Oaxaca have anything to offer those who found village life confining. After eight thousand years of farming and the more recent perturbations of climate change, the land was weary of the heavy weight of humanity.

Just a short distance from Almoltepec lay Guila Naquitz, a cave where scientists found evidence of the first agriculture in the Americas in the form of squash seeds over eight thousand years old. A more famous product of early agriculture also came from this region a few thousand years later, when paleo-Indians began cultivating a wild plant called "teosinte," whose seeds were tasty and nutritious. Teosinte contained only a single row of kernels, but over the millennia, as Indians selected those plants with the most kernels for planting, strains of the crop emerged with scores of kernels arranged on cobs, and maize, one of the world's staple foods, was born.

Continuous farming for thousands of years, however, had taken its toll. Population pressures and inappropriate agricultural policies forced farmers to eliminate fallow periods in efforts to get every scrap of production out of the land. By the end of the twentieth century, many of the valleys had been reduced to barren salt plains, marked by a white crust that, from the air, gave the appearance that the land itself was suffering from cancer. Throughout Mexico, desertification and deforestation had ruined farmlands, forcing millions to abandon their livelihoods and traditional lands. In mountainous areas like Almoltepec, the problems of salt buildup were compounded by erosion, as population pressures forced the Indians to farm plots on steep slopes.

With no valve to relieve Mexico's demographic pressures, the federal government found itself forced to deal with increasingly restive landless and jobless peasants. The rural poor became ever more radicalized, many of them joining brushfire insurrections that sprang up in poor states like Chiapas, Oaxaca, and Guerrero. Faced with the far more dangerous consequences of unrest in the major cities, the federal government focused its resources on placating urban populations and the richer industrial and agricultural regions, such as Monterrey.

Mexico was one of many countries that straddled the gap between industrial nations and the developing world. With its cheap labor and favorable location next to the world's largest market, it teetered on the verge of becoming an exporting power. In other respects, however, even in the late twentieth century, Mexico retained the flavor of a banana republic. A tangled web of politicians, police, the military, and powerful drug traffickers made a mockery of the courts and the rule of law. In 1997, a group of political scientists, economists, and ecologists led by the historian Paul Kennedy of Yale University, identified Mexico as one of the

world's so-called pivotal states, because of its geostrategic importance and its precarious balance between success and failure. As
in other pivotal states, such as India, Egypt, and Indonesia, Mexico's greatest threats were not external but internal. The need to
open the economy and bolster the courts in order to create jobs
for the million Mexicans entering the job market each year collided with the needs of influential politicians and other powerful
figures who had much to lose if true reform came to the country.

In essence, corruption and the closed network of the elite left
the country extremely vulnerable. The fragile equipoise that held
Mexico together began to break down as the government found
itself unable to reconcile the demands of the global marketplace
for openness with the backroom dealings of those who controlled
politics and the economy. The seven-decade stranglehold of the
Institutional Revolutionary Party or PRI ended in 1997, when opposition parties won control of the national congress. Unfortunately, though this democratization gave voice to more people, it
actually aggravated instability, raising expectations without ad-
dressing the poverty of the countryside, which underlay much of
the discontent. In fact, the leftward tilt of many of the newly en-
franchised populists—such as Cuautemoc Cardenas, the first
elected mayor of Mexico City—had the effect of scaring institutional investors, making it more difficult for the nation to raise
funds in the markets.

Oaxaca found itself with more autonomy than it really
wanted, given its impoverished resource base. The situation only
got worse during the economic upheavals of 2006, when the
forced repatriation of tens of thousands of expatriates sent desperate workers and families to villages already bursting at the
seams. When the pestilence that followed the depression swept
through the region, health authorities had neither the infrastructure nor the resources to contain the epidemics, which decimated
many villages.

In such chaos, the strong consolidated their power. For a
while, drug gangs and other elements of organized crime brazenly
operated in Oaxaca and throughout Mexico. Large landowners

supplanted the gangs when, supported by public outrage and vigilantism, they helped drive out criminal elements. (The hold of the drug lords in particular was already weakened, for the worldwide religious revival had mobilized public opinion against their products.) The impotence of the local governments in the face of these crises had the effect of dampening zeal for the radicals and their leftist message. The landowners exploited this weakness to make deals with their former revolutionary adversaries, which, in essence, allowed them to restore the feudal system that had prevailed in parts of Mexico since colonial times.

The landowning elite, which consisted of both families and huge agribusinesses, profited enormously when, at the end of the twentieth century, the government gave individual peasants and Indians title to lands that formerly had been held communally. The breakup of the *ejido* system, as the communal ownership had been called, was deemed a crucial step in the modernization of Mexican agriculture. Once the poor had title to land, it was reasoned that they would have better access to credit, and would make improvements, such as investing in higher-yielding seeds. Moreover, with the passage of the North American Free Trade Agreement, those farmers who planted high-value crops, such as fruits and nuts, would have access to the huge American market.

In Oaxaca, however, with its scarce water and depleted, overburdened soils, the privatization of the *ejidos* did not produce the envisioned bounty. Many peasants ended up with title to lands that had become virtually worthless, and found themselves in worse shape than before. Those with good lands fought endless battles with squatters, egged on by peasant radicals. This only encouraged individuals to sell to conglomerates and wealthy landowners, who could recruit private armies from the landless poor and effectively protect their holdings.

The land-holding elite also found it easy to recruit workers for wages that amounted to outright indenturement. Some of the feudal elite took a paternalistic interest in the welfare of their workers, but others took advantage of having near-absolute power over the desperate poor. In the markets of the villages surrounding the fenced and patrolled agribusinesses, women gossiped about girls sold into slavery, children in company "schools" that amounted to sweatshops, harsh punishments for misconduct, including torture and summary executions for those suspected of opposing the system. These stories reached Almoltepec and helped convince the villagers that there was something to be said for living on land that nobody else wanted, even if conditions were harsh and prospects limited.

These sentiments were only reinforced by stragglers who returned to the village after trying to find work in Mexico's beleaguered cities. Mexico City is now smaller than it was in the twentieth century. An exodus that began as a trickle prompted by diminishing opportunities, health problems associated with pollution, and acute water shortages, had increased smartly as a result of the plague years. The exodus gained additional strength when a blanket of ash and poisonous gases from the erupting volcano Popocatépetl killed tens of thousands and left much of the southwestern part of the city uninhabitable.

Even though diminished in size, Mexico City continues to suffer the problems afflicting other megacities. Its water problems have gotten worse, the water table dropping and toxins and sewage poisoning the aquifer. New migrants to the city found themselves unwelcome, even among family members who had previously established themselves in the city. After a series of crime waves at the turn of the century had threatened to drive out foreign investors and undermine the very viability of the city, the police evolved into a brutally efficient force. They treated squatters and those who could not find shelter as threats to public order. Nor could those forcibly evicted from Mexico City hope to find any better welcome in the other cities of water-starved Mexico.

Every starved, bedraggled Indian who made his or her way back to Almoltepec would recount anew the horrors of the world beyond the hills. By the second decade of the new millennium, the villagers were convinced that the rewards of leaving were few and the risks great. The more entrepreneurial and restless Mixtecs, who in earlier times would have gone off to seek their fortunes elsewhere, now stayed put and turned their attention to the village and its problems. This simple shift in focus launched the town's climb toward self-sufficiency.

At the heart of this self-help transformation was one elegant invention of the previous century. In the 1980s, a visionary economist from Bangladesh named Mohammad Yunus perfected a technique for making loans to the very poorest members of society. This simple but immensely powerful idea—known in Bangladesh as the "Grameen Bank"—substituted peer-group pressure for collateral. The bank would loan money to a group of poor people. Once one member of the group began repaying his or her loan, the next loan would go out, and so on. Because every member of the group had an interest in the success of the others, Grameen became a tool of social transformation as much as a bank. By the beginning of the new millennium, Yunus' invention was recognized as the most powerful tool for social progress invented during the twentieth century, and he was rewarded with the Nobel Peace Prize.

The idea was adopted by the World Bank in the 1990s, and under the bureaucratic term "microcredit" continued spreading around the world. It came to Almoltepec early in the twenty-first century, through the philanthropic spirit of a villager who had prospered in the dry-cleaning business in the U.S. and returned to Almoltepec to retire. He had read about the idea and put up $2,000 as a kitty for the first bank. He did not particularly want the money back, but he knew that the repayment rates for Grameens around the world was roughly 98 percent. It appealed to the businessman that his philanthropy was rooted in solid business principles.

The first Grameen in Almoltepec came together after the patron presented the idea to the local priest. (Catholicism was still the dominant religion in the area, but in isolation the local version of the faith had slowly incorporated many elements of the old pantheistic beliefs of the Mixtecs. The resultant belief system would be unrecognizable to the Vatican.) The two men began interviewing the poorest of the poor in the village. Following the advice of Mohammad Yunus, they politely put off those who came to them and instead sought out those too shy and miserable to come forward. They would encourage these people, mostly women, to think of some venture they would launch if money were available. Eventually a group of thirty women was assembled. After deciding among themselves who would go first, they parceled out the first loan—$125, so that a single mother, whose plot was too small to farm, might buy a foot-powered sewing machine and set up a small tailor shop. Once the woman successfully began making the first payments, the next loan went out, this time for cheap cellophane-packaging equipment for a woman who collected medicinal plants. At first the men of the village were suspicious and resentful of the idea, which seemed to favor women and thus altered, to their perceived detriment, the economic balance of power between the sexes. Almoltepec had seen so much hardship, however, and its prospects were so limited, that the men ultimately embraced the concept. As neighbors watched their friends bootstrap their way out of poverty, new self-policing groups formed, and tiny enterprises spread through the region.

Emboldened by their success, the older Grameen Banks began using their profits and borrowing power to invest in small power plants, cellular phones, and seed banks for farmers. As the years went by, the newly empowered Mixtecs began to address municipal problems like sanitation and social problems like family planning. In the 1990s, the community still had one of the highest birthrates in Mexico, but by the early part of the twenty-first century, the average number of children per family had dropped from seven to two; by 2050, population in the village has stabilized.

Thus, amid the tumult of the twenty-first century, one of the poorest, most isolated villages in a failing nation found a way to survive, thanks in large measure to one powerful idea. More unsettling perhaps is the notion that the plagues and unrest of the earlier part of the century played a crucial role in Almoltepec's struggle to find a sustainable future. With its earlier high birthrate, Almoltepec might never have achieved that elusive goal. Every household in the village had lost at least one family member to disease, malnutrition, or civil unrest in earlier decades. Nor would the village have flourished if its best and brightest still had the option of migration. By 2050, Almoltepec has found a stability of sorts.

Chapter 15

NEW YORK CITY:
ADVERTISING ADAPTS

IF LIFE IS THE art of encounter, the city still remains the place of encounter, although there is now a great deal less spontaneity to urban life. Memories of devastating plagues that accompanied the chaos of the early decades of the century still cast a pall over chance meetings. This has turned on its head the remark of the great twentieth-century social critic Lewis Mumford, who noted that one of the delights of a city was that you never knew what might lie around the next corner.

It is all the more remarkable that people did not abandon the city altogether. In fact, many large cities around the world did slide into the type of decay glimpsed proleptically in the twentieth century in places ranging from Kinshasa, Zaire, to Camden, New Jersey. New York, however, did not collapse. This does not mean it prospered through the rough times. The city contracted, but its unique creative vitality provided it with a type of immunity from catastrophic decline.

In fact, New York's continued survival is the product of the same tangible and intangible assets that permitted the city to outlive the writers of several premature obituaries—starting in the nineteenth century, when Gotham's fate seemed sealed by the advent of railroads, since a cheap transportation network decreased the city's importance as a manufacturing center. On the tangible side of the ledger, the city had as assets an installed base of tunnels, constructed over a span of more than two hundred years, to transport people, water, electricity, and sewage. This massive underground infrastructure could be adapted to changes in technology and would be almost impossible to replicate in a crowded world with scarce capital.

Its intangible power derives simply from the fact that people continue to live there whom other people want to be near. In the arts, in finance, in the media, in publishing, and in policy, the city remains a center of discourse for those creative minds with something interesting to say or the throw weight to make a deal happen. The continued survival of New York City testifies to the profound need among people for human contact, a need that traces back to the origins of our species. Despite the risks that urban life now entails, and even though technology has for many decades permitted telecommuting and video conferencing, people still want to exchange ideas face to face during important meetings and critical negotiations.

This is why, one summer day in 2050, a group of creative minds from one of the city's largest advertising agencies decide to ignore the inconvenience and schedule a brainstorming session as the first step in launching a campaign for a new perfume. It is the kind of session that presumably could take place in cyberspace or even through the more primitive medium of a conference call. But people long before recognized that not everything can be reduced to bits and bytes, and that face-to-face meetings convey riches of information, verbal and nonverbal, that dwarf the capacity of any information technology.

This reckoning has figured prominently in the advertising creative team's decision to meet face to face. By 2050, values and circumstances have changed sufficiently so that meetings are very different from their twentieth-century antecedents. Advertising has changed as well. These changes reflect alteration in the life of the city itself

*　　*　　*

At first glance, midtown Manhattan, like London, appears to have changed little since the previous century. A few skyscrapers have been torn down, but their absence is mourned by no one. Where 666 Fifth Ave. had once stood, there is now a delightful garden park. The Plaza Hotel still commands the southeast corner of Central Park, and the older, stolid façades of Fifth Avenue continue to convey affluence and power to those passing by.

From the air, however, midtown Manhattan looks very different indeed. Many buildings are now almost camouflaged by greenery. Virtually every flat roof houses trees or a garden. Avenues and side streets are flanked by phalanxes of maples, lindens, tulips, and oaks. Buildings with roofs too steep to support greenery are covered with high-tech surfaces that absorb the sun's rays.

On the ground too life looks different. The paucity of strollers taking in the light, bright warmth of the summer's day belies the pleasing greenness of the city. Many of those who do walk the streets wear surgical masks. Fuel-cell-powered buses silently patrol the avenue, and empty taxis whir by, slowing hopefully as the driver spies the fugitive pedestrian. People walking the sidewalks swerve to give others a wide berth, a habit so deeply ingrained it is subconscious, and it is not considered rude.

A witness from the twentieth century would be surprised by the way people are dressed, although radical change in fashion is probably one of the most predictable aspects of the future. A society that during the twentieth century variously, if temporarily, embraced Nehru jackets, muumuus, bell-bottom trousers, and other clothing trends should not be surprised if by the middle of the twenty-first century many of their children and grandchildren favor long flowing garments that look like monk's robes or jellabas. Some are colorful, but many are drab, and most look worn. The fashion suggests a clerical takeover, but it represents neither a religious nor a political statement. The garments are simply a response to practicality. Specifically, the dress of the 2050s is one of many adjustments people were forced to make in the aftermath of devastating plagues earlier in the century.

Not everyone adopted the robes. Holed up in their island nation, the insular British do not feel the need to make many of the drastic adjustments other societies have undertaken. More conservative folk elsewhere also favor clothing styles that would be familiar to those living in the twentieth century.

The garments are popular simply because they are the most convenient form of dress, given the unique problems of urban life. Entering a building or office, for instance, has become something of a chore. First one has to negotiate air-lock doors, which minimize the intrusion of unfiltered air into buildings. Almost all buildings maintain positive air pressure, which means that the pressure inside the building is higher than that outside. This procedure was used in earlier decades to prevent casual contaminants from entering a space during the delicate stages of fabricating semiconductors, and other operations that required so-called clean rooms. Now whole buildings use the techniques. Office suites have positive air pressure as well, so that people going to work have the disorienting sensation of diving as they enter their offices on the upper floors of buildings.

Workers also sometimes have to contend with cumbersome sterilization procedures when they enter their offices, which further dampens interest in casual strolls at lunchtime. On those unpredictable occasions when the Centers for Disease Control issue an alert concerning the outbreak of a new virus or an old flu, health officials around the U.S. impose containment protocols. When they are in effect (and this is so frequent that people simply refer to the procedures as "the protocols"), sterilization mandates that a person leaving a sealed space subject his clothes to irradiation and himself to a brief, microbe-killing, exposure to ultraviolet light.

Indeed, the drudgery of going through the sterilization routine even a few times a day makes people think twice about going into the office when the Centers for Disease Control have imposed containment protocols. For those whose jobs require that they attend meetings, the protocols demand that they meticulously plan what they need for the day.

The protocols are only an emergency measure. The governing health philosophy of the time is that the immune system needs to be regularly challenged by exposure to pathogens, lest a person's defenses turn against the body itself. The health authorities impose containment protocol only when some particularly dangerous pathogen breaks through ordinary barriers, and then for as short a time as possible, since the procedures so disrupt commerce. Indeed, many health officials recognize that the calming psychological impact of the procedures is as important as their actual effect on the spread of infection. The death of over 1.5 billion people in the early decades of the new millennium (750 million from disease itself, and another 750 million from the attendant agricultural chaos, civil unrest, and economic and social upheavals that accompanied the pandemics) has left a profound impression on society. Builders and retrofitters, for instance, advertise the installation of prophylactic defenses against rogue microbes when marketing a skyscraper.

The sterilization procedures might seem extraordinarily alien to someone from the twentieth century, but they are a natural outgrowth of less extreme measures that began being instituted in various facilities before the millennium. Besides those working in "clean rooms," airplane travelers to Hawaii and other places fearful of exotic pests had to sit through the pesticidal spraying of cabins before being allowed to disembark. Not long after 2000, ordinary hospitals began using some of these and other techniques for controlling biohazards as more and more resistant forms of bacteria incubated in medical facilities. By the time the CDC instituted the full suite of controls used in the sterilization procedures, most Americans had had some experience with one or more of the components of the procedures.

Although the easy-on, easy-off robes owe much to practicality, a good number of people have other reasons for adopting the style of dress. The long, flowing garments level rank and affluence in a society that has become intolerant of greed and privilege. Those who have money are not interested in attracting attention, and the mood of the times frowns on conspicuous consumption. The robes mark the wearer as a serious, humble person, not prone to vanity—esteemed qualities, even in New York City.

There are also a good number of people who appreciate the religious connotations of the robes, even if it is not the style to wear one's faith on one's sleeve. Scientists and other professionals have been humbled greatly by the events of the earlier decades of the century. First there was the mysterious death of huge tracts of forest, and the unanticipated collapse of whole ecosystems, then the epidemics, then the collapse of basic models of medicine and other sciences. Appalled by what the blind application of science and technology had done to the earth and its inhabitants, the scientific community had a crisis of confidence. Even physicists began to question whether science could arrogate to itself the role of deciding what constituted reality or the basic laws of the universe. As faith in reason declined, a general religious efflorescence spread through the educated classes as well as the poor. Intellectuals, professionals, and scientists gravitated to a faith called Maya.

Scientists of various stripes have struggled to reconcile the need for rigor and the beauty of science with a world that has in the most dramatic fashion told mankind that there is an extremely heavy price for pretending to know everything. Out of this has emerged Maya, a new belief system that explicitly recognizes the limitations of science and its subordination to nature. The attraction of Maya for hard scientists is that it attempts to justify its de facto deification of nature by using the tools of scientific rigor. It owes its name to the Hindu veil of maya, the illusory fabric of reality, but it traces its scientific roots to James Lovelock's Gaia hypothesis, first articulated in the 1970s. Lovelock argued that the planet functioned as a type of organism in which biological and physical systems interacted to maintain conditions suitable for life.

Among the articles of faith of Maya is the notion that the best science can do is offer up powerful metaphors that enable humanity to manipulate nature. Over time, through the application of human imagination, a discipline might replace these metaphors with yet more powerful images of reality, but Maya accepts as an a priori truth that nature is ultimately unknowable.

It also accepts that nature is the source of all. In contrast to the New Age search for higher consciousness, adherents of Maya seek what might be called lower consciousness—embodied in the notion that, just as our individual development retraces the evolution of life on earth, humans can reconnect to that umbilicus leading to the origins of the universe.

Not all scientists turned to Maya, of course, nor did all the disciplines suffer a loss of prestige. Epidemiologists and ecologists emerged from the plague years with their standing somewhat enhanced. They had predicted the coming crisis, and since their paradigm recognizes the power and interconnectedness of the natural order, the leading ecologists are treated with the same reverence as great teachers and religious leaders.

The plague years and the economic panics of earlier decades have had many other impacts on urban life. The xenophobia and anti-immigrant fever of earlier decades have reversed movements toward the assimilation and integration of New York's mosaic of different cultures. People of different ethnicities meet in the workplace and now maintain cordial relations, but tend to withdraw to families and enclaves in the evenings.

Such circumstances present those in the advertising profession with a difficult work environment. Most people in 2050 have nowhere near the discretionary money that characterized the glory days of the consumer society. Nor are they either willing or able to take on debt to make nonessential purchases. Society frowns on ostentation of any sort, and in this era in which kin and peer groups provide vital support networks, few people can risk being shunned for the sake of some material indulgence. To work in advertising in the middle decades of the twenty-first century is to be viewed with suspicion as one involved in an unsavory endeavor.

A look at the creative team gathered for the brainstorming session reveals instantly how advertising has adapted to this new era. Most of the group are dressed in robes, with the exception of one elderly gentleman who is wearing a suit. Although the field is a throwback to the era of the consumer society, the creative team from the Avatar agency has adopted the camouflage of the times.

From an advertiser's point of view, the tenor of the times leaves very little room to maneuver. Advertising is a profession whose sole raison d'être involves subtle psychic engineering, attaching subconscious needs and wants to often unnecessary products; but many of the field's traditional appeals are now off limits. Overt sex is out, for instance, a victim of changed mores that see unfettered sexual expression as a threat to the family and thus to the community at large. Whereas late-twentieth-century pundits looked to sitcoms like "Ellen," in which the main character declared herself gay, as indicators of a trend toward more openness in sexual relations, increasingly unstable times mooted the debate by changing the risk-reward ratio underlying attitudes toward sex. The costs of sexually transmitted diseases such as AIDS, and the burden on society of unwed pregnancies and single-parent families, came to be viewed as increasingly onerous. In fact, sexual behavior had already begun to change before the end of the twentieth century. As in the case of ostentation, peer pressure more than laws brought about the change. As people turned inward, toward family and community, ancient cultural taboos gradually reasserted themselves.

Although the idea would have seemed preposterous in the twentieth century, Islamic fundamentalism was a better predictor of the future of the role of sex in the community than either feminism or the rampant pansexuality of the end of the century. Sex cannot be denied, of course, but it has been driven underground into much more coy and hypocritical expressions. Everybody in advertising in 2050 longs for the good old days, when all you had to do was devise a campaign around a photo of Claudia Schiffer naked and you could sell anything from jeans to cologne

Youth culture is another victim of changes in the new century. Part of this shift has to do with a natural graying of the population, with people living longer and having fewer children. Again, as attention shifted from celebration of the individual to the integrity of communities and families in unstable times, the elderly and experienced gained renewed respect, and the young found themselves with fewer freedoms and more responsibilities. Audiences in the New York of 2050, for instance, would be truly mystified by films such as *Rebel Without a Cause* or *Natural Born Killers,* which seem to glorify destructive, disruptive behavior and celebrate alienation.

In this more community-oriented era, which places a high value on civic virtue, both politics and political advertising have changed as well. Those running for office spend a lot more time in direct contact with the voters, meeting with community and neighborhood groups, and a lot less time on television. Ironically, the very ubiquity of information and communication technology has bred a counterreaction. Despite the risk of casual infection in the aftermath of the plagues, people place a high premium on personal contact with those who might affect their lives, in no small part because they can never be sure whether images delivered over the Net are real or confected. In part, political advertising has fallen victim to this same distrust of a medium that can effortlessly recombine images and texts to create any reality the designers want. Also, the distrustful, Balkanized polity made it difficult to get away with the breathtaking hype and misrepresentation typical of political advertising at the end of the last century.

Given all these restrictions, it is somewhat remarkable that advertising has persisted at all. However, advertising has always drawn both the resourceful and the mercurial, and those in advertising in 2050 respond to this brave new world by zealously trumpeting the mores of the times. The advertising community has adopted stringent rules about what is permissible in a campaign and what is not. Despite suspicion and disfavor in the community, advertising still performs a vital service for companies who have to compete for a buyer's attention.

Vanity cannot be completely suppressed, despite the overall piety of the times. Women, for instance, still wear perfume, the proximate occasion for this gathering of creative minds. The brainstorming session is taking place in a conference room in the

Cargill Building, which in the previous century was known as the General Motors Building, on Fifth Avenue. On the walls are pretentious homilies testifying to sober times: "Ritual is the repository of memory," reads one, "custom the sediments of wisdom."

The group consists of four people: an elderly man, two young men, and a young woman. One young man has a shaved head, identifying him as a devotee of Maya, pan-Buddhism, or one of the other Eastern sects. He wears a saffron tunic over loose trousers cinched with a bright-orange cloth. Two of the others wear frayed monk's robes; the older man has opted for a plain business suit. As in the society at large, younger members of the creative team defer to the judgment and experience of the older member of the group.

Meetings have become events by 2050, if only because they entail so much more inconvenience than in the past. A voyeur from the twentieth century would find meetings in 2050 an incomprehensible combination of stultifying formality and rituals that seem to owe their origins to the more risible affectations of the so-called New Age. Quite often, for instance, meetings begin with a moment or two of relaxed silence, as people settle into the room and adjust to one another's presence. This is done with none of the self-consciousness characteristic of so many New Age gatherings of earlier times, but functionally serves the same purpose as those fumbling attempts to find some common ground for the group, some way to open intuitive and other nonverbal channels of communication.

Opening the session, the older man speaks a bit about perfumes in general, about how they are the purest vehicles for advertising. The interaction between skin chemistry and a perfume is unique to the individual, but advertising can associate a pleasing odor with a mystique that taps collective longings and allows a woman to dream of what might be. The others have heard this before, but listen deferentially until he has finished. To get the discussion going, he nods to one of the young men, who has prepared some ideas.

The young man takes a remote control and calls up his campaign, which, through holographic technology, hovers over the conference table in three-dimensional form. An image appears of a woman seated against an old bent oak on the shores of a still pond. Tiny ripples evoke warm summer days blessed by refreshing zephyrs. Her children are in the background, playing in succulent green grass. A fawn delicately laps the water a few yards away. The young man clicks the remote and a new image appears. An old man with long white flowing robes is now part of the tableau. He is holding an open book and looking benignly down on the family. The remote clicks again and the last image appears, showing the group arrayed around the old man in a rapt circle while he reads from the book. Steeped in quasi-religious imagery, the campaign has more in common with illustrations out of *Watchtower,* the magazine of the Jehovah's Witnesses, than with anything out of a late-twentieth-century women's magazine.

The introduction of religious themes into advertising began toward the end of the twentieth century, as marketers tried to cash in on renewed interest in religion in ads for products ranging from the apéritif Campari (one ad focuses on a priest looking miserable at a garden party where he is forced to drink white wine), to the image of the Dalai Lama in an ad for Apple computers. These early forays, however, were opposite in spirit to what would come later. They represented an invasion of formerly hallowed ground by advertisers eager to mine the cultural landscape for powerful symbols, and they were decried by some religious figures as part of the vulgarization of society. By the mid–twenty-first century, power has shifted from marketers to religious and community leaders. Advertisers never directly use religious symbols, and instead invoke the spirituality in subtle ways.

Such is the approach taken in the young man's perfume campaign. "We are talking to a woman who sees herself comfortably ensconced in the values of the day," notes the young man, summing up his concept, "a woman who dreams of a refuge and the comforting presence of elders—in short, the woman of the fifties."

The others take this in for a moment, and then begin offering questions and suggestions. Would he recommend a religious leader or an ecologist as the comforting older figure? Why not thunderclouds on the horizon, to add drama to the notion of the refuge? The discussion is intense and invested with a theatrical sense of moment. There is some more back and forth, and animated conversation about archetypal concepts such as the notion of a refuge, of nature's power, of what women long for. The meeting extends well into the afternoon as alternatives are discussed. Such face-to-face sessions are infrequent, and those attending, sustained by an adrenaline rush, want to get as much as possible out of the occasion.

The meeting ends with handshakes, which are a special gesture of trust in this microbe-conscious age (ordinarily, people content themselves with a friendly wave; air kisses rule the day, and even Japanese-style bowing is making a comeback). After the session, the three younger members of the group repair to the advertising club for a drink. Since the plague years in the early part of the century, professionals have preferred the security of private clubs to bars as places to meet people outside of their families. Clubs, with their careful vetting of applicants, offer better protection against casual exposure to infectious agents, and also serve as a nexus for networking. With its proliferation of professional/social organizations, New York of 2050 is somewhat redolent of Victorian London.

Inside the advertising club, the mood is sepulchral; dark woods, ample couches, and overstuffed chairs suggest the flavor of clubs in the past. The members, mostly older men, sit in silence, reading or meditating in one of the many quiet alcoves designed for that purpose. The creative types settle into the comfortable chairs and order glasses of sherry from the ancient steward who appears as soon as they sit down. Alcoholic beverages have survived the prudish temper of the times, both because of the health benefits of moderate drinking, and because the mild disinfectant properties of such beverages reassure those gathered for social reasons outside of the home.

After some gossip and discussion of the session they have just had, the conversation inevitably comes around to the question of the frustrations of working within the limits of codes, formalities, hypocritical rituals, and other controls. The young woman complains that people seem to be afraid of everything. This draws a sharp reply from one of the young men, who sternly notes, "The reason we are afraid of everything is that in the twentieth century they were afraid of nothing."

This is true. During the heyday of the consumer society, advertising and marketing agencies were the equivalent of nuclear powers in the realm of the mind and heart, manipulating ideas, images, and feelings with only glancing acknowledgment of their power. Now the profession feels the full weight of a moralistic culture. Advertising has bent to the times. Although it is down, however, it is not out.

Humans will always be vulnerable to temptation. If times change for the better again, the pattern of generational forgetting that allows humanity to keep repeating the mistakes of its past might even erase the cultural memory of the horrors of the early decades of the century.

Chapter 16

CENTRAL AFRICA:
NATURE OUT OF BALANCE

AFRICA'S SANGHA RIVER CUTS through some of the most remote and inaccessible parts of the continent, none more remote than when it enters the northern part of what in the twentieth century had been known as the Congo. The region to the east of this part of the river, called the Ndoki, was once one of the most remote rain forests on earth. Even as late as the 1990s, this canopied realm, guarded by vast swamps and unnavigable rivers, remained so inaccessible that its wildlife did not flee at the sight of man. The Ndoki escaped the massacres of wildlife that plagued the rest of central Africa. In the twentieth century, it was one of the last remaining places on earth where man could observe life as it was in the Pleistocene, before *Homo sapiens* itself became a natural force on the order of a comet or volcano. Gorillas and chimps, hunted throughout their habitat, and among the shiest creatures on earth, would simply stop and stare when the occasional scientist mounted expeditions into this enchanted refuge.

In 2050, there are no such remaining places on earth. A slow trip by air over the Ndoki reveals nothing but scrubland. The chimp and gorilla are gone, as is the forest. The area looks more like the Sahel than the Zaire basin. In some places the brush grows so thickly that a human venturing into the area would have to tunnel through the tangled branches.

Although chain saws had never entered this forest, tree-felling contributed to the demise of the Ndoki. Deforestation throughout Africa accelerated regional climate change. As Africans discovered too late, the rain forest is to some degree a self-sustaining system, one crucial element of which is a canopy of greenery that helps to capture and recycle moisture, and to protect the moist understory from a desiccating sun.

Unwittingly, modern man was re-creating devastation not seen in central Africa since fifteen hundred years ago, when a population explosion of ancient Bantu tribes deforested much of the Congo basin. The tribes back then did not outlive the forests, and their numbers collapsed, allowing the ecosystem to recover. Now the catastrophic cycle is unfolding again.

By the end of the twentieth century, the Ndoki had crossed a point of no return. Rainfall fell below two hundred centimeters a year, the minimum threshold of moisture necessary to support a wet tropical forest. In just a few years, the ecosystem underwent a rapid collapse. Gilberteodendron trees disappeared first, depriving monkeys and other primates of their tasty fruit. Then followed otranella, *omphalo carpum, Balanites wilsoniana,* myacanthus, *Truculia africanus,* and a host of other rain-forest giants, whose fruits supported creatures ranging from elephants to mangabeys.

On certain days, those entering the remains of the forest now notice that many leaves are coated with what looks like red dust. In earlier decades, scientists curious about the dust were dumbfounded to discover that it came from the Sahara, blown south by harmattan winds. As it invaded territories that had been moist tropical forest for millennia, the dust served as a memento mori, a chilling signal of the impending death of a great ecosystem.

First the outer edges of the barrier swamps began to dry, ending the Ndoki's isolation from the rest of central Africa. Seeking refuge, the more mobile of the Ndoki's resident creatures embarked on an exodus toward the equator. Unfortunately, as these animals left the shelter of the Ndoki, which had been protected from invaders as much by local taboos as by law, they ran into a gauntlet of poachers and tribal peoples looking for meat. Those that survived guns, bows, poisons, and wire snares discovered that even where there was sufficient rain, logging had stripped the forest of many of the crucial fruit trees. Sapoli and sipo trees had become window frames in Spain and Japan; peracopsis trees were transformed into veneer; gilberteodendrons became planks. Without these pillars of the canopy, ficus trees, whose figs serve as a source of quick energy for chimps, gorillas, and monkeys, also diminished.

Forced to search for food, chimp bands invaded territories already occupied by other chimps. This in turn set off warfare between the groups as the stronger ones systematically hunted down other chimp groups, killing them with teeth and hands. Conflict between bands is an ancient chimp behavior and, under the direction of one or more chimp "generals," even involves elements of strategy and coordination. In this topsy-turvy world, however, conflict was perpetual, and the toll of the carnage matched the deaths caused by human hunting.

Conservationists and scientists began rallying to save these forests in the late twentieth century, and they watched with deep and helpless sadness as the quilt of life came apart. Later this sadness would be replaced by apprehension: by the early twenty-first century, humanity had learned at great cost that the retreat of the rain forest also stirred other creatures, far less savory than chimps and gorillas. These were viruses, bacteria, protozoa, and other pathogens that had lurked in the forest for millennia, opportunistic creatures that thrive amid climatic chaos and environmental change.

Some of these parasites, having evolved to prey on primates and other large mammals, found humans to be agreeable surrogates when their normal hosts disappeared. At first a trickle of new diseases began to emerge. Hemorrhagic fevers such as Marburg virus and Ebola found an equilibrium of sorts with their monkey hosts, but when they invaded naïve organisms they became horrifyingly destructive, perforating membranes so that people became like sieves, leaking blood and fluids internally and externally. Ebola killed so quickly that its very virulence limited

the damage it might wreak. New forms of encephalitis and menin-
gitis also emerged, as did novel intestinal viruses and other ailments. The trickle of new diseases soon became a flood, while
old scourges gathered new strength in the weakened immune systems of man and beast.

Ultimately, humans learned the harsh lesson being delivered
by the rain forest. Over time, bacteria and other infectious agents
tend to find some balance with their hosts—it is not in the reproductive interest of a pathogen to kill its meal ticket too rapidly.
Thus, over time, a bacteria will find an accommodative, or even
mutually supportive, relationship with another creature, in its guts
or, in the case of plants, roots. But change, whether brought about
by humans invading new territory, altering the environment, or
changing their behavior, creates enormous opportunities for
agents of pestilence to invade new territories. Ordinarily benign
agents can become lethal; germs adapted to one creature may
find a happy home in others. Change comes with a price; unfortunately for humans, change, more than anything else, was what
the twentieth century was about.

In 2050, the wreckage of change is everywhere evident. It is
evident in Kabo, in the ruins of a logging company strung out
along the banks of the Sangha River and long ago abandoned by
Nouvelle Bois Sangha, a defunct timber consortium. Its concrete
buildings now serve as shelter to a ragged and sickly group of
BaNgombe pygmies and an assortment of people from various
Bantu tribes. Until Bois Sangha began deforesting the area, yel-
low-fever-carrying mosquitoes remained in the trees, feasting on
monkeys and other primates. Tree-cutting brought them down to
earth, so to speak, and into closer contact with the large bipedal
primates who now dominated the area.

Farther south, the wreckage of change is evident in Ouesso, a
former river-port, now also largely abandoned. Along the river are
arrayed the crumbling remains of once-grand mansions, built in
the early and mid–twentieth century by traders and lumber
barons. Here and there a few people huddle around campfires,
but for the most part the city seems devoid of life.

Not far from the city lie the remains of the airport. The ragged forest crowds in on the pitted airstrip, and trees and vines have erupted through the ruins of four different half-completed terminal buildings, which remain as rotting monuments to the corruption of successive Congolese governments. Each terminal building had been launched with groundbreaking ceremonies and grand promises, but the fugitive ambitions of self-important rulers were no match for Africa's unique mixture of thievery and lassitude. No aircraft has landed in the airport for decades.

To the west and south of the jumbled, depopulated, picked-over remains of Ouesso and its airport are the edges of the retreating forest. Gaps in the forest canopy reveal salines, open spaces where animals used to gather to lick salt. African gray parrots squawk in the surrounding trees, and a palm vulture sails across the opening.

Here the growth is thicker, although the region was long ago stripped of its ancient mahoganies and other commercial woods. A healthy rain forest looks chaotic to the observer, but its ruckus conceals an interlocking and interdependent series of plants, trees, insects, and animals. Now, however, there is no hidden order underneath the crazy-quilt surface, just continual turmoil as creatures compete in changed circumstances.

With elephants gone, there is no creature to distribute the huge seeds of otranella or balanites. Similarly, hornbills, another large distributor of rain-forest seeds, have all but disappeared from the region. Like a Mafia family reacting to the imprisonment of a don, other trees grab the opportunity to invade rival turf. *Musanga leoerrerae*, an opportunistic tree species, has aggressively filled the void, much to the benefit of a number of species of cercopithecus monkeys, who prosper as other primates decline. And so the ecosystem has lurched along like a drunk struggling to find his balance. The disorder will continue until, sometime in the distant future, the forest finds a new equilibrium.

Deeper in the interior lies Sembé, situated at the southern end of an abandoned road that runs northward to Souanké, near the Cameroon border. The jungle long ago reclaimed the buttoned-down German plantations that were abandoned shortly after the end of the colonial era in the twentieth century. With the commercial timber already harvested and the colonialists gone, African governments showed little interest in the region. The jungle has gradually erased the last traces of the road.

By the end of the twentieth century, the Bakota, Bakouele, and Fang peoples of the region had begun to reconstitute the councils of elders, in the absence of any central government presence. The Bantus renewed their ancient relationship with the BaNgombe pygmies, with whom they would trade vegetables and other crops for bush meat, the common term for game caught by the pygmies in the forest. From the outside, the relationship looks exploitative, but it creates a market for pygmy hunting, tracking, and gathering skills and thus helps keep alive their culture. By 2050, the area is as isolated as it was before Africa's colonial period.

North of Sembé lies the village of Bayonke. As was typical in central Africa, the BaNgombe pygmies and the Bantu communities have sorted themselves according to an informal apartheid, clustering in separate compounds. Both use leaf and mud for their simple houses. The thatched roofs are made of palm leaves sewn into mats.

Now a third group has joined the African community in this village. They are distinguishable by their lightweight protective clothing on the back of which are stenciled the bold letters "CDC." At this point in history, the presence of the CDC in a remote African village is a sure sign that something is very wrong. In the aftermath of the plague years, the CDC, and its equivalents in other countries, grew in power to rival the size and influence of defense departments, which in a sense they were. The CDC had satellite offices scattered around the world, and when some microbial threat emerged would regularly dispatch teams to investigate.

The CDC team consists of a veterinarian, an anthropologist, a microbial ecologist, an epidemiologist, and a lab technician. They have built their own compound out of lightweight, portable materials. Solar technology, fuel cells, and satellite communications have enabled the group to establish a sophisticated research facility as well as a small clinic.

The scene inside the research facility would be familiar to the visitor from the twentieth century, although it would also be obvious that epidemiological research has been torqued by the unique stresses of the twenty-first century. Decades of experience with resurgent infectious disease have produced highly efficient, commonsensical ways of protecting researchers, and isolating patients and microbes. Decontaminating portals, filtration systems, lightweight protective clothing, positive air pressure to reduce the chances that some microbe might invade if a seal failed, and the strategic use of sterilizing light all combine to give researchers a refuge from dangerous life forms at large in the world. The visitor from the twentieth century would admire the different ways in which medicine has optimized all these procedures, but would not be very surprised by the nature of the precautions. On the other hand, those familiar with the imperial disdain with which Western medicine regarded indigenous, folk, and other non-Western therapies would be very surprised by the behavior of the CDC team in the Congo.

In one corner of the facility, a bearded anthropologist handles what looks like native cooking implements: a bowl, a ladle, and a bone knife. The man believes that objects hold meanings, and that by handling them he will help open channels to his own subconscious that will help him better understand this particular pygmy culture, which in turn will lead him closer to understanding the medical mystery the team has come to investigate. Someone taking this type of approach to investigation in the previous century would likely have found himself derided in Congress for wasting government resources. Proponents of hard-nosed empiricism would be even more horrified by some of the other "soft" techniques embraced by the team.

The CDC team has journeyed to this remote part of the former African republic as part of a worldwide effort to deal with a menacing and as yet unidentified contagion. As has happened so many times in the twenty-first century, a new disease has made its appearance, seemingly simultaneously throughout the world. It appears to be a hemorrhagic fever that jumps back and forth between pigs and humans. Researchers elsewhere have come up with what they think is the so-called index case—the first case to be documented—a Midwestern missionary who walked the Sembé-Souanké road and then returned to a farm in Kansas.

Because it was several months between the missionary's return and his sudden, awful death, the health authorities were deeply afraid. He may have unwittingly exposed thousands to the contagion—no one knows exactly how it was transmitted. Worse, scores of pigs have moved in and out of his farm. After the health authorities were humbled by epidemics in the early part of the century, any new outbreak of disease raises the question, Could this signal the return of nemesis? "Nemesis" is the label given to viruses whose characteristics enable them to evade human containment procedures: a relatively long dormant period, so that the microbe can spread stealthily among a population; the ability to travel easily from human to human and between humans and other creatures; and innocuous initial symptoms followed by a rapid kill, which makes it difficult to diagnose and treat.

Sensitive as they are to the threat of a nemesis virus after years of epidemics, researchers still recognize that, beyond any particular disease, the deeper threat lies in the perilously stressed immune systems of both humans and animals that serve as incubators for microbes, and in ecosystems disturbed by human activities and climate change, which make the world a factory for the breeding and dissemination of disease. After decades of contending with these threats, vigilance has been tempered by weariness and fatalism. A disease emerged, the world responded—sometimes in time, sometimes too late to prevent a pest or microbe from raising havoc, burdening societies with health costs they could not afford, dragging down economies, and otherwise distracting people from the ordinary affairs of life.

So it is with this new hemorrhagic fever. Around the world, millions of pigs have had to be slaughtered, ruining thousands of farmers and the businesses that depend on them. So far the disease does not seem to pass directly from human to human, but bitter experience has shown that this could change as well.

The CDC team has also been sobered by the circumstances surrounding the emergence of the new disease. This part of central Africa is one of the most isolated areas of the world, and the people who live here have been virtually cut off from the outside world for seventy-five years. Earlier they survived AIDS, TB, and the subsequent epidemics of the plague years. For generations they have been entering the forest and hunting wild boar, yet the CDC investigation has revealed that they had no prior experience with this new scourge, which starts out like a flu and within a couple of hours leaves its victims drowning in their own blood. Despite the isolation of the place where the disease emerged, despite restrictions on travel, quarantines, and screening procedures, and despite all the other barriers to the spread of disease that societies have imposed following the resurgent epidemics, this new disease has still raced around the world. It is another discouraging indicator that, in the competition between man and microbe, the bugs still hold most of the cards.

The team uses all the weapons of epidemiology, biotechnology, and plain medical-detective work to try to determine what they are up against. A microbial ecologist has examined every possible vector through which the disease could have been transmitted. Through satellite communications, they can draw on and contribute to the pooled talents of a global network of researchers.

The team uses other methods as well. The paradigm of disease has opened up in concert with the paradigm of physics. If there is a medical analogy to Einstein's EPR experiment, which pointed toward a reality beyond that described by classical physics, it is the placebo effect. Investigating the efficacy of drugs during controlled testing in which some patients would unknowingly be given sugar pills instead of real medicines, researchers discovered that the mere fact that someone thinks that he is being given a miracle drug can have more effect than the medicine itself. Conversely, some of the targeted medicines produced by biotech which specifically attacked pathogens at the point when they infect a cell, mystified doctors because they proved no more effective at increasing health than cruder and more primitive drugs.

The importance of state of mind and other ineffable factors caused doctors to wonder whether the Western concept of disease as a blind war between pathogens and antibodies in which the patient is a passive participant was too limiting. Consequently, less doctrinaire and more result-oriented doctors made efforts to broaden the ambit of their search for ways to manage pathogens. This meant bringing along an anthropologist who relied on unorthodox methods.

Traditional doctors now pay far greater attention to the perceptions and insights of the pygmies themselves than was the practice in the past. Through observation and trial and error, the hunters and shamans have accumulated enormous knowledge of the forest and its denizens. They know what forest pigs eat, what makes them sick, and what diseases they catch. Though sometimes encrusted with myth and concealed in taboos and superstition, and sometimes fragmented because much had been lost during earlier periods when some of the young had turned their back on tribal ways, this basic knowledge of the ecology of their world has given investigators an enormous head start in their own research.

Consequently, the CDC team pays respectful attention to the shamans and wisdom keepers of the tribes of the area. The attempt to span both worlds requires the epidemiologist to balance the rigor of Western science with an openness to belief systems based on magic and the spirits of ancestors. Such a feat was extraordinarily difficult for scientists of the twentieth century, but the more humble researchers of the twenty-first accept the effort as crucial to learning.

Thus, when the anthropologist goes off to watch a BaNgombe dance in which the shamans summon the spirits to explain their plight, the doctor on the team does not scoff. On the way to the pygmy compound, they stop at the clinic. Out of deference to the feelings of the patients, and still confident that the microbe does not travel from human to human, they do not wear the protective space suits.

They enter the clinic, which has a rudimentary disinfectant entryway dividing less infectious patients from the outside world, and then a separate, more formidable barrier further isolating another group of patients. Within the compartments, each patient is sequestered inside a large bubble. Doctors have long recognized that hospitals serve as excellent places to create tougher microbes, but the logistics of central Africa, much less the budgets of the overburdened health authorities, do not permit the luxury of portable isolation units, with their elaborate filtration units and pumps. Instead, the research team has been forced to keep the patients together. Despite high-tech touches, the scene greeting the two scientists is like something out of an Africanized Brueghel.

Sunken-eyed patients lie on cots, breathing shallowly through masks. A trickle of blood slowly drips from one emaciated man's ear. His hands and feet are black, even his palms and the soles of his feet, which would normally be pink. Sores cover his chest, some of them so deep that they appear to penetrate the chest cavity. As they pass, he gives them a pleading look. The doctor tries to put an encouraging smile on his face, but succeeds only in looking helpless.

Later, as they enter the compound, a graying but compact man comes out to greet them and leads the Western healers to a place of honor. In the center of the compound, a bonfire burns. A group of pygmies are smoking some plant rolled into cigar-sized stogies. They chant softly. In the center of the group stands someone completely covered by a large raffia-leaf mask. Suddenly the mask collapses in a heap on the ground, and the pygmies melt into the forest at the edge of the compound.

The anthropologist explains the ceremony, that the dancers are following the spirit, the thing that is under the raffia leaves, into the forest, and that when they come back they will be possessed by Enanyi Njenyi, which is what the BaNgombe call the spirit.

It is now pitch-black. After a while, the pygmies reappear and begin circling the mask, singing. No one approaches the pile of raffia leaves. Suddenly it begins rising from the ground.

The raffia-leaf-covered figure or spirit hovers in the center of the singing group. The elderly man leaves the two foreigners, approaches the circle, and joins the group of men singing and chanting. He then returns to the two outsiders and invites them to smoke a large cigar rolled out of leaves. Both inhale deeply and enter a type of stupor. This kind of research would have cost the doctor his job and reputation in the preceding century, but neither man shows the slightest discomfiture.

As they stare into the circle of men around the fire, both researchers see the same thing, although in their blurred state they are not sure whether they are looking at an enactment, a fata morgana, or something entirely different. Whatever it is, the tableau they see catches their attention. The raffia-leaf spirit figure looks as though it is picking up something from the forest floor. It sprinkles the dust in the air, then on a dancer dressed as a pig, and finally on the dancers themselves. All flee in horror from the dust—or whatever it represents.

The two scientists sit in silence pondering the dance. Could the dust be some fungal spore from the forest floor? Or does it represent some other toxin released by the changes in the forest? Or is it merely some fanciful creation of the dancers themselves, representing nothing at all? Still, with few other leads, it is worth investigating.

Epidemiology is a crucial discipline in this century of disturbed environments, but science itself has been disturbed by events that it failed to anticipate and which many people believe it helped bring about. Unlike their predecessors, the medical researchers of the era are open to other ideas, other therapies, and even other systems of thought, some of them anathema to the quantitative, materialistic paradigm of twentieth-century science.

Chapter 17

KANSAS:
TROUBLE ON THE FARM

ONE ROLE MODEL FOR the farmer of 2050 is Job; the other is Tantalus. Prices for crops have never been better, but prosperity seems to lie always just out of reach, and every attempt to grab the brass ring is stymied by windstorms, hail, floods, droughts, heat waves, blights, or some frightening new disease afflicting livestock. In a quiet corner of Kansas, these tides are etched in the face of a middle-aged farmer as he walks purposefully toward his pigsty. He watches a towering thunderhead make its slow way over southern Kansas as evening approaches the Great Plains, the worried look already on his face taking on additional hues of apprehension and irritation. It is a characteristic mix of emotions for farmers in this tumultuous era.

The farmer needs rain, of course, but often as not he gets a downpour, and all too often at the most vulnerable stages of a crop's maturation. Through history, the whims of nature have made farmers a thoughtful lot. Over the decades of the twenty-first century, however, nature has shown an ever-increasing capriciousness that has worn down the reserves and self-confidence of farmers even as it has increased the prices they get for crops in an overcrowded and insecure world. At a point in history when people once again turn to religion more than science for answers, farmers tend to be the most religious of all.

They are not like the Luddites of the nineteenth century who, following the example of their leader, Ned Lud, roamed the English countryside smashing textile machines; but the farmers of 2050 are keenly aware of the limits of technology. Nor have they become hippies. Despite the myth that farmers are close to the earth, agriculture has always entailed profound interventions in nature's workings. From breeding plants to ripping up ecosystems and replacing them with fields, it has always been an unsentimental business. In 2050, farmers are no less interested in agricultural research than they were in the twentieth century. One major difference, however, is that the farmer of 2050 is much more attuned to the tolerances of soils and ecosystems. The arrogant notion that the limits to farm productivity involve capital and energy rather than nature has long since disappeared.

The farmer of 2050 relies on birds, friendly insects, and other biological controls as well as bioengineered seeds that have had resistance to pests bred into them to reduce crop losses. They minimize irrigation to conserve water and soils, and they seek out grains and vegetables appropriate to a climate that seems to have gone haywire. As the farmer, a God-fearing man named Higham, walks, he pauses to inspect the health of a field of pearl millet. His grandfather switched to the African crop from corn because of its extreme tolerance of drought and heat. Although the farmer does not know it, the crops that now suit conditions in Kansas originally evolved to survive in the Sahel. This year, he has planted a quick-maturing strain which is almost ready to harvest. The long heads, which resemble giant caterpillars, produce a grain that can substitute for wheat or rice, and the plant's hardiness more than compensates for the lower price it commands. His other crops—sorghum and spelt—would also have been considered rarities in Kansas in the last century, but they too are now commonplace in the Midwest, favored for their ability to withstand pests and extreme conditions.

Higham walks through the fragrant air of the summery Kansas evening and enters the barnyard. Hastily pulling a breathing mask over his face, he hurries over to the pigsty, where a young man and woman, also masked, are hovering over an old sow. Glancing only briefly at the pig that lies bleeding from its eyes, ears, and nose and breathing heavily, he snaps at his adolescent children to stand back.

The three of them stare at the dying pig with a mixture of fatalism and melancholy, only a small part of which is an expression of sympathy. Even without calling a veterinarian, Higham and his children know the obligations entailed when an animal is discovered with an unknown ailment, and they know the hardships and dangers that will follow. For the humans it means quarantine and testing, for the livestock slaughter and cremation.

Knowing the economic pain and social isolation that would lie ahead once he reported the disease, a twentieth-century farmer, even a responsible one, would have been tempted to slaughter the pigs and be done with the problem without telling the authorities. In 2050, this response is all the more tempting, given the greater uncertainties of agriculture, but it is inconceivable, because the farmers of 2050 know all too well the horrible risks of putting self-interest over communal good.

In the earlier decades of the century, the human epidemics got the headlines, but some of the diseases, particularly new variants of morbilla—a class of viruses that includes measles—emerged in animals before jumping over to humans. Other epidemics ravaged crops, which had their own special vulnerabilities.

At the beginning of the twenty-first century, most of humanity still depended on high-yielding varieties of rice, wheat, and corn. As noted earlier, the high-yielding rice and wheat strains had been created by interbreeding plants that had sturdy stalks with plants that produced heavy heads of grain. With a stronger stem, the plant could support more grain; hence the higher yields and the Green Revolution.

The trouble was that the process of transferring genetic material in plants was not exact. Even in the twentieth century, scientists wondered whether, along with stronger stems, the breeders of high-yield crops were also transferring vulnerabilities to some blight or pest. In 2015, farmers discovered that along with the stumpy stalks for wheat came susceptibility to a fungus. Worse yet, so many farmers around the world had abandoned local strains of crops and switched to high-yielding varieties that plant breeders had only a limited stock of variants through which they could search for resistance to the blight. In the best circumstances, it took months to select and breed a response to the blight.

Worst of all, even when the blights hit, some poor farmers continued to plant vulnerable crops, not wanting to waste precious seed, in essence playing Russian roulette with the world's food supply. Thus the contagion continued to spread even after alarms traveled around the world. Farmers learned the costs of going it alone—an expensive lesson, costing millions of lives through malnutrition, migration, and social upheaval, as well as countless billions of dollars.

The experience put the fear of God into farmers. Around the world, farmers and agribusinesses developed the equivalent of a military code of conduct, although it is unstated and enforced only by peer-group pressure. Farmers understand that a new disease is as much a threat as an invading army.

Despite the pain humanity suffered, farmers were not blamed for the blights and crop failures. Public anger focused more on huge agribusinesses, middlemen, and trading houses that were accused of hoarding and price gouging; individual farmers were perceived to be victims of events, along with ordinary people. One result of these crises was a resurgence of small family farms, as many agribusinesses were carved up in bankruptcy or forced to divest themselves of farmland by angry politicians. The small farmers were better able to adapt to changing circumstances, swiftly changing their mix of crops, and drawing for cheap labor on family members no longer so eager to abandon farms, given the cruel realities of the labor market.

Farmers actually rose in public esteem through these years. Everybody with a bit of land, even city dwellers, now resorted to vegetable gardening as a hedge against the vicissitudes of markets and nature, and this shift turned people's attention toward those upon whom the food security of the world depended. By the middle of the twenty-first century, many communities treat farmers with the respect ordinarily reserved for religious elders.

In some respects, that is what they have become. They hold themselves to far more austere codes of behavior than might ever be imposed by a government. God or the gods, depending on whether the family is Christian or pantheist, is once again a presence in people's lives, and the wages of sin weigh heavy in their imaginations. Shame, that powerful weapon of cultural norms longed for by conservatives in the twentieth century, and embodied in the Book of Ezekiel—"the fathers have eaten sour grapes, and the children's teeth are set on edge"—once again enforces community mores. The typical farmer would rather go broke than bring dishonor on his family.

Their homes reflect their austere values. The beleaguered farmer's house bears a strong resemblance to the farmhouses of the Amish (who in 2050 plow lands that, after generations of intelligent rotations and soil-protective methods, are even more fertile than they were in the twentieth century), with the notable difference that he is far more accommodating of technology than those simple folk of Pennsylvania and Ohio. Farmers are linked to weather information and agricultural extension services through computer, but their simple, efficient homes offer little in the way of entertainment. The bookshelves are almost bare, except for the Bible and a few books. One of the titles, *The Last Days*, is an interpretation of the plague years as God's retribution for mankind's descent into avarice and venality. The dining room is spartan, furnished with a simple maple table and functional wooden chairs. The young people of the 1990s found the austerity and uncompromising world view of their parents oppressive, but the young of 2050 accept parental authority, which has resurfaced in response to the hardships of the century. The farmer himself knows only a little about the indulgent, materialistic times of the previous century. He would have been stunned by the vanity of the technological optimism that prompted Americans to dream of a risk-free society.

Harder to endorse in rural communities are the xenophobia

and racism, which impose an undercurrent of suspicion and hostility during informal encounters between people of different
races and religions. A powerful sense of public decorum and rigid
formality smooths interactions between groups when they meet in
the course of a workday, and for the most part there is less friction
between groups than characterized the latter part of the twentieth
century. For most people, the world beyond their communities is
a frightening place best avoided. The farmer, a decent man in
most respects, does not allow even the slightest contact between
his daughter and the children of the non-Christian families in the
region ("non-Christian" means some variety of pantheism in Midwestern farm communities). He and his wife educate the children
at home, which minimizes contact in any event.

Now, with his pigs dying of an unknown ailment, Higham
knows that the outside world is about to intrude. Federal and state
governments, not trusting the farmers to police themselves, impose their own overseers on the agricultural community. Panicked
legislatures in many countries give agriculture departments
sweeping powers to abridge both due process and individual
rights if it is necessary to protect crops and livestock. As has always been the case when an institution is granted special authority, these powers have been abused.

The farmer accepts this fatalistically. In a sort of religious
equivalent to convergent evolution, the drumbeat of crises has
driven not only Christian fundamentalists but even the pantheists
to accept life's reversals as God's will. As space-suited specialists
invade his barnyard, his reaction to the swirl of events is to pray,
and his terror, several months later, when his daughter appears
red-eyed and announces that she does not feel so good is muted
by his certitude that his family's woes are part of God's design. He
is a man who has not forgotten the harsh lessons of the century.

The farmer of 2050 is more sophisticated than his counterpart
of the previous century in only one respect: his understanding of
the interaction of crops and ecosystems. Perhaps more than any
other group, farmers embody a new paradigm that is emerging as
the successor to the myth of progress. The thrall of religious faith,

which emerged in response to the harrowing decades of disease, economic upheaval, and civil disorder, narrowed the farmer's focus and somewhat limited in him the natural human desire to innovate and experiment, but it did not crowd out reason entirely. Rather, faith, in all its resurgent forms, acts as a governor, re-establishing the historical role of religious passion that has been repeatedly interrupted during Western history.

Chapter 18

ANTARCTICA STIRS

Approaching Antarctica from the air has a quality of drama appropriate to the silent, looming immensity of the continent. After one has been flying for hours over the roughest waters on earth, icebergs and floes give notice that the continent is near. Then, as one continues toward McMurdo Station, the main American base in Antarctica, the northern mountains of Victoria Land heave into view, rising ten thousand feet or more above the Ross Sea and oozing great tongues of ice from every couloir and notch. The vast, silent, treeless continent conveys the awesome inertia of a place where motion is noticeable only on a geological time scale, as though the extreme cold of the polar world has slowed down the pace of life itself.

As one continues southward over the Ross Ice Shelf, the continent's two great ice sheets appear. On the left lies the West Antarctic Ice Sheet, as large as China, and nearly three miles thick in places. Viewed from high altitude, its ice streams are visible. These glaciers-within-a-glacier allow ice to flow through the great ice sheet, and they look from the air like frozen rapids.

These streams, however, are rapids reified. On human scale their motion is almost imperceptible, but relative to the immobile ice sheets, the massive conveyors of ice, fifty miles wide and thousands of feet deep, are moving quite rapidly. Indeed, if time-lapse photography could somehow collapse thousands of years, the whole continent would look alive as the ice flowed and cracked, redistributing its mass according to the laws governing gravity and friction.

Farther south, the endless expanse of the East Antarctic Ice Sheet comes into view on the right, pushing up against the very tops of fourteen thousand peaks in the Transantarctic range. Indeed, this aerial perspective is the only vantage point from which the human eye can begin to appreciate the scale of these ancient ice sheets. The mountains are like the rim of a bathtub the size of a continent, while the ice, averaging over two miles in thickness, stretches to infinity to the east.

The scene begs the question: What could ever alter this seemingly immutable landscape of blinding white against a heart-breakingly blue sky? The notion that the puny machinations of humanity might bring change seems laughable. But, by 2050, change has come to Antarctica.

Ernest Shackleton's hut sits in its protected hollow on Cape Royds just as it has since 1907, when the British explorer last left it. Boots, mittens, and shoes are neatly piled, as are case upon case of stores: Moir's gooseberries in bottles, tins of Irish brawn, Aberdeen marrow fat, boiled mutton, tripe and onions, parsnips and scarlet runners all look ready to eat. The tin of Colman's mustard is as recognizable to the buyer of 2050 as it was in 1907. Generations of visitors have respected the inviolability of this accidental museum of early Antarctic exploration, while the cold and dryness of the climate have preserved the clothing and food-stuffs.

Outside the hut, however, there are tiny, subtle signs of change. Corn and hay that lay outside perfectly preserved through the twentieth century have now turned to compost.

Farther east of Cape Royds, near Franklin Island, an entire colony of emperor penguins has disappeared. The birds need 255 days of sea ice to complete their cycle from mating to the fledging of the young. But beginning in the 1990s, the sea ice began forming later and breaking up earlier, forcing the fledglings to dive into the ocean before they were ready to cope with life in the open waters. After losing a succession of yearlings, the colony began dwindling rapidly, through mortality and migration, as some of the birds began moving out in search of more stable ice, abandoning a colony that had persisted for many thousands of years.

Other, bigger changes have taken place as well. Indeed, a cascade of dramatic climate events in Antarctica and around the world continues to set humanity's teeth on edge. As the world community discovered to its discomfiture in the decades following the millennium, the laws of geophysics that govern climate are massively indifferent to human attitudes.

Beginning in the late 1980s, geophysicists, atmospheric chemists, modelers, and a host of other specialists began warning that the release of CO_2 and other so-called greenhouse gases could change the energy budget of the planet with unknown consequences. Perhaps the most memorable warning came from marine geochemist Wallace Broecker of Columbia University's Lamont-Doherty Laboratory, who, sounding like an Old Testament prophet, said, "Climate is an angry beast. And we are poking it with sticks."

Human failure to act was the result of a variety of disparate if not contradictory causes. The arrogant belief that we could fix climate if we broke it conspired to delay action, as did the self-deprecating notion humans were too puny to alter the systems that run the planet. Economic self-interest and ingrained habits united people and industries against taking action. Those who felt they had something to lose in efforts to control greenhouse gases—energy companies, manufacturers, etc.—were unwilling to change their ways as long as there was a smidgen of scientific uncertainty that might be exploited to paralyze policy makers.

Indeed, there was uncertainty about climate change, but by the end of the twentieth century, the confusion centered on what kind of change might happen and how long it would take, not on whether change was on its way. This cozy academic and policy debate continued until it was rudely interrupted by nature herself. The surprise, when it came, undermined the confidence of scientists and left elected officials and policy makers around the world floundering for answers.

At first scientists were reluctant to connect the various events of the early decades of the new century: seemingly innocuous anomalies such as the disappearance of fogs off the coast of California were followed by massive coral die-offs throughout the Pacific. In the North, polar bears died off by the thousands as the sea ice in the Arctic retreated before the cubs were ready to move onto the ice.

By the 2020s and 2030s, however, the changes were so big and dramatic they became impossible to dismiss. Withering droughts and heat waves hit large parts of the grain belt in the U.S. Farther north, the great boreal forests baked in unaccustomed heat, causing wildfires to erupt and devastate millions of acres. In the tropics, fires raced through forests as well, particularly in Malaysia and Indonesia, as droughts turned ordinarily moist wood to tinder. The changes had varied and bizarre effects. As the upper layers of permafrost liquefied, for instance, buildings across much of Russia toppled, ridding the nation of thousands of ugly, poorly built structures erected during the communist decades. Everywhere, the altered climates provided opportunities for a host of pathogens and pests, fueling the plagues of the era.

In Antarctica, the most dramatic changes occurred at the edges of the continent. In the late twentieth century, scientists discovered that the apron of sea ice had shrunk by 25 percent, or 5.65 million square kilometers, since the late 1950s. Beginning in the second decade of the twenty-first century, satellite imagery revealed huge seasonal holes in the sea ice. These areas, called "polynas," had occurred before, but never on this scale. In some parts of the coast, ice cover was reduced by 60–70 percent. Moreover, as the polynas stayed open season after season, air temperatures rose over the areas of open waters by as much as thirty-six degrees Fahrenheit, from an average of four below zero during winter months to just above freezing. For large areas over the Southern ocean, an arctic climate switched to maritime in the blink of an eye.

All of these events had some precedent in the recent climate record—El Niños in 1982 and 1997 fueled massive fires in Borneo, ice retreat in 1995 trapped polar bears on Wrangell Island—but now it seemed that the climate upheavals were not only extreme but also persistent and global. Around the world, people wanted to know why. With tremendous foreboding, scientists began to speculate on whether climate was in the process of "flipping," a type of extremely rapid climate change only discovered at the end of the previous century.

The notion of a flickering climate instills dread in 2050, because, until the mid-1990s, most climate specialists assumed that change, if it came, would be gradual. In 1986, the conventional wisdom was that it took a thousand years for climate to change from an ice age to a warm period. By 1991, that figure had been reduced by an order of magnitude to one hundred years, which was worrisome enough. Just two years later, however, a Pennsylvania State University geophysicist named Richard Alley published a paper arguing that in some parts of the world the transition took between two and five years.

Alley found this evidence in deep ice cores taken from Greenland. Subsequent research looking at glaciers in Chile, seafloor sediments off Santa Barbara, California, ancient pollens in New York, and other evidence from elsewhere in the world confirmed that around the world climate changed drastically in periods ranging from two to fifty years. Roughly 11,500 years ago, climate suddenly chilled, and then, fifteen hundred years later, warmed. What also captured the attention of climate specialists was the magnitude of the change. To put a change of this magnitude in perspective, a mere two-degree drop in global temperatures during the thirteenth century started the Little Ice Age, described in the introduction, which wiped out the Vikings' Greenland colony, spurred glaciers to advance crushing villages in the Alps, and caused periodic episodes of starvation and mass migration.

No one wanted to speculate on the enormous cost should climate warm in some places by upward of fifteen degrees. Scientists knew that climate could flip, but they did not know whether these drastic changes only happened at the end of an ice age. There was still hope that change of this scale and speed would not occur during the warm period that had persisted since the last ice age. Despite the urgency of these questions, the evidence of change remained tantalizingly ambiguous even as the years went by and the stakes rose. Scientists had only the sketchiest ideas of what a flip would look like.

One place scientists began looking for answers was Antarctica. Over the decades, paleoclimatologists, marine biologists, marine chemists, oceanographers, and geophysicists converged on this seemingly immutable continent, their efforts closely followed by a global press corps. In Antarctica, the scientists faced the chore of sorting through whether the changes afoot were the result of human activities in the previous century, a response to changes in deep ocean currents that began a thousand years ago, a vastly attenuated response to events set in motion by the end of the last ice age, ten thousand years ago, or some combination of the above. Antarctica is a living museum of time, a place where the past hovers close upon the present. This conflation of epochs makes the task of deconstructing the continent's symphony of time scales maddeningly difficult.

In the phrase used by climate specialists, Antarctica is "thermally isolated" from the rest of the world. This means that for fifteen million years the continent has largely generated its own weather, sealed from atmospheric events elsewhere by the great circumpolar current in the Southern ocean and its companion stratospheric winds, which act as a barrier to storms and weather fronts from more temperate climes. Once the ice sheets formed, they became somewhat self-perpetuating: a stabilizing mass of ice the size of a continent (so big that the ice sheets smother active volcanoes and flatten the tops of eight-thousand-foot mountains) that also reflected enormous amounts of solar radiation back up into the atmosphere during the summer months could blunt the edges of minor variations in climate.

Despite this inertia, scientists began to worry about the stability of the ice sheet in the late twentieth century, a concern that was prompted as sea level began rising around the world. At about two millimeters per year, the rate of rise did not seem that large, but as the century drew to a close, the rate at which sea level was rising appeared to be accelerating. Geophysicists could account for about 40 percent of the rise as a result of the melting of mid-latitude glaciers and the expansion of the oceans as waters warmed during the latter part of the twentieth century. But a number of scientists suspected that the mysterious unaccounted-for 60 percent was in some way coming from Antarctica.

They feared also that a much larger increment might come from Antarctica should the West Antarctic Ice Sheet (or WAIS, as it is called) break up or begin floating. Concern focused on WAIS because it is the world's last remaining marine ice sheet, meaning that it is heavy enough to sit on the seabed. In the case of WAIS, this meant displacing eight thousand feet of water. Because a marine sheet can stay in place only as long as it has enough mass to displace the ocean water that would otherwise lie underneath it, scientists consider such ice sheets inherently unstable.

Ice sheets remain in balance only as long as the amount of annual accumulation roughly matches the amount of ice shed through the calving of icebergs and evaporation. Though it is the size of China, WAIS has shrunk greatly since the last ice age. The question for scientists was whether there was some tipping point at which the process of collapse would speed up and lead to rapid and large changes in sea level. Records of ancient corals in the Caribbean, for instance, suggest that on several occasions in prehistory sea levels rose by several meters in periods of less than two hundred years, implying that WAIS has greatly shrunk or collapsed in the past.

To determine whether WAIS was again in danger of catastrophic collapse, scientists focused on two major issues. The first was the behavior of the ice streams. Though ice seems rigid, in great masses it behaves like a very slow-moving liquid. As ice accumulates on top, its weight tends to cause the sheet to spread. If the sheet is in balance, the accumulation will be matched by losses through evaporation and the flow of ice into the sea and onto ice shelves. Once a sheet gets more than thirteen hundred feet thick, the stresses caused by the weight of the ice tend to force rapid spreading. Since at its thickest WAIS is over fourteen thousand feet thick, ice is continually moving from its interior toward its edges, and the principal means by which an ice sheet sheds interior ice is through what are called ice streams.

In essence, these sixty-mile-wide ice rivers are glaciers bounded by ice rather than rock. Since they extend many thousands of feet to the bottom and move as much as three miles a year, they transport enormous amounts of ice from the interior of the ice sheet to the ice shelves. The amount they move depends to some degree on the resistance of the material over which they move, water and sediment tending to speed the flow, and rock tending to retard it. Trouble begins when the ice streams transport more ice off the sheet than is accumulated. Over time, this sets in motion a series of self-reinforcing events that cause ever more ice to move off the sheet, which in turn can lead to the catastrophic collapse of the ice sheet.

Critical to the process is the position of the so-called grounding line. This phrase refers to the boundary region marking where the ice sheet sits on the bottom, blocking the intrusion of seawater underneath it. If the ice streams transport more ice off the sheet than is accumulated over time, the grounding line will move inward, toward the center of the sheet. It will also move as sea level elsewhere rises, which changes the amount of water the ice sheet needs to displace to remain anchored on the bottom. Moreover, as the grounding line moves deeper (at its deepest, WAIS rests on sea bottom eighty-three hundred feet below sea level) and the ice gets thicker, the stresses to flow outward increase. At some point—no one knows when—the retreat of the grounding line completely destabilizes the ice sheet, and either through floating, a massive calving of icebergs, or both, the world as we know it changes.

In the late twentieth century, the U.S. National Science Foundation mounted a long-term interdisciplinary effort to take the pulse of the ice sheet. This effort was joined by a number of other organizations as sea levels continued to rise at accelerating rates. Over the years, people around the world became familiar with the notion of grounding lines and ice streams, and news organizations would regularly report on changes. The dynamics of ice sheets became the subject of conversation in the bazaars of Bangladesh and Indonesia as the steady sea-level rise and the destruction of protective coastal barriers made life ever more insecure for the billions of people who lived on land less than fifteen feet above sea level.

As of 2050, WAIS has not yet catastrophically collapsed. Few people can take comfort in this stay of execution, however, because, with every passing month, catastrophic collapse seems more likely. The news is of a steady retreat of the grounding line and of surges of the ice streams that dump increasing amounts of ice onto the Ross Ice Shelf and into the waters surrounding Pine Island, another crucial area through which the ice from WAIS ends up in the ocean.

The fate of the ice sheet is cause for concern, but it is not a problem that could be blamed on human folly in the twentieth century. The stage was set for the collapse of WAIS by rapid rise in temperatures ten thousand years earlier, when a pulse of warmth started migrating down through the sheet at the rate of about a foot a year. Warmer ice deforms more easily, and so, as this pulse reached the bottom (a process that itself takes several hundred years), it accelerated the surges in the ice streams.

In the twenty-first century, world attention shifted from the ice sheets to the other major component of the Antarctic system— its sea ice. This fragile, friable apron effectively doubles the size of the continent during the depths of the Antarctic winter, and then, each summer, shrinks to less than a quarter of its maximum size. Despite its enormous size, however, the sea ice is only about one and a half feet thick on average. This makes Antarctica's ice cover very vulnerable to changes in the ocean temperatures beneath it: warmth from the tropics invades the Antarctic region in the form of a vast deep-water current that wends its way south in the Atlantic and then enters the Antarctic region underneath the circumpolar current. The warm water is part of what marine geochemist Wallace Broecker dubbed the "great ocean conveyor," a Möbius-strip-like system of a deep, cold, and salty ocean current linked to a warmer, more shallow current. The amount of water moving through this system (twenty million cubic meters per second) equals one hundred Amazon Rivers, and is responsible for redistributing between 30 and 50 percent of the heat the earth receives from the sun. In simple terms, the conveyor absorbs heat from the sun at the equator and, over a long, slow cycle of fifteen hundred years, redistributes it to the poles.

This warmth—a relative term, since it keeps the deep current just a degree or two above freezing—then gets transferred to the atmosphere, as a number of forces, including the effects of the earth's rotation, cause the current to rise once it nears the continent. When it nears the surface, this current gives off its heat to the atmosphere and then sinks again, to begin a new journey around the globe.

Although water moves through the conveyor on a millennial scale, one of the crucial periods in this cycle is the relatively brief period when warm water rises and gives off its heat under the sea ice. The stability of the system depends on the temperature and salinity of the layers of water under the ice. As long as there is a relatively fresh and buoyant layer of water above the current of warmer water coming in from below, ice will continue to form. As ice thickens, however, salts become concentrated in the underlying water, to the point where the upper layer of water is as dense as the warm layer below. When this happens, warm and cold waters begin to mix, which in turn releases all the heat formerly trapped in the current. This melts the surface ice, forming a polyna amid the ice.

By the early twenty-first century, this process was happening on a massive scale. Something was mixing the waters, and the heat formerly trapped in a nine-thousand-foot column of water was venting to the atmosphere. The maddening thing, however, is that even in 2050 scientists still do not know what is driving these changes.

Scientists know of linkages that connect changes in winds and currents over the North Pacific to the North Atlantic. They have uncovered other connections between El Niños in the Pacific and analogous shifts in climate halfway around the world, in the North Atlantic. They have explored correlations between El Niño events in the tropics and changes in the edges of the sea ice in Antarctica. In normal times, this knowledge helped farmers plan what crops to plant and when, and it helped municipalities anticipate floods and snowy winters. Every new piece of information was integrated into global climate models, which became ever more able to replicate how climate had changed in the recent past—at least until climate began to go haywire.

Despite the vast increase in knowledge, each new breakthrough added a layer of complexity to the global climate system, so that the goal of finding the key to global climate has continued to recede into the future. Climate seems to be determined by global-scale systems moving heat through air and water, but also by subtle and intricate interactions at the boundaries between warm and cold, between air and land, between air and green matter, between air and water, between the different layers of warm and cold water, between sun and land, sun and snow, and hundreds of other points where heat is absorbed and gases exchanged, reflected, and otherwise distributed around the globe.

The more scientists discover about the myriad linkages connecting the components of the system, the harder it becomes to identify what it is precisely that has produced the surprises. Meteorologists and oceanographers could explain why fogs disappeared from the California coast after the fact, but they cannot predict where the next surprise may occur.

For the scientific community, it is a profoundly unnerving time. In 2050, scientists working on climate questions suffer no want of resources as a fidgety world seeks answers. But people and policy makers become ever more impatient as overwhelmed researchers hedge their answers on whether worse shocks are in store. There is no lack of models, but, rather, too many, leading to widespread confusion, both in the public and in the policy community, about what is going on. If scientists are reluctant to provide answers, demagogues and street-corner prophets have no such hesitation, offering a potpourri of paranoid, paranormal, and religious explanations for the world's plight.

The climate chaos has profoundly affected every culture. Even during periods marked by relative tranquillity, most people are reluctant to believe that normalcy has returned. Different societies came through the tumult of the previous decades with varying degrees of success. No group entirely escaped the ravages of resurgent microbes or the volatility in the global markets, but these crises eventually quieted into chronic problems that were manageable if not solvable, encoding their harsh lessons in the austere, devout, quasi-pantheistic values that are a leitmotif running through otherwise wildly disparate cultures.

By 2050, some parts of the world are in recovery mode. As life in water-rich parts of central Canada, Norway, the Russian Far East, parts of Chile, and other geographically and demographically favored places—marked by abundant water, good land, relatively low population density, mountains, and other features that provide some measure of climate stability—returned to a semblance of normalcy, so did the temptation to revert to the consumer values of the previous century. If the temptation is there, however, so are periodic reminders that the forces unleashed during the previous century still buffet the world. Antarctica continues to send its cryptic signals to humanity. With its omnipresent threat of inundation and more climate chaos, the continent looms over the future like an angry, unforgiving god.

PART III

THE CASE
FOR
INSTABILITY

THE CASE
FOR INSTABILITY

COULD IT BE OTHERWISE? Is there an equally convincing case to be made that the next century will be one of near-utopian prosperity and tranquillity, or of some middle ground between the remarkable stability of the past few decades and global upheaval? Certainly there are those, ranging from the late social critic Herman Kahn to Bill Gates, making that argument. The end of a millennium inspires hope as well as dread, even if the millennium is a significant date only to those who use the Christian calendar.

The optimistic case might be summarized as follows: Broad global trends reveal that food continues to become cheaper, that people are living longer, and that millions of poor around the world continue to move out of absolute poverty. Democracy is spreading around the world and markets are opening, speeding up the pace at which human ingenuity betters people's lives. As noted earlier, some optimists, like Julian Simon of the University of Maryland, dismiss environmental change and resource scarcity as a factor in future prosperity. A long line of thinkers, starting with the nineteenth-century economist David Ricardo, argue that, should limits arise, governments and the markets will adapt, as they have in the past. It is true that critics often ignore that consumer societies tend to become more efficient over time, as entrepreneurs seek out opportunities for profit, and businesses optimize processes to meet the demands of growth. Technological optimists like Vice-President Al Gore seize upon this and project a future in which developing nations "leapfrog" the West. Because emerging nations tend to lack energy, transportation, and sanitation infrastructure, goes this argument, they have the opportunity to adopt clean, efficient solutions such as solar or wind power, low-cost mass transit, and water-wise sanitation systems without investing in the costly nineteenth-century solutions adopted by Europe and the United States.

The fantastic potential of clean, efficient technologies has transformed Amory Lovins, the alternative-energy guru who founded the Rocky Mountain Institute in Colorado, from a dour pessimist in the early 1970s to a raving optimist. Nicknamed "cornucopians" to contrast themselves with more dour Malthusians, this group argues that the next century could see a world where billions of poor greatly raise their living standards while simultaneously reducing the burden that they place on earth and its ecosystems. In a new book entitled *Factor Four,* Lovins; his wife, L. Hunter Lovins; and the German physicist Ernst von Weizacker argue that humanity can live twice as well on half the resources through achievable changes in means of manufacture, construction, and engineering. Today, for instance, there is much discussion of fuel-cell-powered vehicles as an alternative to the internal-combustion engine. Fuel cells, which are in essence batteries that continuously recharge by converting hydrogen to power, have the potential to increase efficiency enormously in both transportation and power generation and produce as an effluent pure, distilled water.

In fact, the potential for technological transformation is perhaps the most persuasive dissuader of those who predict Armageddon. Societies do adapt. As the Chinese proverb puts it, "If you do not change direction, you end up where you are headed." The "silent spring" predicted by Rachel Carson in 1962 as pesticides killed off bird populations did not come about because many nations recognized the danger and banned DDT and other destructive pesticides. Some countries, like China, did not heed these warnings and ended up where they were headed. Over the decades, bird populations have plummeted in much of China from the lethal effects of pesticides.

Partly because of past evidence of the human ability to recognize and avert disaster, even some of the most pessimistic observers of the present believe there is the possibility of a "soft landing" in the various scenarios of environmental, demographic, and financial disaster. Donella Meadows was one of the authors of the 1972 bestseller *The Limits to Growth,* which argued that humans were pushing the limits of earth's ability to absorb human impacts on the biosphere. That same group of systems analysts, including Donella Meadows, updated their argument in the 1992 book *Beyond the Limits.* This maintained that trends in the world in the intervening twenty years fulfilled the dire predictions of their earlier work, and that the global situation is even more precarious today, because the impact of exploding human numbers has foreclosed options and shortened the amount of time available to come to grips with rising threats to the environment. Despite the apocalyptic flavor of these books, Meadows believes that it is still possible to avert disaster—"if," she says, "humans manage brilliantly starting very soon."

It is not hard to find prescriptions for what "managing brilliantly" means. To slow the loss of wildlands and the extinction of plants and animals, conservationists have rallied around the notion of protecting critically endangered habitats, focusing on so-called biodiversity hot spots—places that have extremely high concentrations of unique species, as well as protected corridors that preserve the migratory routes and nurseries essential to the health of an ecosystem. To ensure the future of agriculture, the International Food Policy Research Institute calls for nations to pursue research on crops and pest and water management, to disseminate that research through agricultural extension, and to protect the genetic diversity of the crops. To reverse the resurgence of infectious disease, the Centers for Disease Control would focus on research, investments in sanitation, and an infusion of resources into public-health extension services in the developing world, as well as the establishment of a network of crisis-response teams to react to outbreaks when they occur. These are all reasonable programs.

In the economic realm, some of the very experts who predict that the incredible increase in foreign-held dollar holdings portends future instability in the global currency markets also argue that the resolution of this unsustainable path need not be catastrophic. Wynne Godley of the Jerome Levy Institute at Bard College remarked that even if U.S. debt obligations held by foreign nations reach 30 percent or more of Gross Domestic Product— levels characteristic of debt-laden third-world countries—a resulting fall of the dollar might bring about a severe recession in the U.S. but, if the financial community acted prudently, need not destabilize the U.S. and the global economy.

Reducing the widening and potentially destabilizing gap between rich and poor is an equally tough problem. Various proposed solutions require some interference in open markets, which have become a type of god in global economy. Even here, however, some believe that there is a way to preserve basic human values without sacrificing prosperity. The billionaire George Soros holds that capitalism must be tempered with other values. He argues that, if the nations of the world encourage "open societies," in which all members have some influence, the marketplace of ideas and values could decide when the interests of society outweigh the sanctity of the marketplace.

Another cause for optimism is that human attitudes about fundamental matters like family size and the environment seem to be changing around the world at an extraordinarily rapid rate. As late as 1992, at the Earth Summit in Rio de Janeiro, Brazil, the question of human population was barely discussed. Delegates from India and Malaysia dominated the discussion, arguing that the problem was not human numbers but industrial nations' consumption and pollution. Just two years later, at the International Conference on Population and Development in Cairo, Egypt, a stunning change was evident in the delegations from 180 nations gathered there. Gone was most of the rhetoric that equated population programs and birth control with rich-nation racism, and in its place was a widespread recognition of the problems that high birthrates placed on economies of poor nations. Two years later, in 1996, population statistics throughout the world began to show a dramatic decline. For the first time in over twenty years, population was growing more slowly than projections anticipated, confusing demographers and policy makers alike.

The fall has nothing to do with policies that came out of Rio or Cairo but, rather, reflects rapidly changing decisions about family size throughout the developing world. The global phenomenon of urban migration plays a role in this calculus, because the expenses of housing in the cities turn additional children into liabilities, not the asset they can be in the countryside. Yet urbanization does not fully explain the change. Hundreds of millions of men and women—poor and middle-class, literate and illiterate, rural and urban, in countries where women's rights are respected and in countries where they are not—have decided to have smaller families, as evidenced by an almost universal drop in fertility rates.

This change in attitudes about family size has been matched by rapid change in attitudes toward the environment. Again, in both rich and poor countries, people seem to have awakened to the connections that link their health and prosperity to the health of natural systems. In the U.S., voters consistently support spending for environmental improvement, even though it reduces consumption (and therefore, in the minds of classical economists, individual well-being). In polls and votes, Americans seem to be saying that a sound environment is important to their well-being. So do the impoverished residents of the kampongs of Jakarta, the Penans of Malaysian Borneo, and millions of ordinary people in Russia, Poland, Czechoslovakia, and other states some of whose earliest protests against their rulers were prompted by the threats to their health and well-being of the laissez-faire environmental policies of communism. This emergent value has only just begun to surface, but in countries ranging from the U.S. to Brazil, politicians are finding that they ignore it at their peril. In Chile, long a bastion of unfettered free-market capitalism, a newspaper poll revealed that respondents ranked the environmental movement first in positive forces for change, even above the Catholic Church.

One final, oft-cited argument for optimism has to do with the nature of change itself. So far, the collapse of communism, a process that continues in China, has been extraordinarily nonviolent. How many times in history has an empire fallen without civil war or invasion? (The reverberations of the collapse of communism continue as of this writing, however, and could yet produce violent upheavals.) How many times previously have beleaguered rulers surrendered power without violence? In retrospect, it is easy to make the cynical argument that communist rulers acquiesced because they were well positioned to prosper in the Mafia-dominated economic free-for-all that has followed. Still, it has become harder to get away with atrocities with the whole world watching, and that in this respect the globalization of information and also of the economy enforces more civilized behavior.

Put all of this together, and isn't it possible that humanity might slip past the dangers described in the previous pages? Let us assume that these changes in values are occurring. Let us assume that the weather will remain benign for the next fifty years (a very unlikely proposition even without greenhouse forcing, because of the disruptive effects of continuing deforestation). Let us also assume that the prescriptions to prevent the various environmental, social, political, and economic train-wrecks described in the previous pages are doable. Though necessary and worthy, they will not be sufficient to stave off the coming chaos.

The feedback between such problems as environmental stress, urban and international migration, the rise of infectious disease, volatility in food and financial markets, etc., means that solutions to one problem are hostage, to greater or lesser degrees, to solutions to other problems. Moreover, larger than any of these specifics is the question of whether the increasing pressure of human numbers on the biosphere can be reduced without upheaval.

One way to reduce such pressure is to stabilize population, but, despite the drop in birthrates, there is an enormous demographic momentum in a global population in which more than half the world's people are younger than twenty-six. It is impossible to imagine stabilizing population unless every young man in the third world suddenly decides to become a priest, chemicals like PCBs really lower sperm counts, or some form of disaster befalls humanity.

Even if this change were accomplished, it would pose a profound challenge to the market economy as this is currently configured. Where would profits come from in a world in which the number of consumers was fixed or declining? In a 1997 editorial, *The Wall Street Journal* stated flatly, "Falling birth rates of the 1990s threaten to devastate growth in the next century."

One possible source of economic growth with population stability comes from the material aspirations of the billions of poor who have yet to achieve the standard of living of the industrial nations, and from continued material improvements in the lives of the affluent. This, however, leaves the world in the same fix it is in today, since those material improvements will almost surely come at the expense of already stretched ecosystems.

More likely, population will continue to increase for the next several decades. This means that, to maintain a stable world, increasing human numbers must be accompanied by a reduction in the byproducts of rising standards of living such as pollution, competition for resources, and the destruction of forests and wildlands—a tall order that would require fundamental changes in both consumer behavior and the economy.

If increasing human numbers are going to lessen their impact on earth's overstressed ecosystems, the consumer society must be replaced by some successor system more in harmony with the biosphere. Cornucopians such as Vice-President Gore argue that this is possible, that a shift among the present industrial, transportation, and energy infrastructure to more earth-friendly technologies would stimulate a huge round of capital spending that could drive economic growth even as it addressed problems of pollution and resource scarcity.

Such a shift is likely to occur at some point in the coming

decades. However, more often than not, shifts of basic technologies on a global scale are either preceded or accompanied by upheavals such as war or economic depression. The industries supporting horses, buggy whips, and carriages that gave way to the automobile had not nearly the importance to the overall economy as the multitrillion-dollar installed base of equipment and infrastructure tailored to the needs of the internal-combustion engine. Eventually, this nineteenth-century technology will give way to its successor, but its very durability despite the technical availability of more efficient alternatives indicates the degree to which the internal-combustion engine and fossil fuels are embedded in the industrial economies. It is more likely that the internal-combustion engine will be toppled from its perch rather than voluntarily relinquish the throne, as the long-playing record did before the advance of the compact disc.

A more serious impediment to a smooth transition is the nature of the consumer society itself. If the term "consumer society" merely described buying behavior, people could accomplish this transition as values and purchasing tastes changed. But the consumer society goes much deeper, drawing on human needs more profound even than comfort and safety.

The genius of the consumer society is that it captures religious needs largely disenfranchised by modern Western life, and translates those spiritual longings into material appetites, the satisfaction of which through purchases further expands the consumer society's reach. In effect, the consumer society is a system that integrates both religion and economics into a culture in which material wealth is valued far more than spiritual wealth. Cultures can and do change, but the question is, Can the consumer society evolve into its successor without upheaval? I believe that it cannot.

One of the perverse laws of the universe is that we least understand those phenomena that have the greatest bearing on our lives and future. So it is with consumer societies—along with population growth, one of the two great phenomena to emerge in this century. For all the scrutiny the consumer society has received over the decades, it is all too easy to focus on the materialistic aspects of consumer behavior, particularly the consumer society's surface manifestations of waste, greed, conspicuous display, and a host of other unattractive activities and values. This is what happened at the 1992 Earth Summit, which became a futile exercise in finger pointing as emerging nations argued that rich-nation consumption, not the exploding populations and rising aspirations of developing countries, were what had put the world in its current environmental pickle.

The arguments are not trivial: the average American has roughly eighty times the impact on the global economy than the average person from India. Environmentalists fear that, as billions of peasants around the world adopt the consumer values of the West, the world's already overburdened ecosystems will collapse under the weight of expanding human numbers leveraged by ever-increasing material consumption. If China develops its vast coal reserves to meet its energy needs, that nation will soon be putting as much CO_2 into the atmosphere as the entire industrial world, nullifying whatever steps the rich nations take to limit greenhouse-gas emissions.

There is no question that rising consumption combined with rising human numbers poses a profound problem for the world, but upon examination, the spread of consumer behavior cannot be so neatly reduced to an indicator of increased consumption and waste. For one thing, as the world has seen in Eastern Europe in the years since the fall of the Soviet Union, the spread of consumer societies can have the effect of reducing waste and making a society more efficient. Communism in Russia and the Eastern bloc managed to produce all the ills of the consumer society, but almost none of the benefits. The Trabant, the people's car of now defunct East Germany, produced as much as thirty times the polluting emissions of the equivalent-sized cars sold in West Germany. In fact, by closing antiquated East German factories and converting other coal-fired plants to natural gas, Germany has been able to lower the nation's overall CO_2 emissions by 10 percent since 1990. The consumer society cannot be dismissed as wasteful.

The consumer society is also something more than a society

made up of people who want to buy consumer goods. Given the opportunity, nearly everybody on earth wants to buy goods that make life healthier, easier, and more convenient. Nowhere was this proposition more powerfully demonstrated than in New Guinea during World War II, where Stone Age indigenous peoples became so enamored of the bounty brought along by invading armies that many would build airstrips with the belief that such signs of devotion would prompt the gods to deliver more cargo. Noble as their efforts were, the Cargo Cultists failed to grasp one important aspect of consumer societies: true consumers not only buy goods, they also organize themselves to produce them. When Cargo Cults flourished, only a handful of industrial nations—the U.S., Canada, Australia, followed by Japan and most of Western Europe—had the necessary markets, political structures, and values to qualify as consumer societies. With the triumph of capitalism and democracy over communism, however, the entire world is busily trying to join the club.

India is trying to free its markets and eliminate red tape so that it can hop on the global merry-go-round of buying and producing consumer goods. In such a religious and tradition-bound country, this process has been halting. The protesters who stoned Kentucky Fried Chicken outlets in several cities did so in part because they felt that the Western enterprise would induce the poor to abandon their healthy and inexpensive vegetarian diet for fast food that would put a strain on peasant pocketbooks and health, and would place additional burdens on Indian food production, which even today must strain to feed nine hundred million mouths. At the same time, video vans that roll through rural villages urging the poor to buy Colgate toothpaste instead of using traditional cleaners such as charcoal and the bark of the *neem* tree have for the most part been greeted with enthusiasm. Are these transformations necessarily bad?

Neo-Luddites, so-called deep ecologists, and a burgeoning crop of radical Christian thinkers led by Jesuit priest and writer Thomas Berry would emphatically argue yes. One attribute of a consumer society, goes this argument, is that it treats nature as raw material to be manipulated by technology for the short-term benefit of humanity, which believes itself to be separate from the rest of the natural order. With no appreciation of natural limits, the consumer society ultimately will destroy earth's life-support systems and itself in the process.

Values, however, are a crucial component of the consumer society. Because consumer spending amounts to so much of the U.S. GDP, buyers can have an enormous effect on what gets produced. As the power of advertising makes clear, most of these purchases are profoundly influenced by the buyers' values and aspirations. Since the early 1970s, automobile buyers have shifted from purchasing ostentatious gas hogs to simple economy cars and then back to ostentatious, gas-hog sport-utility vehicles as the American self-image has interacted with notions of scarcity, confidence in the future, and considerations of comfort and safety in unpredictable ways.

It is worth considering what would happen if people around the world suddenly awakened to threats to the biosphere and demanded that industries protect ecosystems and adopt clean technologies and sources of energies. What would happen if technological progress brought us abundant sources of clean, cheap energy? Could the consumer society become sustainable, to use the word that has become the mantra of the eco-conscious community?

This future is unlikely. It is in the nature of businesses to optimize efficiency, and the consumer society is supremely adaptable to buyer tastes, but the consumer society is unsustainable. At its core, the consumer society functions more as a religion than as an economic system.

A look deep into the workings of the consumer society reveals a startling paradox, involving the relationship between reason, the irrational, and religion in a consumer society. Anti-religious in its nature, and ostensibly built upon reason and technology, the consumer society actually draws upon both religion and irrational forces. This paradox is what makes the consumer society such a formidable presence in the late twentieth century, even if many of its converts find its fruits empty and unrewarding.

One of the broad trends of Western history has been the gradual diminution of religion as an influence on behavior. In the so-called primitive religions, gods and the spirits of the ancestors encoded in ritual and taboo influence every aspect of life, ensuring that people follow the lessons of survival worked out over millennia by trial and error. The ancient Greeks exiled the gods to Olympus, allowing themselves a much freer hand to do business. Monotheism and then Christianity went the Greeks one better, pushing God off the planet altogether and up into the heavens. With the gods and God out of our hair, all of creation was at man's disposal. When the religious codes of the Roman Church still proved an impediment to business (prohibiting interest, for instance, which put Christian diamond merchants in medieval times at a competitive disadvantage to Jews in the Antwerp marketplace), the Reformation solved the problem by equating worldly success with godliness. Add the factors of progress and willingness to break with tradition and the elements were in place for the emergence of the consumer society, the most supremely adaptable culture the world has yet encountered.

What vast purpose has been served by the inexorable diminution of religion as a force in daily life? Clearly one result has been to allow humans greater latitude to intervene in nature and otherwise take control of the way we conduct our affairs. As humanity has turned away from religion for guidance, it has turned to reason and science, attempting to impose rational management on aspects of life formerly determined by tradition, taboo, or some other expression of cultural authority.

If reason has sapped the passion from modern religion, it has also channeled that power in surprising directions. One signal artifact of consumer societies is that more and more people define themselves either through purchases, through their role in producing goods, or through their role in persuading other people to make purchases. Each of these activities has become invested with aspects of devotional duty, completing the long slow trend toward sanctifying commerce that began with the dawn of monotheism. If the Reformation made it acceptable to strive for worldly success, the advent of the consumer society made holy the acquisition of worldly goods. The true heroes of the consumer society are not those who save but those who spend.

Each consumer purchase—in the aggregate, $6.8 trillion yearly in the United States—helps expand the hegemony of the consumer society and, by extension, the hegemony of the rational management of human behavior and resources. This is what the consumer society is about; its accomplishment, if that is the appropriate term, is the increase in the power of reason as a force in life. The consumer society does this by capturing religious needs pertaining to such profound needs as the urge to understand one's place in the universe, and translating them into material appetites, the satisfaction of which further extends the hegemony of reason.

Everybody knows that the promises of advertising are false and its logic is specious, but it still works, because advertising and marketing—the connective tissue between the productive side of the consumer society and the inchoate realm of needs and wants—tap into deep and powerful needs. A vast panoply of products are sold through the implicit promise that the purchase will connect the buyer to some desired community or attribute. Rather than actually test himself in combat or in the wild, the corporate bureaucrat can try to satisfy the inner warrior through the purchase of a Humvee or a luxury hunting package tour in Alaska. Even the intangible satisfactions of religion itself are up for sale. Faith becomes an image of faith, in the form of a crucifix worn as an accessory.

And, of course, redemption can be purchased through philanthropy as well. In this transaction, a tycoon can in one gesture erase the sins of a lifetime of marauding and self-interest by making gifts in his declining years, and then find himself celebrated for his goodness far more than humble souls who limited their material ambitions and tried to honor their God in their actions on a day-to-day basis. The consumer society is thus built on a substrate far more complex than a simple desire for convenience and material wealth.

But there is more. The true genius of the consumer society is in its relationship to discontent. As volumes of monographs, books, and articles on the alienation of modern life and the emptiness of materialism have told us, it is impossible to satisfy religious needs through material purchases. The attempt to do so only leads to discontent that manifests itself on the individual level through various forms of anomie, and on the societal level through recurring outlaw movements—protest movements, the counterculture of the late 1960s, New Age mysticism, etc. These periodic explosions of discontent are intrinsic to the consumer society, a product of the basic engine that makes the whole system go in the first place. Rather than suppress these inevitable eruptions, it harnesses them as new forms of consumer interest. Outlaw energy that would bring down the system becomes domesticated into purchasing decisions that help expand the system.

This is the paradox alluded to earlier: the consumer society taps as a source of energy the discontent it helps create. This is what makes the system so supremely resilient and adaptable. Unfortunately, a system that transforms all attempts to change it into consumer interest loses the ability to recognize danger and adapt. If every public expression of fear, anger, or outrage is assimilated as a market opportunity, the system cannot change.

Such a system is both stable and unstable. It is unstable because it produces turmoil and indeed requires it to function, but it is stable because, like the Greek demigod Proteus, it continually changes form without altering its basic substance. What does it mean for the world as the consumer society conquers new cultural frontiers and brings ever more people and ever-larger pieces of the world under its control?

The consumer society is a pyramid sales scheme on a global scale. It is about growth and the exploitation of new markets. Its hallmark is its extreme adaptability. Over the decades, the managers and marketing geniuses who tend the consumer society have optimized corporate abilities to identify, target, and exploit eruptions of consumer interest wherever it surfaces. The result is the Orwellian situation in which one division of a corporation can respond to consumer concern about inner-city violence in its publications, while another division promotes recording artists who celebrate murder and call for killing cops.

Like George Soros, conservative thinker William Bennett believes that the best way to restore some balance is to bring nonconsumer values back into the system. Soros is more concerned with emerging economies around the globe, whereas Bennett worries about the decline of the moral sense at home in America. Both firmly believe that it is possible to have commerce and values, and they are right, although some of the recent precedents, such as the awkward marriage of religion and markets in Iran, would hardly gladden the heart of a capitalist.

Difficult as is the fit between Islamic fundamentalism and a market economy, it is much more difficult to imagine the merging of a consumer society and the values necessary to make peace with the biosphere. Try to imagine the consumer economy without growth. Even the President's Council on Sustainable Development cannot do that. In their wisdom, they define sustainable development as "sustained economic growth." Try to imagine the impact on today's economy if consumers no longer defined themselves through material possessions, and instead returned to religion, nature, and other traditional nonmaterial sources of satisfaction.

Since the system depends on spending and perpetual growth, it is difficult to imagine that the consumer society can ever become sustainable, perpetual growth being impossible on a finite planet. The consumer society can embrace an ethos that seeks efficiency, but any value change that fostered the simple life and a search for nonmaterial satisfactions would ultimately bring it down.

The market system that underlies the consumer society is amoral. It is also blind, since there is no way of knowing what humanity will need in the future to survive. For decades, the market regarded the Pacific yew tree as nothing more than a nuisance.

Rather than sell the yews felled during timber operations, companies would burn them. Then researchers discovered that the bark contained a compound called taxol that helps treat various types of cancer. Unfortunately, the market's recognition of the value of Pacific yews has not yet led to a resurgence of the tree. Now the scarce remaining trees are in danger from timber pirates lured by the high prices the tree's bark commands.

There is no way the market can know what humans might need in the future, or what ecosystems might need right now. Economic activities convert natural systems into capital in almost complete ignorance of the real costs and benefits. Though nature is readily converted into capital, the reverse is not so easy to accomplish, even when the value of the natural resource finally becomes recognized.

Around the world today, from the rise of Islamic fundamentalism to other expressions of radical religious discontent, there are stirrings of a reaction to the consumer society and a search for something beyond material satisfactions. Do these stirrings represent a true threat to the consumer society, or are they just another manifestation of the discontents that the consumer society produces and then domesticates?

Humanity will make the transitions to stable population growth, to an economic system that neither beggars the earth nor marginalizes the great bulk of humanity, and to a value system that recognizes the limits of materialism, but these transitions will not come about smoothly. One thing we can know about the future is that it will be less stable for more people than it is today.

Paleontologist Richard Potts of the American Museum of Natural History argues that, since humanity is adapted to instability, as a species we are well prepared to deal with instability in the future. He also notes that we have become creators of the circumstances that created us: that our pollutants affect the climate the way volcanoes did in earlier times, and that human-induced global warming may bring about rapid shifts that humans have lived through many times during our evolutionary history. In effect, humanity has become a stimulant to the endocrine system of the planet.

That humanity has survived, however, leaves the impression that humanity sat out the cataclysms of fire and ice that periodically devastated the planet suffering no more than inconveniences. In fact, the history of the human ancestral line has been for hominids to appear, flourish for a couple of million years, and then yield the stage to a more adaptable descendant. Even during the more recent past, there have likely been repeated population crashes within the histories of *Homo erectus* and *sapiens* as climates careened from wet and moist to dry and vice versa.

A temporary 40-percent reduction in human numbers, which might have been the norm during periods of extreme instability in prehistoric times, might seem like a small blip on a long, successful evolutionary journey when viewed from the distant future; but our children may take a different view if they live through a period during which 2.2 billion people succumb to various calamities and plagues. I am not suggesting that this is going to happen, but only that we should not take comfort from the fact that, more than any other species save the insects, humans, as Potts put it, "are adapted to that aspect of nature that is most volatile."

Humanity finds itself at a remarkable conjunction. Present-day humans have been the beneficiary of a rare syzygy: fifty years of political stability on top of 150 years of good weather that falls into an eight-thousand-year period of relative climate stability. It could be argued that civilized man has never really known true instability, and that the industrial and information ages have flowered in a period of almost uncanny tranquillity. Humanity has taken advantage of our long respite from climate instability. We have invented technologies and social systems to insulate us from the vicissitudes of nature. We have bet the world that our fortress will protect us when climate and the environment again become temperamental. We never imagined that our very success would hasten the return of bad times.

What can be done? It is very late in the game. I chose the clues described in the first part of this book precisely because they represent long-wavelength, difficult-to-reverse phenomena. If a doubling of carbon dioxide carries with it climate chaos, we are likely stuck with these consequences, if only because, given the momentum of the global economy, there is very little time left to halt the increase in CO_2. The lifetime of these molecules in the atmosphere is roughly one hundred years, which means that once CO_2 finds its way into the atmosphere it tends to stay there for a very long time. Similarly, the destruction of the world's ancient forests and the fragmentation of its ecosystems cannot be reversed easily, and humanity will have to deal with whatever upheavals accompany this global ecological imbalance.

Despite this, there is no cause for despair. The global climate is such a complex system that some unanticipated reaction of its many components may mute the predicted impact of ever-increasing greenhouse gases. Even now, some as yet unidentified mechanism seems to be taking a small amount of CO_2 out of the atmosphere, so that the buildup of greenhouse gases is occurring at a slightly slower rate than was predicted based upon known levels of global emissions.

Moreover, there is much that people and nations can do. We may not be able to head off some measure of instability, but humanity has the power to moderate the impact of the coming upheavals. Nothing will happen, however, unless people around the world recognize the dangers lurking just beyond the turn of the millennium.

We have seen in this century how bad ideas, turbocharged by the integrated global market and the heft of six billion people, can transform the planet. Something so seemingly innocent as a health-conscious interest in sushi has virtually stripped the North Atlantic of bluefin tuna. Asian folk beliefs in the aphrodisiac properties of tiger parts and rhino horn have driven both great animals to the verge of extinction in the wild. Misunderstandings about natural systems embedded in classical economics have encouraged nations to destroy most of the world's original forests and wetlands and view the results as a positive contribution to gross domestic product. We have reached a point in history where we can no longer afford the luxury of bad ideas. To paraphrase Sigmund Freud, the character of our ideas is now the destiny of the planet.

If bad ideas can transform the globe, so can good ideas. Even before Congress acted, public outcry over tuna fishing methods that inadvertently drowned thousands of dolphins forced the world's largest tuna canning companies to boycott fish caught by those methods. Even if Congress acts to end the boycott, it is likely that consumer pressure will continue to enforce the ban. Now a number of prestigious restaurants are employing a similar boycott to give some relief to beleaguered stocks of swordfish in the North Atlantic. More and more people seem to care about not only what they eat, but where it was raised and how it was caught. Consumers seem to be creating an ad hoc and ecological analog to kosher dietary restrictions.

The extraordinary reversal in attitudes toward family size shows how attitudes can change rapidly in vastly different cultures at the same time. As indicators of environmental stress and climate chaos become more compelling, and as people wake up to the threat of an unstable world, it is possible that there will be a sudden shift in values.

Even if the world enters a period of economic instability, the pain of straitened material circumstances might be muted if this rocky time strengthened family ties and renewed interest in things spiritual. To the degree that such an awakening translates into altered purchasing decisions and political action, the face of various societies might change very rapidly. Something as simple as renewed respect for the workings of natural systems, awareness that the weight of six billion people has made humanity the most consequential creature on the planet, would work wonders in tempering humanity's self-destructive tendencies.

Throughout humanity's history, ecological lessons have been culturally encoded as taboos. Around the world, aboriginal peoples protected certain forests and creatures not so much because they had developed a sophisticated science of ecology, as because they felt that violations of taboos would produce empty harvests and barren wives. This fear of the consequences did more to protect natural systems than any biodiversity treaty, and today it is surfacing again in more modern form as more and more people around the world recognize that heedless tampering with earth's life-support systems is a very dangerous game. This represents a healthy reversal of the trend to view nature as an infinitely stocked refrigerator created solely for man's pleasure and needs.

Over the millennia, humanity has proved to be an artful dodger of fate, a defier of limits, a surmounter of seemingly insurmountable obstacles, and a master escape artist from traps laid by nature. Only the very brave or foolhardy would assert flatly that our resourceful species has finally exhausted its bag of tricks. Still, it is very late in the game.

ACKNOWLEDGMENTS

THIS BOOK IS THE product of a twenty-five-year journey probing the consumer society—America's bequest to Western Civilization. To some degree this project was prepared for by my previous books and articles exploring humanity's relationship to the natural world and the origins of the consumer society. As such I have benefited from hundreds of conversations and interviews with scientists, artists, and thinkers over the years. In this book, however, I have gone far beyond reporting for previous books and articles, even in those cases where I revisit material from earlier projects. While space does not permit the full acknowledgment of all people I talked to in the five years I have been working on this book, there are a number of people who deserve special mention.

First and foremost I am grateful for the editorial advice of Alice Mayhew, who probed and challenged my thinking at every stage of writing. Her colleague Elizabeth Stein provided constructive criticism and comment at various stages of the writing, as did Lisa Weisman. The book is far better for their suggestions. I also owe a great debt to Esther Newberg, my agent at ICM. Jim Wilcox read the manuscript in its final stages and had a number of helpful ideas.

I cast a wide net in preparing for this book. Conversations with Tundi Agardy, Spencer Beebe, Dirk Bryant, Bill Conway, Lisa Curran, Thomas Eisner, Mike Fay, Nels Johnson, Tom Lovejoy, Russ Mittermeir, Charles Munn, John Robinson, Ralph Schmidt, Nigel Sizer, Lee White, and E. O. Wilson, among others, helped me in a variety of chapters ranging from the nature of stability to the subtleties of the biodiversity crisis. I also benefited greatly from a few days at the Santa Fe Institute thanks to a gracious invitation from Murray Gell-Mann. I was particularly helped by conversations with Brian Arthur, Baruch Bloomberg, Michael Caher, John Casti, Stuart Kauffman, and Christopher Langton.

In preparing the sections on the integrated global marketplace and investment banking, I benefited from conversations with James Bennett, Robert Costanza, Craig Davis, Amy Falls, Tully Friedman, Wynne Godley, James Grant, Leon Levy, Jeffrey Sachs, and Ben Weston.

One of the more complicated pieces of research involved my speculations on how changes in the fog regime in central California might affect the Redwoods. Among those who helped me in this endeavor were Daniel Axelrod, David Cayen, Mark Finny, James Gardner, Charles Goldman, David Graber, Kate Gregory, Ralph Gregory, Malcom Hughes, Jere Lipps, Bert Shorne, Tom Sweatnam, and G. T. West.

I have explored the issues of megacities and infectious disease in a number of different articles over the years. In rethinking these issues for this project, I would like to single out conversations and interviews with Neal Boyle, Rita Colwell, Paul Epstein, Martin Hugh Jones, Jaime Lerner, Ross McPhee, Stephen Morse, Jonas Rabinovitch, David Sattersthwaite, Carolyn Stephens, and Tim Weiskel.

Climate change and ozone depletion are other issues I have been exploring for a long time. Here again, a number of people showed great patience as I revisited various aspects of the issue, including Wallace Broecker, Tom Karl, Jeremy Leggett, Paul Mayewski, Bill Moomaw, Sherwood Rowland, and Harvey Weiss. The National Science Foundation gave me invaluable support during a visit to Antarctica, and while there, a number of scientists were generous with their time. From the NSF I would specifically like to thank Cornelius Sullivan and Lynn Symarski. Among those in Antarctica who were very helpful were Bob Bindshadler, Don Blankenship, Gerald Kooyman, Carol Raymond, Charles Raymond, Ted Scambos, Christopher Schuman, and Kendrick Taylor. Back in the United States, I followed up on the issues raised in Antarctica through interviews with Richard Alley, Lloyd Burckle, Peter de Menocal, Arnold Gordon, Douglas Martinson, and Dorothy Peteet.

For help on the chapters on food and migration I would like to thank T. Maya, George H. L. Rothschild, and R. Wassun of the International Rice Institute; Mark Rosegrant and his colleagues at the International Food Policy Research Institute; David Barkin, Lester Brown, Jorge Bustamente, Daniel Esty, Jack Goldstone, José Gómez de León, Heather Hanson, Thomas Homer-Dixon, Michelle Leighton, Václav Smil, and Noel Vietmeyer. Special thanks to P. J. Simmons for inviting me to a number of provocative seminars at the Woodrow Wilson Institute at the Smithsonian Institution.

Conversations with William Dowell and Richard Ostling, two colleagues at *Time,* spurred me in new directions in the section dealing with the rise of Islamic fundamentalism. I would also like to acknowledge the help of Lyman Kellstedt, for his suggestions about areas to explore in Christian fundamentalism. At different points in the writing, David Bjerklie played the very useful role of devil's advocate.

During many trips to other remote places, I have had the good fortune to encounter scientists, diplomats, and other expatriates whose insights extend far beyond their immediate discipline or job. Mark Atwater, Christophe Boesch, Mike Chambers, Mike Fay, Steve Galster, Harry Goodall, John Mackinnon, Richard and Nancy Malenky, Charles Munn, and Dan Phillips all fit that category.

When I began writing this book, Jerry and Ani Moss offered me a place to hide out and write, and when I was doing my final revisions, Joan and James Blaine did likewise. Thanks to all these good friends.

There are a number of people who do not fit neatly into any category, but whose encouragement and insight have helped me over the years. These include Roger Kennedy, the Very Reverend James Parks Morton, Strobe Talbott, John Tierney, and Timothy Wirth.

Finally, I must acknowledge the support and extraordinary

tolerance of my wife, Mary, who gave birth to two babies and met the demands of her job as an attorney, and yet still encouraged me to go off by myself at crucial times during the researching and writing of this book.

I gratefully acknowledge all of the above, but any list in a project this long in the making is incomplete, and I apologize to anyone whose help I might have omitted.

INDEX

Printed in the United States
By Bookmasters